Understanding education

Understanding education

Toward a reconstruction of educational inquiry

WALTER FEINBERG
University of Illinois at Urbana–Champaign

CAMBRIDGE UNIVERSITY PRESS

Cambridge
London New York New Rochelle
Melbourne Sydney

Published by the Press Syndicate of the University of Cambridge
The Pitt Building, Trumpington Street, Cambridge CB2 1RP
32 East 57th Street, New York, NY 10022, USA
296 Beaconsfield Parade, Middle Park, Melbourne 3206, Australia

First published 1983

Printed in the United States of America

Feinberg, Walter, 1937–

Understanding education.

Includes index.

1. Educational research. I. Title.
LB1028.F34   1983   370′.7′8   82–12790
ISBN 0 521 24864 7 hard covers
ISBN 0 521 27032 4 paperback

For Jay, who understood more than he could say
and who did more than he could know

Contents

       Notes   235
       Index   267

Foreword

Through a refinement of the idea of social reproduction, Walter Feinberg provides us with a bold attempt to reconceive and restructure the domain of educational inquiry. A number of contemporary educational scholars and critics have also viewed education from this perspective, for example, Apple, Bowles and Gintis, Greer, Katz, and others; but, to my knowledge, none has looked outside his own particular type of investigation to see in the idea of education as social reproduction the potential to unite in a fundamental way a variety of useful forms of educational inquiry that are presently disconnected. Feinberg's vision is comprehensive and his book seminal. It sets the stage for a basic reconsideration of the nature of educational inquiry much in the same way that Peter Winch's book, *The Idea of a Social Science,* did in the philosophy of the social sciences.

Feinberg's contribution is an original and important one. He argues that educational inquiry should be viewed as inquiry into all the dimensions of social reproduction, the empirical and descriptive, the normative and critical, and the historical and interpretive. He views the study of education as a study of the processes of social reproduction of intergenerational identity amid change in any society. He identifies two fundamental functions of education: First, education in its many forms is the reproduction of social skills both general and technical – the transmission to the next generation of those objective modes of acting, behaving, and doing that constitute the peculiar social-cultural life and occupations of a particular society. Second, education reproduces social consciousness, those intersubjective shared understandings of what legitimates, makes significant, and constitutes the rights and privileges associated with the social skills of the society. Educational research, then, is essentially the study of the structures of these social knowledge codes, of the various means of their social reproduction, and of the ways individuals engage in the process with the recognition that "we are both bound by past forms of reproduction and the creators of new ones."

This comprehensive and compelling view of the domain of educational inquiry presents a challenge to educators. It is an opportunity to reconceive and restructure educational research and scholarship in a way that will allow researchers from any and all orientations to see how their work connects with and contributes to an understanding of the ''whole cloth'' of education. It is also a reminder that the educational scholar cannot escape moral responsibility and must make judgments and evaluations regarding this essentially normative process.

JONAS F. SOLTIS
William Heard Kilpatrick Professor
of Philosophy and Education
Teachers College, Columbia University

Acknowledgments

I wish to thank Gabriele Lakomski, Ralph Page, Alan Peshkin, Philip Steedman, and Steve Tozer for their comments on various parts of the manuscript. I am also indebted to the late Helen Freeman for a number of helpful conversations. The assistance of Stephen Norris in analyzing the material presented in Chapter 2 was very valuable, as were the comments of Michael Apple and Ernest Kahane, who read an earlier draft of the entire manuscript. David Yick and Audrey Thompson's editorial assistance on the final drafts of the manuscript is very much appreciated as are the comments of students in a seminar that I taught on value theory and education.

I have been especially fortunate in having had as a colleague Eric Bredo, who gave many hours to discuss issues raised in this book and helped to clarify my thoughts on a number of occasions. I profited greatly from these sessions and from the qualities of character and mind that he brought to them.

Research for this project was aided in part by the University of Illinois Research Board, the Department of Educational Policy Studies, and the Bureau of Educational Research.

W.F.

1 Introduction: Educational studies and the disciplines of educational understanding

The conflict in educational scholarship

The young Marx concluded his thesis on Feuerbach by boldly proclaiming that hithertofore "Philosophers have only interpreted the world . . . the point, however, is to change it." Fortunately for Marx this thesis did not have to be approved by a committee of educational philosophers before it appeared in print. Had it required such approval, Marx would have been seen as a hopeless generalist and told that he lacked sufficient commitment to the intellectual pureness of the singular disciplines that form the proper basis for educational thought.

It is more likely, however, that long before such an embarrassing situation arose, some friendly faculty member would have taken the young scholar aside to inform him that one-liners like these are not acceptable to educational philosophers, and that given his inadequate commitment to disciplinary purity there would be little point to think of continuing in philosophy or even to changing fields to history, economics, sociology, or any of the other disciplines that form the core of educational thought. He would have been bluntly told that the point indeed is not to change the world, but to know it, and in order to know it one must be able to reflect upon it through the concentrated lens of a single discipline. Generalists with missions would be well advised to study educational administration and to seek a career as a school principal or superintendent. A new suit, a clean shave, and a more winning smile would be necessary, but beyond these requirements, and a few courses in finance and interpersonal relations, he could easily manage the intellectual demands of the field. The mocking displeasure that marked this advice would likely have given Marx reason to wonder about educational scholarship. For Marx's thesis on Feuerbach was not motivated by a drive to maintain the purity of a discipline, but to weld a bond between the theoretical and the practical spheres of human activity. This motivation was later to be shared in their own way but with a different emphasis by

Sections in this chapter appeared in an earlier form in *Educational Studies,* Vol. 11(4), Winter 1980.

Dewey and by those scholars known as the educational foundationists who followed him.

The above fantasy signifies the central dispute in educational studies, a dispute that has been expressed many times in different ways, but that can be captured by a single question: Is the understanding of a practical activity such as education best approached by modeling one's inquiry after the established disciplines, or is there something about the object of educational understanding itself that cannot be captured by any single discipline or even by adding together the insights of many disciplines? Each side of this dispute has its advocates, and it is an issue that has been raised in more than one of the allied disciplines. On one side of the issue stand the traditional foundationists who believe in the primary importance of an integrated course of study in which the insights of various disciplines have been sifted and sorted for that which speaks to the practical work of schooling. On the other side are those who believe that to subordinate a discipline to some unquestioned end, such as the improvement of schooling, is ultimately to distort its insights and to turn it into a tool of propaganda and ideology.

Among these latter scholars, it is said in criticism of the traditional foundationists that their work is tied too closely to the concern of immediate practice. It is said that they have been unable and perhaps unwilling to look critically at the relationships between schooling and other, more powerful institutions, and thereby to see the crucial ways in which schools are bent, shaped, and molded by dominant interest groups and classes. It also has been said that they have watered down the insights of the disciplines by looking at the past from their perspective in the present. It is said that they have served as apologists for the public schools and have given educational scholarship a bad name. Now whether or not these charges are accurate will vary from case to case, and I do not want to take up these in this book. There is good reason to believe, for example, that many traditional scholars, although not ignoring problems of racism, sexism, and discrimination, have placed an unwarranted faith in public education to correct these evils.

Whatever one may think of this debate, whichever side one may support, there is little doubt that the older form of scholarship has been in retreat, and that until recently the emphasis on methodological rigor within a discipline had spirited new insights and helped redirect the educational debate. Historians have shaken us from the belief that schools were always the bastions of equality and freedom that many believed them to be. Economists have forced us to consider the powerful influence that the nature and distribution of work has on the nature and distribution of education. Some scholars have confronted us with strong evidence to the effect that a person's social class background still has a strong influence on advancement, an influence that mutes other factors such as talent and effort. And philosophers have carefully analyzed the meaning of such concepts as education, indoctrination, and equality, setting the stage for discussions about whether a purportedly "educative" activity is meeting the standards that this term implies.

In light of these disciplinary achievements one can reasonably ask if there is anything that can be said for the older generation of foundation scholars, for those generalists who believe that educational scholarship, perhaps because of its relation to practice, but perhaps for other reasons as well, was in some fashion unique and required an understanding to which disciplines might contribute but which they could not override. This question can be joined by looking first at the criticism as it has been developed in one field – educational history.

It has been said, at least among the circle of educational historians, that the older scholars relaxed their objectivity and let the past speak not for itself, but for the present. The history of education, it is said, became the prehistory of the undaunted movement toward a comprehensive compulsory system of public schooling that served to instill the values of equality, freedom, and human rights into the consciousness of a new generation of Americans. It was thus the gloss of the present that guided the understanding of the past and hence distorted it.

For the historian, the charge of presentism described here seems to be the most biting of all. Yet presentism is a charge pressed against many but admitted by few. The old foundationists, scholars like Counts, Cubberly, and Kilpatrick, are said to be guilty of presentism because of an unswerving commitment to the public school. The older generation of "pure" historians, scholars like Bailyn, Cremin, and Curti, are said to be guilty of presentism because, writing under the background of the cold war, they presented an image of American society in which democracy had learned to exist peacefully with an ever-expanding role for the expert, and that in providing such an image they also provided a justification for the power and the glory of the expert society. Similarly the newer revisionist writers, people like Katz, Karier, and Spring, are said to be guilty of the same presentism because, in their concern to address the issues of racism and discrimi- nation, they perceived the educational past as but a prelude, an unbroken con- tinuum that has now reached its nadir in the present. In doing so, it is said, they have helped to undercut the very basis of public support that the schools so desperately need – a conclusion that in spirit brings us back to the concerns of the older foundation scholars.

What are we to think about this cycle, about this strange ritual of the historians in which each must gesture to the purity of the discipline before addressing education through concerns that have been informed by present conditions? Might one not begin to think that perhaps the activity of education is so intricate a part of the human enterprise that our understanding of the past is largely initiated because of our uncertainty about the present? And might one also think that where one stands in the present will influence what is seen of the past and also the way that it is interpreted? Ironically, historians have not overlooked this insight either. Presentism always belongs to someone else. One person's present-ism is another's unique framework and individual values; values that generate historical description, but about which the historian has little to say.

Presentism is not a problem. It is a condition. The problem is when the interpretation of the past is put forward without any reasonable consideration of obvious and alternative interpretations (the kind of consideration that should be second nature to philosophers) and when it is assumed without question that ideas and events had the same meaning for those who lived in the past as they do for those who are writing about them from the present. The dangers of educa-tional history are these and not any abstract sin called "presentism."

If educational history runs the danger of failing to provide alternative explana-tions, of indelicately mixing facts and values, of confusing exposition, in-terpretation, and evaluation, and of embedding criticism within description, educational philosophy may be said to be endangered in a different way. While philosophers may have provided us with clearer understandings of such impor-tant concepts as indoctrination and equality, they have failed to consider the historical context in which such concepts took on importance. The concept of equality of educational opportunity, for example, is analyzed in isolation from any meaningful context and hence without any consideration given to the rela-tionship between the development of this ideal and the development of newer forms of technology, changes in the structure of work, and the breakdown of an older, more stable rural structure. Similarly, the idea of human rights is analyzed by these same philosophers without consideration given to the concern to main-tain an active and articulate public to serve as a check on government, a concern that clearly formed an important part of the context for the early discussions about human rights in the American experience. As philosophers have ignored the historical context in which these concepts were developed, so too have they lost the practical significance of the concepts that they have undertaken to ad-dress. Thus in examining the idea of human rights they have often failed to ask whether or not such rights are sufficient to sustain an articulate public in an age in which great disparity in wealth coupled with advances in communication tech-nology have made the manipulation of the many by the few all too common. By failing to understand the contextual background, philosophers have often ne-glected to consider some of the very basic functions of education, as we will see in Chapter 6.

Because of their implicitly held belief in the integrated nature of educational studies, it was easier for the older foundation scholars to act in recognition of the premise that history needs philosophy and philosophy needs history whereas the study of education needs and alters them both. What is more questionable is their belief that a focus on schooling is the best vehicle for integrating these and other studies.

The recognition that educational scholarship is not exclusively defined by public schooling and that not every past educative relationship is best understood as the prehistory of universal, compulsory schooling is one of the key intellectual factors that marks the shift between the older and the newer scholarship. Yet as attempts are made to extend the focus beyond the public schools, it has become increasingly difficult to maintain the integrated nature of educational understanding. We can see this difficulty in the implicit split that has occurred between philosophy and history. Hence, as historical studies have expanded beyond the public school, they have brought about new interest in related areas of study such as child-rearing practices, working class socialization, and other fields that have been conceived of broadly as cultural and social transmission. However, philosophers in attempting to clarify our understanding of the concept of education have distinguished it from related but different concepts, such as indoctrination, training, socialization, and most others that can, in contrast to the focus of the historians, be broadly classified as *merely* cultural transmission. Therefore, as history has moved in one direction, some philosophers implicitly have denied that this direction still constitutes the study of education. Thus, if it was once the case that the public schools provided too narrow a focus for educational studies, it is now the case that there is no single focus, and the apparent success of each of the disciplines has further split them apart.

It might be said that this new-found pluralism is a good sign, that it is evidence of the maturity of educational studies and a recognition that different disciplines are designed to do different things. All this may be granted, but one question still remains to be answered: What is it that makes a study a study of education? As we have seen, some historians believe they have an answer to this puzzle. The history of education, they say, takes as its domain any institution or practice that is concerned with cultural transmission and socialization. Yet it is important to understand that the concepts of cultural transmission and socialization have themselves been borrowed from other foundational disciplines and that there are important aspects of the educational relationship that the traditional use of them leaves out, allowing only the ingenuity and common sense of the historian to bring them back into consideration. Most important, in their focus on habit formation and fixed belief systems, these concepts leave out of consideration the question of the nature of human knowledge, and they have difficulty accounting for the development of new cultural forms.

If it is knowledge that such concepts have left out of the picture, it is knowledge that the philosophers have included with vengeance, often reifying it with such passion that only a graduate of Oxford or some of the better Ivy League liberal arts colleges could truly be thought of as educated. Some philosophers have paid so much attention to "the forms of knowledge" and have spent so much time justifying the liberal arts curriculum[1] that they have forgotten just how well most people are able to function simply by understanding the basic rules of social interaction, rules that the behavior of other individuals and the arrangements of dominant social institutions reinforce daily, providing all of the evidence needed to stamp such knowledge with the philosophically prized label of a *justified true belief.*

A new focus for educational understanding

There is one movement in education that does have potential for reunifying educational studies, and this book is intended to help further that unification. It is a movement that has had some influence in a variety of fields, including history, economics, sociology, curriculum studies, and, to a lesser extent, philosophy. This is the movement that, initiated from the potitical left, emphasizes the reproductive role of education. However, whereas most of the recent studies on this issue have treated social and cultural reproduction as but a finding of empirical research and have not been concerned with clarifying the domain of educational understanding, I argue in the book for taking it, rather than schooling, as the domain of educational studies itself. That is, I believe that education is best understood by recognizing that one of the functions of any society is that of maintaining intergenerational continuity – that is, of maintaining its identity as a society across generations and even in the context of many possible and significant changes, and that it is the activity and institution of education, both formal and informal, that carries on this function. This recognition should enable us both to understand education in a different way and to build upon some of the more recent critical studies.

This insight is not new but is shared by Plato, Dewey, Marx, and other traditional scholars. Yet to suggest that social reproduction is the appropriate object for educational research is not to say, except in very general terms, what it is that is being reproduced, or what it is that should be reproduced. It is only to provide, in general outline, an idea of what educational scholarship seeks to understand.

In order to bring the object of social reproduction more clearly into focus and to anticipate the later discussion of it, I want to look at an example of a study in which social reproduction is also central, not as the *focus* of educational research, but as the *finding* of the educational researcher. I am referring to Bowles and Gintis's important work, *Schooling in Capitalist America.*[2] Here the authors see as one of the major limitations on American educational reform the role that schools are expected to serve in reproducing the relationships of production that are so important in the maintenance of a capitalist society. Such things as the hierarchical character of schools, the different personality traits developed by children from different social classes and in different curricula, and the relative immobility of certain classes within the society are explained by them in terms of the function these serve in maintaining the capitalist relations of production.

For our purpose the point about this research that is important to observe is that it functions not simply as a neutral empirical analysis of the relationship between education and production in capitalist society, but also as a critique of those relationships. And this is to Bowles and Gintis's credit. However, the question that I want to explore is: What is it besides the relationships of production that is being reproduced in the society such that Bowles and Gintis might *expect* that their analysis will be taken as a critique rather than as a neutral description of the way the educational machine works? Let me provide an example in order to illustrate this puzzle, and then we can move on to exploring the major point further.

In the British Broadcasting Corporation's television series *Upstairs Downstairs,* which follows the life of an upper-class family and its servants from about the turn of the century to the Depression, there is an episode that takes place during the boom times of the 1920s in which one of the servants, Frederick, decides to take leave of the household and pursue a career in the movies. The butler, Hudson, who represents the bearer of traditional culture, is deeply disturbed by his underling's announcement and tries, unsuccessfully, to dissuade Frederick from his decision.

Now, what is going on in this exchange is a clash of world views, one in which the value of a career is being pitted against an older ideal of station and place. For Frederick, a career in the movies represents the possibility for individual growth and riches, for personal reward, and recognition. For Hudson, it represents the breakdown of the traditional structure and the wrenching of a person from an environment of mutual service where self-identity is achieved through serving and being served by a visible household community.

Frederick's decision is to Hudson both imprudent and foolish. It represents a challenge to Hudson's sense of rightness. For Frederick, however, careers rightfully belong to all who have the drive, the skill, the intelligence, and the daring to grab them. They are the prizes that await the talented who are willing to venture outside the security of the household. Hudson's is a world not of equal chances but of mutual service, one in which the ideal of "my station and its duties" still has meaning. We know that Hudson's world was in the process of breaking down and that it had already crumbled for the majority of British workers whose station had been transformed into a position in the wage-labor force. Even those upstairs felt this breakdown. For some, like Georgina, it was expressed in a purposelessness that at times crossed the boundary into decadence. For others, such as the head of the household, James, it eventually lead to a recognition of his own violation of the norm of mutuality and then to suicide.

Through all of this, Hudson persists as the bearer of the culture to the bitter end. But what he is left with is a distorted picture of the way the social world is and the way it works. Yet does Frederick's flight from service, represented by his decision to pursue a career in the movies, represent a truer picture than Hudson's? And what are we to say about the moral justification of Frederick's decision? Frederick is not heard from again, and so we can only guess at the answers to these questions. It would not be too difficult, however, to understand Frederick's decision as one in which the ideal of mutual service had turned into the horror of a dead-end job, and where the only service remaining was to stand witness over a decaying corpse. The vigor of life was to be found elsewhere. It was to be found in the idea of growth brought from ''the new world'' and transplanted in the old. To take leave of that world of mutual service was not, as Hudson perceived, to violate life's moral boundaries. It was to recognize and to support a new morality, one in which talent, vigor, risk, and ingenuity are rewarded *without limits*.

Given this clash of world views, we can now ask: How is it that *Schooling in Capitalist America* can be understood as the critique that Bowles and Gintis intended it to be? For surely, Hudson would not understand it as critique, or at least not the critique that the authors intend; rather, it is Frederick's moral vision, one that accepts the empirical and moral view of equal opportunity found in liberal thought, that allows the description given in *Schooling* to work as a critique. Given Frederick's world view, *Schooling* can show that his vision is as listless and moribund as Hudson's. In other words, in order to critique liberal society, Bowles and Gintis must rely upon the fact that the moral consciousness of that society has been reproduced in the intuitions of its members. Frederick represents a moment of this reproduction.

This conflict between Frederick and Hudson can be used to sketch the major features of education as social reproduction in anticipation of Chapter 8, and to display the aspects of social life that the educational process strives to reproduce. There are two things that are at issue in this conflict. The first is the skills that are thought appropriate for an individual with a certain background to acquire, and the second is the way in which it is *thought* proper for skills of different kinds to be related to one another. These two issues suggest the fundamental aspects of education as social reproduction. First, there is the reproduction of skills or what I call, for reasons that I intend to clarify later, skill clusters. Second, there is the reproduction of consciousness that includes an understanding of the rights and privileges associated with the ''legitimate'' exercise of a given skill cluster. Every society will have some arrangement whereby it strives to reproduce these two aspects of its life across generations. And even where more critical forms of education are undertaken, they will involve a reflection back upon these primary moments. Yet the reproduction of skills and the reproduction of consciousness are not divorced from one another but are connected in a number of ways that provide rich areas for both social change and educational understanding. We will look more closely at some of these connections in Chapter 7. It remains here to draw out some of the implications of this focus for educational scholarship.

Education as social reproduction

Every society has certain ways in which some skills are clustered together into a particular social role and other skills excluded from that role. Moreover, whereas certain values and understandings may be widely shared among all members of a society, there will be others that will be quite specific to those who exercise a specific social role.

Formal education, with which traditional educational scholarship has largely been concerned, can be understood as a consciously designed and institutionalized system of instruction that functions to establish or maintain a structured set of skill clusters and the consciousness (understandings and values) associated with them. Later, for purposes of shorthand, I will refer to this structured set of skill clusters and consciousness as the knowledge code of a society. For now, however, it is important simply to note that the study of formal education is but one aspect of the study of social reproduction in general. Formal institutions arise at specific times in specific places to perform specific functions in relation to the reproduction of specific skills and the reproduction of a specific consciousness.

With this brief sketch of the domain of educational understanding, we can return to two themes that have been identified with the older group of foundation scholars – the integrated nature of educational studies and the relationship between theory and practice. Given the perspective of hindsight, it is not difficult to see that these themes were connected too closely to a belief in the liberating possibilities of public schooling, and that too little notice was given to the nature of the society in which schooling occurred. However, the themes themselves can be extracted from any particular set of beliefs. I will begin with the question of the integrated nature of educational understanding.

The important point about the integrated nature of educational understanding is not the particular way in which various disciplines might decide to cut up the conceptual domain of education. Rather, it is that by recognizing that there is a reasonably clear domain for educational studies, the nature of the disciplines and their problematics are altered in a similar direction. A clearer understanding of the domain provides educational studies with a more coherent research program regardless of the particular discipline through which it happens to be articulated at any given time. Where any particular study may begin will obviously be influenced by the discipline and background of the researcher. However, all of the studies would be designed to inform us about the nature of the knowledge code of a given society and the way in which that code is processed by different individuals and groups, through different frames and with different implications for the reproduction of specific skills and modes of understanding. For traditional pedagogical research, this means that problems of teaching and learning would be examined not only to decide upon effective methods of teaching, but also to understand the way in which a given knowledge code influences our understand-ing of pedagogical ends and means. For example, it would mean that learning theory and research would try not only to account for differences in achievement, but also to account for how those differences influence the way in which various groups of youngsters come to understand their own role in the larger scheme of things. It would examine the way in which knowledge in the classroom is defined for different groups of students and the influence that this has on their self-understanding – on their understanding of the kinds of people and learners they are, and how this understanding may or may not facilitate their later acceptance or rejection of their social role. The integrative quality of educational studies also points beyond the classroom and suggests that the body of research in education should attempt to understand the transmission process in the context of an exam-ination of the knowledge code of a given society and the relationship of different individual and group frameworks to that code.

An integrated notion of educational studies would be concerned to understand the aims and processes of social reproduction as they occur within different settings at different times and through different frames. It would be concerned to understand how dominant and subordinate frameworks interact with one another to produce generational variations in work and consciousness, and it would attempt to identify the possibilities for progressive changes in light of the re-straints of historical factors and contemporary material condition. It is this last point that brings us to the second theme of the foundationists' concern – the relationship between theory and practice.

Ultimately, educational scholarship as the study of social reproduction molds the disciplines because it recognizes that value considerations cannot be divorced from the way in which reproduction is understood and that the researcher is also a product of a certain set of values that have been socially reproduced. The con-cepts used, the problem studied, and the factors highlighted are to be understood in part by an understanding of the prominent values and concerns that dominate both the society and the researcher who dwells within it. Thus, educational scholarship requires a degree of reflection that some other areas may not, and it requires an ability to capture values that influence the direction of education but that are all too often concealed in the descriptive posture of social science research. It is for this reason that the early chapters of this book attempt to highlight values that are generally concealed by the dominant research traditions.

Yet educational understanding requires more than simply the reflection upon, and identification of, a set of values. It requires, as the foundationists recog-nized, the articulation and assessment of those values in the realm of practice in which only some of them can be realized.

It requires, however, that this be done without losing sight of the larger goal of human liberation. It is at the intersection of the ideal with the possible that practical activity is judged. As Marx observed, "men make their own history, but they do not make it just as they please. They do not make it under circumstances chosen by themselves but under circumstances directly encountered, given and transmitted from the past.'' In other words, we are both bound by past forms of reproduction and creators of new ones. To forget this simple fact as we attempt to understand the educational process, past and present, is to misconceive the nature of that enterprise, to inevitably distort our perception of it, and to run the risk of misdirecting it in the future.

The purpose and organization of this work

The purpose of this book is to understand the way in which social reproduction constitutes the domain of educational studies. It is also to shift the focus of educational scholarship from schooling per se to the process and forms of intergenerational continuity and change. However, this general purpose can only be served by examining specific instances of education and relating these to more universal themes. Thus education will always involve the reproduction of skills and the reproduction of consciousness, but there are any number of specific skills and modes of consciousness that may be possibilities for reproduction at any given moment. Although the focus of this book is on the process of reproduction, much of its attention is directed toward the thoughts of people who have written about schools. Thus whereas the focus is shifted from schooling to intergenerational continuity and change, recognition is given to the fact that in contemporary society schooling is a major institution for guiding or reinforcing social reproduction. By examining the work of influential educational researchers and scholars, we can begin to understand the mode of consciousness assumed to be appropriate to reproduce in schools.

The point needs to be emphasized that in shifting the focus of educational understanding from schooling to social reproduction, we are not proposing to neglect the analysis of schooling itself. Rather, the recognition that in contemporary society schooling constitutes a major vehicle for social reproduction means that much attention will be devoted to the practices that are carried on in schools. This focus does suggest, however, that a full understanding of the educational function of schooling in contemporary society requires that it be placed in the social and historical context in which the process of intergenerational continuity and change is played out in full. When educational scholars fail to locate the process of schooling in its historical and social context, the result is that they inappropriately place themselves outside the process itself and fail to see just how their own activity is internally related to the practices of schooling. In other words, they neglect the fact that their own work serves as an important factor in determining the skills and consciousness that are to be ''legitimately'' reproduced in schools. Moreover, they also fail to see that their own voice has been legitimized by the very institution and process that they have now turned to examine.

Part I of this book examines the way in which this self-misunderstanding of the educational research community can distort our understanding of schooling. It is the research community that is concerned with finding effective means to realize ends that are generally taken for granted. By looking closely at the work of this community, we can begin to identify these taken-for-granted ends that constitute the object of social reproduction. Hence, the early chapters in this work examine the empirical tradition as the dominant movement in educational research. Chapter 2 explores the IQ controversy as one example of empirical research. The point of this chapter is to demonstrate that quantitative empirical research relies on an unacknowledged interpretive dimension that is generated by assumptions about the value and reproduction of certain kinds of knowledge and by further assumptions about its proper rate of growth. Chapter 3 looks more closely at the political and value assumptions that underly the researcher's interpretation of variations in IQ scores. The fourth chapter looks at behaviorism, a movement in empirical research that appears to be in conflict with the IQ movement. This chapter explores the many values that are shared by both IQ researchers and behaviorists. Chapter 5 then examines the empirical tradition more broadly and in light of the taken-for-granted goals of the educational system as a whole.

The IQ controversy has a long history in American educational research, and many significant challenges have been directed against the view that IQ tests measure intelligence. While some of the earliest of these challenges came from philosophers such as John Dewey or journalists like Walter Lippmann, the more recent ones have come from scientists such as Noam Chomsky, Stephen Gould, or Jerry Hirsh. Contemporary philosophers have not been mute on this issue. Yet most of the philosophical challenges have been directed at the assumptions about the scientific grounding of IQ tests, and very little has been said about the interpretive and the value issues that the tests involve. Educational philsophy, the area that one might expect to have the greatest concern with this issue, has largely been silent when it comes to analyzing the underlying values behind specific empirical research. This silence is a sign that much of the earlier philosophical tradition and its critical thrust has been lost. Chapter 6 examines the recent philosophical tradition in education and analyzes its failure to serve as a critical counterpoint to the empirical tradition.

Chapter 7 turns away from traditional, empirical research and looks at a consciously critical tradition that has arisen recently in educational history. Although this tradition has developed many penetrating insights into the nature of the educational system, its inability to provide an explicitly theoretical context for its analysis has left it conceptually unstable and open to quick and easy criticisms. In this chapter some of these possible criticisms are explored, as are the different frameworks from which educational judgments can be made. This chapter leads into Part II of the book, in which a theoretical framework is developed that hopefully can be used to understand the nature of the educational process and to advance a critical examination of the norms that govern it.

Chapter 8 explores the idea of education as social reproduction and develops some of the concepts that are involved in understanding education in these terms. Chapters 9 and 10 critically examine claims that are made about the access that different individuals and groups have to the knowledge code. Thus one of the concerns of these chapters is the question of who shall be educated and at what level. Both chapters are also concerned to explore some of the factors that are involved in accepting or rejecting a given code. Chapter 9 develops this analysis in a specific area – medical education – and examines some of the factors that are involved when a prevailing knowledge code functions "successfully" without significant challenge. Chapter 10, on education in developing societies, looks at the other side of this issue and examines some of the factors that may be involved when a knowledge code begins to split apart.

The final chapter, on general education, concludes the book by reexamining the features of social reproduction in contemporary times and by proposing conditions required to reconstruct the role of education in contemporary Western society. In this chapter the concern is to open up possibilities for the development of a new code. Thus the focus is not on who shall be educated but rather what, given the tensions in the old code, will constitute the practice of education? In this chapter the treatment of the theory and practice of education is blended because of my belief that the way in which people come to understand their world has much to do with the practices they undertake to change it.

Those readers who would prefer to develop an overview before reading the chapters sequentially may be advised to read Chapters 8 and 11 first. The former develops the analytical framework of this study, whereas the latter provides the normative perspective that informs many of the earlier chapters. The chapters that preceded Chapter 8 are designed to show the limits of contemporary modes of educational scholarship, and a prior understanding of Chapter 8 will enable the reader to see how these deficiencies may be reduced. Chapters 9 and 10 should also be read with Chapter 8 in mind. They are intended to demonstrate how the analysis developed in Chapter 8 can be used to open up new questions and issues for the study of education. These chapters are also intended to show how the study of education as intergenerational continuity and change provides a different texture to the traditional modes of educational research and scholarship.

This last point is most important for understanding the intent of the first part of the book. Although this part is critical of existing modes of educational understanding, the criticism is not designed to dismiss these modes, but to show the need to contextualize them and to provide them with a coherent focus. We cannot, for example, give up the *account* of what is happening that is provided by traditional empirical research, but we do need to see how the *explanations* that often accompany such accounts serve as but an expression of the dominant mode of consciousness. Nor can we abandon the distinctions that philosophers have established between concepts such as "education" and "training," but we do need to understand that the significance of such distinctions requires that they be linked to the everyday activities of social life. Thus while such distinctions can be useful, any full analysis must connect the activities that they represent to the world and its possibilities as we find them. Similarly, the historical–interpretive mode provides an alternative framework that enables us to understand education as a human construction, rather than as simply a natural event. However, one needs also to understand how such a framework is generated and how it both relies upon and challenges the dominant form of consciousness.

There are some obvious ways in which these different traditions can serve as correctives to one another, but in the absence of a clear and common domain they more often ignore one another's orientation. Nevertheless, there is a sense in which each concentrates on a different moment of education as social reproduction. Empirical scholars largely focus on the reproduction of skills, although they do so by taking existing skill clusters for granted. The philosopher, in his or her concern for meaning and values, has begun to focus on key features of consciousness. However, this concern does not include a reflective analysis of the relationship between the pattern of skills found in a society and the form of consciousness that accompanies it. Indeed, the rigid distinction that is made between conceptual and empirical issues leaves the impression that our conceptual schemes are fixed and unrelated to any change in the empirical world. The historians do not challenge this impression directly. However, those of a critical bent do provide an alternative framework in which expressions of the dominant mode of consciousness are to be heard not as description, but as apology, and in the process they raise once-settled issues to the level of deliberation and debate. While this framework helps provide the perspective needed for intergenerational continuity and change to become an object of conscious deliberation, the process by which the framework itself is created remains obscure, and much of the critical force of its analysis appears to rest on conflicting norms.

In their attempt to provide an analysis of the educational process, each of the three traditions rests upon certain values that are usually only implicit in their treatment of educational issues. Once the study of education is seen as the examination of intergenerational continuity and change, and once it is recognized that the goal of such a study is to provide the tools needed for the self-formation of the public to take place, then value issues must be placed in a more prominent position where they can be discussed and debated. The full discussion of such values, however, must be able to see their roots in the pattern of activities through which work and social life are conducted in a given society.

Part I

The prevailing research traditions in education: Contemporary modes of understanding education

2 The empirical tradition and its limits for understanding education

The study of education is commonly thought of as only an applied area of research, one in which the methods of traditional disciplines are used to address school-related problems. Education is taken as an area of applied research because it is thought to have no methodological principles or conceptual domain of its own. Therefore, it must take as its problems those defined by the school and as its methods those developed by the established disciplines.[1] This view accepts without question the belief that methods or concepts developed in other areas and for other reasons are adequate to apply, without alteration, to the activity of education. In this chapter I will show the inadequacy of this belief. Subsequently I will articulate a framework that is more specifically related to education.

On the scope and limits of empirical educational research

There is a generally accepted distinction in educational theory between two different types of educational studies. First, there are those that are concerned primarily with empirical understanding. For example, such studies might examine whether providing rewards for successful learning or meting out punishment for failing to learn increases the likelihood of future learning. This is seen as an empirical issue, and the form of the question will be similar whether the area be traditional educational psychology, economics, or sociology. Second, there are those studies that are primarily interested in understanding the meaning of a concept and the way it is used. For example, the interest here would not be whether punishment improves learning, but rather what is entailed by the concept of "punishment" or the concept of "learning."[2] The distinction between empirical and conceptual studies has served as the boundary between different forms of traditional educational scholarship. The labor of educational scholarship has been divided between the behavioral and the social sciences' quest for general explanatory principles on the one hand and philosophy's attempt to understand concepts on the other hand. In this chapter and the next two chapters we will look at aspects of the empirical tradition. Subsequently, we will examine the philosophical tradition.

17

The applied nature of educational understanding is more apparent with the empirical tradition than it is with the philosophical one because these studies have consistently been addressed to school-related problems and because the guiding motif of such studies has been to develop more effective intervention strategies in order to achieve certain goals. Empirical studies range from research dealing with the IQ scores of different groups of children, to studies about effective teaching methods, to reports about how to most efficiently use the schools to meet the "manpower" requirements of a given society. Some of these studies, such as those concerned with the cognitive or moral stages of child development, are attempts to provide more elaborate maps of normal growth patterns that thereby may serve as guidelines in diagnostic procedures. Others, such as those that examine the effect of intelligence (as measured by IQ tests) on school achievement, are intended to increase understanding of the network of causal relationships that influence a given process and that must therefore be taken into account in developing strategies for intervention and change. Still others are more directly concerned with testing the efficacy of different class-room interventions.

Although traditional empirical studies differ in the way in which research is designed and implemented, they share the goal of developing appropriate interventions in order to better achieve or to correct deviations from a stipulated goal. More important, however, is the fact that the domain of educational research – in both its scope and its goals – is taken as unproblematic. The domain is the school and related areas that influence performance (such as the family background of the child). And the goal is to improve performance, where *improvement* is defined either by the school or by some larger "consensus" about the role of the school. This means that the problems that are set for educational research are normally placed within a practical framework, and that key concepts such as "achievement," "learning," and "education" itself are grounded within a practical rather than a theoretical context. Although the disciplines themselves may be called upon to address school-related issues and may therefore use concepts that have been defined within the disciplines, there is a filtering process that grants primary influence to those methods and concepts that appear congruent with the "practical reality" of the classroom or the school. The preeminence of educational psychology in educational research is understandable in terms of its tendency to leave everything but the individual child or the individual classroom unchanged and to accept as unproblematic the contextual features of the schools,[3] including the potitical economy in which they function.

Because such studies are intended to address practical problems, they are normally evaluated within a practical framework, and as is to be expected, the results vary according to the problem and the type of methods used. However, there is a broader framework by which to understand the limited perspective that this research provides for the understanding of education.

Whatever the particular methods that may be applied in empirical research, the dominant tradition has attempted to understand education through methods that are modeled after those employed in the natural sciences. Such an attempt entails certain assumptions about the nature of knowledge regarding a human enterprise such as education,[4] assumptions that have been recently challenged. Among these is the belief that there is little difference in principle between the methods appropriate for understanding objects of the natural world and those appropriate for the study of human beings.[5]

The challenges to this tradition have raised many questions about the extent to which there is an identity between the objects of the physical sciences and the objects of the social sciences. Such challenges have also questioned whether the ideas of replication and manipulation have the same meaning and force in each of these fields.[6] Yet there is a different kind of problem with the use of the natural science model. This involves the extent to which such studies can be, as their advocates claim, value-free. The practical framework within which these studies are conducted marks a sharp contrast with the natural sciences that are intended to serve as a model for this kind of educational research. In order to understand the limitations that this framework places upon educational understanding, we need to look more closely at the belief that education research modeled after research in the natural sciences can be value-free.

The belief in the neutrality of science means two things. In the first place it means that science treats the world of facts, the world as it *is,* and attempts to find general principles that will help to explain that world. When we are most successful in developing these principles, they can be expressed in the form of scientific laws. Matters of value, on the other hand, are not for science to deal with. This view is reflected in statements like "Science can show us the path to a given goal, but it cannot tell us whether that goal is worth pursuing." In the second place, the claim about the neutrality of science means that the public nature of the scientist's procedures are such as to offer a check against the scientist's own individual values influencing the conclusions of the study. Now whether the claim about the neutrality of science, even in the physical realm, is unproblematic is an issue that others have raised, but that will not be addressed here.[7] What is at issue here is whether, once these procedures are placed within a practical framework, the claim to neutrality can still be upheld.

Consider one very clear and obvious way in which the neutrality claim cannot be maintained successfully. In a practical setting the institutional framework already places the researcher in the service of some set of assumed ends. Even if the only charge is to gather statistical information about some aspect of the educational enterprise, say the relative achievement of black and white students, the researcher has accepted both some received idea about what constitutes important categories for grouping learners and a stipulated measure of what is to constitute achievement. This initial starting point must reflect some received definition, and this is often that of the formal or informal policymaking network. Yet there is another, more subtle, and ultimately more important way in which the practical framework circumscribes the way in which a scientist can be neutral about values.

The difficulty can be seen in the following way. One of the essential characteristics about a human value, although clearly not the only one, is that it is a matter over which some kind of choice can be made. While we may not consciously choose all of the things that we do value, one of the things that makes something a value instead of simply a fact of life or a law of nature is that it is the kind of thing that conceivably could be brought to consciousness and chosen or rejected. Yet of all of the paths that could be chosen, the practical frame largely limits our focus to those that provide the most obvious and immediate opportunity for manipulation. Others that, given a different framework, could be perceived as alternatives either are relegated to background factors that are not considered or else are elevated to causal factors that are treated as if they were unchangeable. This is the case, as we will see, with the controversy over IQ scores and school achievement. Here intelligence as measured by IQ tests is treated as a causal factor, and the standards by which achievement is determined are treated as a background factor. If we accept this view, we are confronted with the choice of teaching children inefficiently or of using IQ tests to group them more accurately into different categories of learning ability and of then applying the pedagogical techniques that are claimed to be most appropriate for each group. That these techniques might have the effect of increasing the differences between the groups is not raised as a problem to be considered. The point here is that the practical framework circumscribes scientific neutrality by limiting conceivable items of choice to those whose manipulability is apparent within an established institutional framework and therefore reduces the number of choices to those that are consistent with that framework.[8] The researchers who take this approach function within that framework, thus their own work constitutes an important component of the educational system.

Within the practical framework there is nothing wrong with limiting the set of choices in this way, and whether an objection should be raised in any specific instance is to be determined by the values that are included and excluded from the set. Yet in order to be able to even perceive the values that are included and excluded we are required to move beyond the practical framework and to take a more critical stance. The adequacy of this stance will be determined in part by how well it recognizes and accounts for the institutional framework and the alternatives that are constituted by it. The point that needs to be emphasized here, however, is the fact that empirical techniques alone limit our understanding of education to the practical frame by sorting and classifying different educational events according to the promise that they hold for manipulation and intervention within a given institution. The claim to value neutrality by educational science is, if accurate, only so within the context of those procedures that it singles out for possible manipulation, and which it therefore *identifies* as candidates for values. The claim is not accurate in terms of those conceivable items of choice that are relegated to the status of background or causal factors and that require a more critical orientation to identify.

The difficulty that empirical educational science has in maintaining the claim to value neutrality is to be understood as a result of assuming that the school constitutes the major domain of educational research and of failing to develop a domain that is conceptually independent of schooling. Thus this form of research begins by *uncritically* embedding its methodology within an already established and ongoing set of practices and problems. To the extent that its concepts are developed independently of the educational process, they are borrowed from the parent discipline and then applied to the school context and the values that are already implicit in that context. The recent controversy over the use and interpretation of IQ test scores provides a clear example of this process, and it is to that issue that we now turn.

The IQ issue as an example of the limitations of empirical research*

Purpose of the section

This and the next sections attempt to understand, as an example of the limitations of empirical research, the normative framework within which the question of the validity of the IQ tests has been debated and that has largely gone unchallenged even by many of the most severe critics of such tests.[9] Rather what *has* been in question ever since the debate came to public attention is whether or not an IQ test is a sufficiently sensitive instrument to detect significant differences in mental ability. Thus, for example, as early as 1922 Walter Lippmann, in criticizing IQ Tests, proposed as an alternative the development of a series of individual vocational tests that would better determine a person's aptitude for a given occupation.[10] Although Lippmann provided a challenge to the preciseness of the tests, he failed to challenge the belief that an accurate assessment of mental attributes (along with perhaps other personality characteristics) alone can tell us how a person should be educated.

Contemporary critics of tests have added to the earlier analysis by raising other questions about the scientific claims of test defenders. They have pointed to serious problems in the definitions of intelligence and to problems in the genetic model that some testers have adopted. They have also noted the cultural bias of

*This section was developed with the assistance of Stephen Norris and part of it was first presented at the Boston Philosophy of Science Colloquium, December 13, 1977. It has been informed by discussions with Jerry Hirsch.

the tests and questioned the assumption that *g*, or general intelligence, can be derived from the analysis of test scores.[11]

As penetrating as much of the criticism of IQ tests has been, the critics generally have overlooked some of the important issues that are involved in moving from the claim that a child has performed at a certain level on an IQ test to the claim that such a child should be educated in a certain way. To address the issue on the empirical level alone is to leave intact the very normative framework that provides the debate with the significance that it has.[12] Yet the debate is taken up *as important* precisely because we understand in a general way what is at stake when an individual or a group is judged as having a higher or lower than average intelligence, and we also know that for many people the stakes are high. The very fact that it is the empirical and not the normative issues that have been raised as significant questions for debate is an indication of the significance that scientific approaches have acquired in addressing educational issues.

Before the normative dimensions of this research can be displayed, it is necessary to show the extent to which areas of choice are blocked as the advocates of these tests render essentially interpretive issues into seemingly simple factual claims. The purpose of this section is to remove the objective aura from some of these claims and hence to understand the extent to which they do indeed require an interpretation and thus to reopen up some of the avenues that have been blocked. Here we look at two such areas. First, we examine some of the problems that *are* involved in moving from a claim about the intellectual capacity of an individual (or group) to a claim about how that individual (or group) should be taught. Second, we examine some of the difficulties that are involved in viewing a response to an item on an IQ test as indicating a certain kind of performance or skill. In this way we can see the extent to which claims put forth as factual are really an interpretation of a certain sort and how the appeal to science has hidden this fact. Once these claims are understood for what they are, then, in the next chapter, we will be able to examine the institutional values that generate a particular interpretation.

Jensen on Level I and Level II abilities

Arthur Jensen concludes his famous 1969 article on what he believes is an optimistic note. He argues that there are two distinctly different kinds of learning abilities. The first, which he labels "Level I" or "associative ability," involves what he describes as the "neural registration and consolidation of stimulus inputs and the formation of associations."[13] "There is," he explains, "relatively little transformation of the input, so there is a high correspondence between the forms of the stimulus input and the form of the response output."[14] In nontechnical terms, Level I learning is what we normally call rote learning, and Jensen claims that it is tested by a number of subtests on the standard IQ examinations, the paradigm being the digit span test.[15]

The second kind of ability Jensen labels "Level II" or "conceptual ability," which he says involves "self-initiated elaboration and transformation of the stimulus input before it eventuates in an overt response."[16] Here he cites conceptual learning and problem solving as good examples where "the subject must actively manipulate the input to arrive at the output."[17] He believes that such ability is "best measured by intelligence tests with a low 'cultural loading' and a high loading on 'g' [general intelligence]," and cites as an example of such a test the Raven Progressive Matrices.[18]

After describing these two different kinds of abilities, Jensen reports his findings as follows:

> Some of the low SES [socioeconomic status] children . . . do very well on our [associative] learning tests, but do not have higher IQ's on less culturally loaded tests of "g," like the Progressive Matrices. It appears that we are dealing here with two kinds of abilities – associative learning ability [Level I] and cognitive or conceptual learning and problem-solving ability [Level II].[19]

Jensen also reports that he has found that "Level I associative learning tasks correlate very substantially with IQ among middle-class children but have a very low correlation with IQ among lower-class children."[20] Level I learning, he writes, appears "necessary but not sufficient for Level II."[21] It is largely from these findings that Jensen draws his pedagogical recommendations.

Jensen begins by observing that schools historically evolved in "populations having a predominantly middle-class pattern of abilities"[22] and therefore they tend to place greater emphasis upon cognitive learning to the neglect of associative learning.[23] Jensen then notes that this emphasis is unfortunate and works to the disadvantage of many low-IQ youngsters. As he puts it: "many of the basic skills can be learned by various means, and an educational system that puts inordinate emphasis on only one mode or style of learning will obtain meager results from the children who do not fit this pattern."[24] He therefore proposes that all the basic skills could be learned by children with normal Level I learning ability, and then suggests that low-IQ youngsters should be taught in an associative way while youngsters with higher IQs be taught conceptually.[25]

Given all of the other controversial aspects of Jensen's article, an article that stimulated much debate about intellectual abilities among different races, it is easy to overlook the problem that this proposal entails. Indeed, if it could be shown, as one more recent research study suggests, that there is really no substantial genetic difference affecting the IQ scores of black and white children,[26] and had the controversy over the black–white variation in IQ scores not been raised, his proposal likely would have been applauded as encouraging the development of diverse programs that are carefully planned to meet adequately diagnosed needs. However, in evaluating his proposal, we need to recognize that there are different kinds of diversity. The kind that is usually applauded recognizes that different objects are meaningful to different culture groups, and it tries to use culturally meaningful material to develop important skills. Whether such skills, upon careful analysis, would be different from culture to culture remains here an open issue. Another kind of diversity, the one Jensen advocates, simply projects youngsters into different social roles and then trains them into behavior patterns and skills appropriate to those roles.

Yet even if, for the sake of argument, we accept not only his reporting about children's test scores but also all of his claims about IQ measuring some kind of intellectual capacity, we are not compelled to accept his pedagogical proposal. The first thing to notice is that the proposal follows easily from the findings only if we interpret the notion of the intellectual capacity measured by the test in a certain way. It follows only if we mean by the claim that "IQ tests measure intellectual capacity" that there is a level of conceptual development beyond which a person cannot go, and that an IQ test measures that absolute limit.[27] A way to think of this interpretation is to envisage Piaget's stages of mental development as analogous to something that is measured by a score on an IQ test, but then to think also that different people are born with different capacities and that these *measurable* capacities determine which stage any particular person would be able to reach. This interpretation is insinuated by Jensen and others,[28] but it is never fully addressed. Yet it is only on this interpretation that Jensen's pedagogical proposals follow in any direct way from his reported findings about IQ scores. The second interpretation is much different in its possible implications, and this interpretation is simply that a person with a higher score on an IQ test can learn faster than a person with a lower one. With this distinction in mind, we can begin to see how implicit normative concerns drive Jensen's interpretation of his research.

Jensen uses the argument for "diversity" to support his view that low- and high-IQ children should be taught differently. He argues that in fact low-IQ children can learn many of the same things that high-IQ children can learn, but that they must learn them in different ways. Whereas high-IQ children can be taught essential skills in a conceptual or problem-solving manner, low-IQ children are best taught in an associative way. However, once we see that the idea of capacity as measured by IQ tests need not display an absolute limit to what a person can learn, but may indicate only speed of learning, then we can see that there is a serious problem with Jensen's proposal. His proposal rests on the assumption that a strong distinction can be made between *the way* in which a child is taught and *what* it is that the child learns. It is this assumption that allows Jensen to speak as if children would be learning the same skills, but through different methods. Now on the level of common sense, this is not an unreasonable assumption to make. After all, children can be taught to read in a number of different ways. Yet on a deeper level, the assumption becomes more problematic. It would seem that when such radically different teaching styles as the ones Jensen proposes are used, children are not only learning something about a particular subject matter, but they are also learning something about *learning* as well. In Jensen's proposal it would seem that while some children are learning how to learn in a conceptual and problem-solving fashion, others are learning how to learn in an associative and rote manner.[29]

The normative or critical force of the observation that Jensen's proposal leaves some children learning how to learn in a conceptual fashion and others in an associative way depends not only on whether someone accepts IQ scores as an indication of intelligence, but also upon the particular interpretation that is given to these scores. In other words, if the score on an IQ test is taken to indicate a conceptual level beyond which an individual cannot go, then Jensen's proposal may simply be taken as following from the natural order of things as he suggests and the observation should not likely be taken as a criticism. However, if the score on an IQ examination is indicative only of the speed at which an individual learns something, then the most that can be said, assuming the accuracy of his data, is that some children show a *tendency* to learn in a conceptual way, and that other children show a *tendency* to learn in an associative manner. This does not, however, answer the normative question of whether, given the possibility of doing so, it is desirable to teach children who display a tendency to think in an associative manner how to think in a conceptual way.

Jensen himself is of little help on this issue since he says almost nothing about what factors constitute conceptual modes of thinking, and therefore we have no way of knowing whether that which he describes as conceptual skills could, in fact, be taught. This neglect is not surprising given the tendency of testers to substitute, for discussion about the *nature* of intelligent activity, discussions about how to *measure* the "intellectual capacities" of different people. Jensen does, however, provide some clues to what he takes to be conceptual skills by citing the kinds of tests that he believes best measure them, but it is only by looking at the questions actually asked in the tests and trying to understand why some responses are accepted as correct and others not that we can begin to get an idea of what Jensen has in mind when he speaks of conceptual skills. Although this question should be viewed as but a preliminary one, it nevertheless must be addressed before one might ask in what, if any, sense can it be said that an IQ test measures the limits for conceptual or abstract thinking. In other words, before one can begin to examine whether these limits are absolute and fixed, or whether at best they simply indicate variations in the speed at which certain skills are learned, one needs to know the nature of these conceptual skills. This requires that we look closely at some of the items that have been identified as testing conceptual rather than rote ability. In the absence of a precise and systematic claim by the testmakers, we are forced to examine the tests themselves and thereby attempt to understand the nature of the conceptual skills that they seem to be calling for.[30] Unfortunately, there are a number of factors that make this task more difficult than it may initially appear.

First, although a number of test items are thoughtfully constructed, others have serious problems. Many have marked answers correct that could easily be viewed as wrong, and others have marked answers wrong that could just as easily be viewed as correct. In many cases there is no identifable criterion for giving credit for one response and not another. In some instances the directions given to the test-taker call for one kind of response whereas the standards for grading the test call for another. Only when such items are reconstructed in a way that seems reasonable can we even begin an examination of the conceptual skills involved in answering them correctly. Yet such a reconstruction itself requires an interpretation of what the testmaker intended, but inadequately executed.

Second, because we are interested in conceptual skills we must select out and eliminate any item from consideration that seems to depend largely on rote learning ability for a correct response. To some extent we can rely here on Jensen's views about which subtests are primarily tests of rote skills, but as we shall see below, the distinction between rote and conceptual learning is more difficult to make than Jensen would lead us to believe.

Third, many items on IQ tests are similar in important ways to items on achievement tests, thereby making it difficult to judge what is being tested. Thus, we must eliminate such items from consideration[31] before looking at those that might call for conceptual responses pure and simple.

Fourth, because Jensen leans so heavily on what are often called culture-fair tests, we need to look at samples of these tests. We have examined the Cattell and the Raven, which, Jensen notes, are especially useful for measuring g. Before examining the conceptual skills that these tests require, we have to determine, first, whether they in fact call for the same kinds of skills as do the standard IQ tests, and second, the extent to which they might eliminate interference arising from material that is more familiar to members of one culture than to members of another.

On the distinction between associative and conceptual learning

In his discussion of the difference between associative and conceptual learning, Jensen fails to provide a clear-cut distinction between these two modes. He does, however, provide some clues. He says, for example, that associative learning "involves the neural registration and consolidation of stimulus inputs and the formation of associations."[32] He also says that in associative learning "there is relatively little transformation of the input, so there is a high correspondence between the form of the stimulus input and the form of the response output."[33] The problem, of course, with these two statements is that they have reference to different things. The first refers to a neurological occurrence that no IQ test is sufficient to tap, whereas the second refers, after the psychological jargon is removed, to the form of the question and the form of the response. Jensen is more helpful, however, when he provides examples of what he takes to be indicators of rote ability in the tests. He refers to the digit memory test, which asks the subject to repeat a series of numbers (anywhere from two to six numbers in each series on the Stanford–Binet, depending on age). The subject must repeat each number in its proper order and must repeat all numbers to receive credit for the item. Hence, if the examiner says "four–seven–nine–three–six–four," the subject must repeat the same numbers in the same order. Thus, what Jensen seems to mean by associative ability is any correct response where the subject is expected to add nothing, either in form or in content, that was not already contained in the original question.

Once the criterion for associative learning is raised to the surface, however, it becomes more difficult to oppose it, as Jensen does, to conceptual learning. To say that the answer to a question is the same both in form and in content to the question itself does not necessarily mean that nothing additional is going on to generate that same response. To illustrate this point, take a slight variation of the digit test just cited, an item that also appears on some IQ tests. Here a subject is given a digit series, but asked to repeat it backwards. Now suppose a subject approaches the task in the following way: Upon hearing the last digit, the examinee makes sure, before responding, that he has learned the digits in their order as given. Then, starting with the last digit, he repeats the digits in their reverse order as far as his confidence will allow. Now he pauses and recalls the digits to himself in their forward order and further digits are added to the reverse listing. This technique would require that the subject keep two things "in mind" at the same time – first, the place left off in producing the incomplete reverse list, and second, the original forward-order list. Surely this could be thought of as an important conceptual skill involving the ability to keep the whole picture in mind while dealing with its smaller parts.

Return now to the forward digit span item. Suppose that upon hearing the direction, the subject realizes, either consciously or unconsciously, that he recalls meaningless symbols best in groups of three and as the numbers are called, he groups them accordingly – 479 364 – and then recalls them as grouped. The fact that the sound pattern in which numbers to the digit span are repeated by the subject often differs from the monotonal way in which the examiner is supposed to present them might be an indication that something like this is going on. In any event, there would be more in this response than simply the parroting back of sounds presented. The subject would have shown awareness of a rule, in this case about himself, and his own style of learning and would have applied that rule to an appropriate situation.

If the digit span test presents problems for determining whether associative or conceptual skills are being employed, other items present even greater difficulty. For example, on the Stanford–Binet test for 13-year-olds, the examiner presents the subject with a grouping of different-shaped beads that are clustered as illus-

Figure 2.1.

trated in Figure 2.1. The examiner tells the subject to watch carefully as he arranges the beads. When the arrangement is complete, he allows the subject to look at the beads for five seconds, then removes them and asks the subject to make an arrangement just like it.

Now if the task is performed successfully, do we know whether associative or conceptual learning has taken place? It could be the case, for example, that the subject memorized the entire sequence of beads and then repeated it when asked. If so, this would seem to be a case of rote learning. However, if the subject noticed that the left side of the chain is a mirror image of the right, then he need only have memorized one side of the chain and then invoked a rule about mirror images. If this was the case, then the response was not entirely dependent upon associative skills.

These are some of the particular problems that we had in identifying items that could clearly be said to test associative skills. However, there is also a general problem with the whole notion of associative learning. The fact that the example of the digit span breaks down so easily suggests that there may be no clear and simple paradigm case of associative or rote learning for human beings as applied to the kind of mental skills found in IQ tests. Indeed, when thinking of a paradigm case of what Jensen calls associative learning, the clearest example that comes to mind is a parrot that has learned to recite a list such as a series of numbers. What Jensen may likely have in mind as a case of associative learning in school is something like the use of flash cards to learn some more or less routine task, like the multiplication tables. However, when we compare this to our case of the parrot it is easy to see that the two are different in important ways. It might, for example, be possible to teach the parrot to recite a list of multiplication rules, such as $2 \times 2 = 4$, $2 \times 3 = 6$, and so on, but there would be nothing that the parrot could add to the list that we had not already taught it. It could not go on with the series, it could not multiply 4 dollars, or apples, or bananas by 2 or 3, and so on. Indeed, if a human being learned to perform this process in the same associative way as a parrot, we might generously say that the person has learned the multiplication tables, but we would not be wrong if we added that he or she has not learned to multiply.

Because of the difficulties mentioned above, the identification of associative items is not nearly the simple task that Jensen suggests. Yet for the purpose of being able to move ahead and examine some of the items that seem less ambiguously conceptual in nature, it is expedient to adopt the surface criterion that nothing shall be contained, either in form or in content, in the answer that was not already present in the question.[34]

Analysis of selected items on standard IQ tests

We turn now to an anlysis of a sample of the remaining items that appear on the Wechsler or Stanford–Binet tests in order to highlight some of the conceptual skills that seem to be called for.[35] In so doing, it is useful to point out that no item carries its own conceptual label, and that a good deal of interpretive effort is often required to establish a reasonable assessment of the kind of skill the testmakers had in mind. This is a point that Jensen fails to address. Yet it is possible to refine many of the items and to get an idea of the conceptual skills that they might be calling for.

The first example is typical of a number of questions on the tests that appear to be concerned with the ability to classify and differentiate. The question appears on the Stanford–Binet test for 6-year-olds and asks the youngster to state the difference between two items in a pair. The first of these questions, which asks the youngster to tell the difference between a bird and a dog, can serve as an example for the others. The scoring procedure for this item, as with many others, lists examples of acceptable and unacceptable responses, and these provide reasonable clues as to the processes that the item is attempting to tap. However, there are some problems with the list of acceptable and unacceptable responses that make it difficult to describe these processes with any degree of certainty. For example, given as a sample of a right answer is. "The dog can run and the bird can't," which seems to be factually wrong. Birds can run. Moreover, given as an example of an incorrect answer is "A bird can go faster than a dog," which in fact seems generally correct. Since no criterion for correct answers is given, examples like these make it difficult to decide precisely what conceptual ability the youngster is being called upon to display. However, if we take what appear to us to be paradigm cases of correct and incorrect responses, we can begin to get an idea of some of the processes that might be demonstrated by this kind of item. A paradigm case of a correct response would seem to be "A bird flies," and a paradigm case of an incorrect response that is provided by the scoring list seems to be "A bird is white and a dog is brown." We take it that the latter is incorrect because, whereas it may apply to particular members of the classes of dogs and birds, it does not apply as a distinguishing feature of the classes in general, and we take it that it is the ability to pick out distinguishing characteristics of separate classes of things that the test is looking for.[36]

A comparable item appears in the Wechsler test, but this item asks for similarities rather than differences. Here the scoring procedure is somewhat more sophisticated than the Stanford–Binet test since there is an implicit attempt to distinguish (on some of the items) between essential characteristics (for which full credit is given) and merely relevant similarities (for which partial credit is given). Unfortunately, however, the child is not told of this scoring procedure, nor is he or she given any indication to believe that an "essential" characteristic weighs more in his or her favor than what is accepted as merely a relevant similarity. Perhaps even more fundamentally problematic is the fact that no criterion is provided for deciding when a difference is to count as an essential difference and when it is to count as merely a relevant similarity.

From a different level of analysis, it is important to notice that the very way in which the question is scored assumes the viability of a certain kind of epistemology, one in which essential and nonessential differences are to be found, context-free. Yet good arguments could be made that the answer to the question of whether a stipulated property is essential or not depends upon the particular context in which it is being considered. When the examiner asks what is the similarity between a banana and an apple, he requires the student to respond that they are both fruits if maximum credit is to be given. Yet clearly, what is to count as an essential characteristic is at least partly a function of who is doing the counting. To a nutritionist the essential similarity might be that one could be substituted for the other for certain kinds of nutritional needs, whereas to a shipper it might be that both can be in transit only a certain amount of time before they rot, and so forth.

The failure of the testmaker to consider the extent to which the question of similarity may be context-bound leads most test manuals to reject certain kinds of answers as being inadequate. For example, the youngster who responds to the question about the similarity between a banana and an apple by saying that he had both of them for breakfast this morning, or that they are each too expensive for his parents to buy, is usually given no credit for such a response. This suggests that when an IQ test asks for the similarities between two items, it is often looking for the ability of a child to remove items from the personal experience in which they might be embedded in everyday life and then to classify them in some way that has *come to be looked upon* as general and context-free.[37]

The process of ''decontextualization'' seems to be required in a number of the other test items as well. For example, on the Stanford–Binet adult tests, there is an item in which the subject is asked to give the meaning of a proverb such as ''No wind can do him good who steers for no port'' or ''Don't judge a book by its cover.''[38] The examiner, but not the subject, is told that ''the proverb must be analyzed, abstracted and applied to life situations. Particularized or literal interpretation is not satisfactory.''[39] The description of the processes involved seem generally accurate as far as the testtaking situation is concerned. What the test obviously fails to take into account, however, is the fact that the meaning of such metaphorical statements is almost always established within a context in which the literal meaning does not work. For example, when someone at sea says, ''No wind can do him good who steers for no port,'' no metaphorical meaning may be intended. The fact that items like these work as proverbs is in part dependent on the fact that they are uttered in contexts where they do not work in any commonly accepted ''literal'' way, but it is also the context that instructs us about how such utterances should work. To understand the intended impact of "All things considered, I prefer Philadelphia," it is important to realize that it is supposed to be inscribed on W. C. Fields's gravestone. Thus whether someone understands a proverb is not strictly a matter of context-independent thinking, even though that is the notion one would get from the test. Indeed, most proverbs are not only context-dependent, they are also situationally and culturally dependent. The surprising thing is that given similar situations and cultures, most people will understand a metaphorical statement like a proverb.

If we put these shortcomings aside, what items like this seem to require is the ability to move beyond a literal to a more general, more symbolic interpretation of a verbal utterance. The process might involve first getting some representative but still literal significance for the main words of the proverb (for example, to someone at sea the wind represents a force or a push, some kind of aid, whereas a port is a destination). The proverb could then be translated with specific reference to its original content (thus, when one is at sea the blowing of the wind is of no real advantage unless one has a destination). Finally, upon recognizing the application of proverbs to more general situations, the subject removes the particular context of the sea and replaces it with a statement of broader context – for example, in life, advantages are of little use unless one has a goal. Yet the fact that understanding proverbs is so common suggests that it is not such understanding per se that the test is seeking to demonstrate, but rather the ability to reconstruct a natural process in a setting where the meaning is not imbedded in the context of a conversation.

Many of the processes that are involved in the previous items are inferential in some not very clear way. A clearer example of inferential processes is to be found in the following item. Here the 14-year-old subject is given the following problem: "My house was burglarized last Saturday. I was at home all of the morning but out during the afternoon until five o'clock. My father left the house at three o'clock and my brother was there until four. At what time did the burglary occur?"[40] Now clearly from the information that is given by this question, the only correct response, unless the testers are relying upon knowledge of a subtle legal distinction, should be that the burglary occurred sometime last Saturday. Yet this response would be marked incorrect and credit is only given, as the test manual says, for "any specific time between four and five o'clock."[41] Thus listed as correct responses, among others, are four-fifteen and four-thirty, which, by any chance calculation, are likely wrong. Yet if we overlook the problem that the tester has failed to share with the subject his assumption that the house was burglarized when no one was home, we can see the intent behind the item is to allow the subject to demonstrate some processes of inferential reasoning. The idea is to take information that is given and to use it to uncover information that is not given.

Much like the understanding of metaphor, which is called for by the earlier item, the process of inferential reasoning is a part of normal life, and it is likely that a reasonably sensitive observer could, even among youngsters who miss this item, pick out occasions in their everyday life when such processes are exhibited. Moreover, A. R. Luria has made a strong case that the development of basic processes such as inferential reasoning is strongly linked to the conditions of social life.[42] This view would give little credence to the idea that (except in rare instances) in tapping inferential processes an IQ test is marking a fixed cognitive limit.

One of the most promising yet at the same time one of the most problematic items in the Stanford–Binet is an item first given to 13-year-olds called a Plan of Search. Although some of the other mistakes that the testers make are little more than interesting but correctable curiosities, the problems involved in this item reveal something more fundamental. The item places before the subject a diamond-shaped figure with a small gap in the angle facing the subject. The subject is then handed a pencil and told to imagine that the diamond shape is a big field in which the subject has just lost his purse with a lot of money. He is then asked to "take this pencil and start here (pointing) at the gate, and show me where you would go to hunt for the purse so as to be sure not to miss it." The subject is then expected to mark out a path.

The directions for scoring this item are stated as follows: "The purpose of this test is to determine whether the subject can execute a plan of search that meets the logical requirements of the problem. The paths must be almost parallel and there must be no intersections or breaks."[43]

Examples of adequate and inadequate responses are then given (see Figure 2.2).

What we need to observe first is that the problem as it is given to the subject has only one logical requirement, although the scoring directions suggest that there are in fact more than one. The one criterion that seems to be implicit in the directions given to the subject is that he should be able to walk the route, that is, that there be a possibility of continuous movement from one part of the path to another. Yet given this single criterion the inclusion of item 2 as a correct response is questionable, since there is in fact no connection between the right and the left parts. Moreover, if 2 is acceptable, then one must wonder why 19 is not acceptable, since other than the absence of a right–left connection it seems to meet the idea of a reasonable search as well as does number 2. Moreover, number 10 is also marked acceptable, even though it too seems to lack the required connections. On the other hand, if the youngster who drew number 10 assumed that the sides could be used as walking borders, his drawing would seem to be all right, and given the minimal logical requirement, number 14 would seem perfectly acceptable. It may involve retracing some paths, but there is nothing in the directions that says that paths should not be retraced.

We mentioned in introducing this item that despite its problems it was one of the more promising items on the test. This was because if it were used appropri-

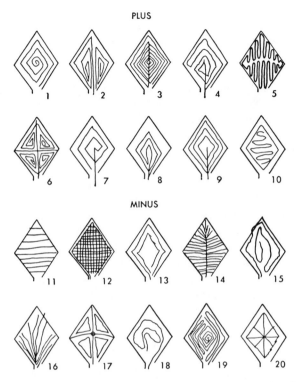

Figure 2.2. Acceptable and unacceptable answers to the plan-of-search test.

ately, it could provide a teacher or a counselor with a good indication of the way in which a youngster sets out to plan and carry out a scheme of action. Through items like this, for example, a teacher might be able to see the extent to which such attitudes as efficiency, thoroughness, and care govern a student's activities. For this is what the item, in an ironically careless way, seems to set out to test. Yet insofar as these criteria are in fact used to judge the IQ of the student, they are slipped in through the back door without the student's knowledge.

The problem with the question is larger than the fact that it is difficult to understand why some items are marked as correct and others are not. The fundamental problem with the question is that it assumes there is in fact a correct plan of search that can be identified independently of any particular aspects of the situation. Consider item 12 in order to illustrate the problems with this assumption. Now there are surely some reasons that could be given for marking item 12 wrong. It appears inefficient, involving crossing each point more than once. Yet it is surely thorough, and more likely than any of the other nineteen plans to enable the subject to find the purse. Well, how do we trade off thoroughness for efficiency in this case? The question is unanswerable unless we know other things. For example, if the youngster were imagining a field with long grass and thinking that there was a lot of money in the purse, and that he had a lot of time, then item 12 should clearly be preferred over all the others. Long grass would make thoroughness virtually an imperative. If the grass is covering the purse up from one angle, it is likely that it will not be covering it up from another. The more money there is in the purse, the more important is thoroughness, and the more time available, the less important is efficiency. The simple point is that in many instances we do not know what a response indicates unless we know the reasons why the response was given, and it is precisely the giving of such reasons that the test does not allow. It is as if reasons were somehow located in the task as presented and the problem is to find the best way to accomplish the task according to those reasons.

Many of the other cognitive processes involved in responding to the Stanford–Binet are also called for on the Wechsler IQ test,[44] to which we now turn. We alluded to some of the verbal items in the Wechsler test when we noted the duplication between some IQ items and some achievement test items. We have also noted certain similarities between some items on the Stanford–Binet and some on the Wechsler. It will thus be efficient to concentrate the analysis here largely on items that are somewhat unique to the Wechsler and that are included in the Performance Tests.

One of the tests, entitled Picture Completion, appears to be very useful in identifying the developed powers to observe details of everyday life as portrayed in still drawings. However, much more is claimed for the test. Wechsler says in his book on adult intelligence that it measures the subject's basic perceptual and conceptual abilities.[45] Even more boldly, he writes:

A type of response often elicited by the picture completion items is one which has no obvious relevancy to the immediate percept. . . . A simple example would be the response ''the hand is missing'' to the pitcher item, or ''bow is missing'' to the violin item. Responses of this kind are sometimes given by normal persons, but when they occur more than once or twice, or when particularly bizarre, are pathognomonic.[46]

Few of these claims appear to be warranted by the nature of the items themselves. We will return shortly to examine some of the deficiencies that are to be found in this test and to discuss the principles that seem to generate them. (The simulated test item of the carriage with the missing wheel can serve as an illustration of the items on this test (Figure 2.3).[47]) For now, however, we want to take an example of some of the more difficult items and examine them at the level of common sense in order to uncover the kind of process that might go into a successful answer. One example would be a picture of a phone where the cord from the receiver to the body of the phone was missing. Unlike some of the earlier items, the missing part is not immediately obvious to many people, and it

Figure 2.3. Simulated item from the Wechsler test (Picture Completion part) courtesy of The Psychological Corporation.

is likely that a person would begin by inspecting some of the different features. Are all the fingerholes included? Are the letters and numbers all there? Is the exchange of this telephone listed in the center circle . . . and so on. In other words, it seems as if the person who does not immediately recognize that the cord from the receiver to the body of the phone is missing would have to be able to analyze the instrument into some of its component parts, to check each of these components, and to remember the ones checked before going on to the next component. This kind of process would therefore seem to require some ability to observe fine detail, and to either break a large structure into a smaller, easier-to-solve components or to intuitively understand how individual parts are related to a functioning whole. People do in fact seem to differ on these skills. Such differences, however, may be a function of training and experience or of some natural endowment, and there is little that the test can tell us about the source of these differences.

When we move from the common-sense level of analysis to a deeper level, however, we can begin to see serious problems with these questions, problems that issue from the same kind of assumption that we saw earlier. It is assumed that there is but one essential feature that is missing from each of the pictures. For example, in one picture of a boy the response that the tester is looking for is "the eyebrow." However, also absent is his cheekbone.[48] The simple fact is that in many items there is more than one missing part, but the test allows for only one correct answer.

In the final item in the Wechsler that we will look at we see even more clearly the epistemological assumptions that underlie the test. The child is given a series of pictures in what is described by the test manual as a "mixed-up order." He is then asked "to arrange them in an order that tells a sensible story." On the surface, these items appear to be asking for a demonstration of a number of useful skills. In the first place, they seem to require the ability to see how individual parts can be related to form a coherent whole and to build that whole piece by piece. Second, it would seem as if the child were being asked to tie that

Figure 2.4.

whole together by some narration. However, below the surface this item is plagued by some of the very same assumptions that were so problematical in many of the other items on both the Stanford–Binet and the Wechsler. These assumptions become quite clear by looking at the directions as they are given to the child. In the sample item the examiner begins by placing three cards in numerical order and saying: "These pictures tell a story about a lady who weighs herself on a scale. The pictures are in the wrong order now. Watch how I put them in the right order so they tell a story that makes sense." After saying this, the examiner then says: "First the lady is walking toward the scale. Then she weighs herself. Finally she walks away."[49] What the examiner does here is to arrange the pictures in the "correct" order and then provide a narration that ties that order together. He then turns to the child, places three different cards in front of him, and says, "These pictures tell a story about a fight – a boxing match. The pictures are in the wrong order now. See if you can put them in the right order so they tell a story that makes sense."[50] The child, however, is not given the opportunity to provide a narration, and he is led to assume that there is but one right order in which the pictures can be arranged.

We can see the problem with this approach by looking at the sample item in Figure 2.4. The first arrangement is the one that the tester identifies as the right answer whereas the second arrangement would be considered wrong. However, suppose that the item was answered in the second way with the following story in mind: "A woman has just weighed herself on a scale when she realizes that she had not put down her shopping bag. In order to get a more accurate weight she drops her shopping bag and returns to the scale.''

The problem with the sample is typical of other the test items as well. The child is allowed to provide no narration. It is simply assumed that the meaning lies in the pictures themselves and that the child has but to discover it. Virtually nowhere, either in this item or in the other items on this and the Stanford–Binet, is the child expected or allowed to provide reasons for his or her response or to explain why one response was chosen over another.

Examination of selected items on "culture-fair" tests

The very same epistemological assumptions persist not only in the standard IQ test, but in the so-called culture-fair ones as well. These tests are important to turn to, even if only briefly, because they have been used by Jensen and others to support arguments for the genetic basis of racial differences in intelligence[51] and to insinuate the idea that IQ tests measure a fixed limit to intellectual capacity.

Before looking at a few illustrative items in these tests, it is useful to observe that defenses of culture-fair tests echo the epistemological assumptions that are to be found in the standard tests. The idea behind these culture-fair tests is that in some situations the standard test picks up interferences that distort what would otherwise be a true reading of intelligence. Once such interferences, usually resulting from verbal language, are removed, then it is thought that we can arrive at a true reading of the person's intelligence. What is interfered with, of course, is the person's ability to pick up or to communicate the meaning that is thought to be found in the items on the test. With many of the culture-fair items however, the object that is supposed to give meaning is reduced to a series of spatial patterns, and this presents special problems, as we will see.

In this section, we want to comment on representative items from two of the tests that Jensen cites as being the least culturally loaded. The first is the Raven Progressive Matrices test and the second is Cattell's Culture Fair test. We have already seen why these tests might be appealing to Jensen. In the first place, they do not appear to include any items that involve simply the exercise of rote skills. In the second place, the items do not appear to duplicate those that are asked on achievement tests, and hence do not in any obvious way depend upon school learning. (This is not to say, however, that they may not be dependent on school learning in some less than obvious way.) Thus, the only questions that remain are whether the tests in fact measure such a thing as "general intelligence" (g) and precisely what the nature of the conceptual skills that they call for might be.[52] We will look at the question of general intelligence first and then turn to the question of the kinds of conceptual skills that these tests call for.

The claim to culture fairness may make sense if one thinks of cultural factors as some form of interference that can "distort" the true reading of a person's

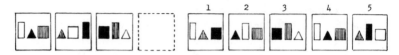

Figure 2.5.

intelligence. Although it is odd to think of intelligence as divorced from culture, the general idea behind the culture-fair test is to rid the measurement of intelligence of this interference. By and large, the interference that the testmaker appears to have in mind is that caused by verbal variation between different cultures, and thus the culture-fair tests attempt to reduce this verbal element as much as possible. What this means in practice is that whereas the directions must be given in words, words are largely eliminated from the test items themselves. Clearly this has some advantages in that it does minimize any variation in performance that might be the result of cultural variation in verbal forms. However, it has one clear disadvantage in that it renders any claim to be testing for *g* extremely questionable.[53] In order to see this point, return for the moment to the Wechsler test. Despite its many problems, one of the clear advantages of that test was that it attempted to tap intellectual performance over a range of different kinds of phenomena. Intuitively, this would appear to be a correct move, for if general intelligence exists, then it should further a consistent quality of performance over problems in very different fields. The culture-fair tests, issuing out of a desire to minimize verbal interference, restrict the range of problems largely to one sort, namely those that involve spatial representations of some underlying pattern that the tester wants identified. Thus, whereas the standard tests have difficulty dealing with the problem of cultural interference, the culture-fair tests have the corresponding problem of restricting responses to an overly narrow range of phenomena. It should also be mentioned before beginning the analysis of specific items that the claim to cultural fairness is based on the assumption that spatial representation does not vary across cultural lines, and this claim has been challenged by a number of researchers.[54] The Raven Test[55] can serve to illustrate the way in which an attempt can be made to tap different cognitive processes without recourse to words. In attempting to assess analogical reasoning, for example, an item uses two circles with different internal designs and a square with the same internal design as the first circle. If the child can perceive that a circle with X design is to a circle with Y design as a square with X design is to a square with Y design, she will be able to answer the item correctly.

The Cattell seems to call for many of the same skills as does the Raven, and like the Raven does attempt to tap many of the skills called for by standard tests. However, it goes beyond the Raven in some ways and presents more serious problems in others.

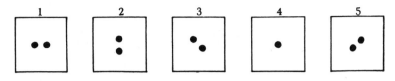

Figure 2.6.

The item shown in Figure 2.5, which requires the subject to discover two patterns running at the same time, such as shape and color (shading) appears to go beyond the Raven. This item[56] requires that the subject be able to hold some things constant while examining others and to remember intermediate results while solving other parts of the problem. It also seems to require the ability to keep two aspects of a problem disassociated from one another until they are both solved, and then it requires the ability to integrate these two aspects.

One of the subtests (Test 2), however, illustrates a serious problem with the way in which directions are given and likely creates confusion for a number of subjects. It asks the youngster to look at a row of five boxes, four of which, the tester explains, "are similar in some way," but one of which "is different from all the others." These directions are generally appropriate for the early items in which one form of similarity does bind four of the items. A simple example is shown in Figure 2.6.

Yet midway through the test the similarity principle shifts from one principle that binds together all items in the series to two principles each of which links together paired items. The item that is not paired with another is the one that the child is expected to select. If this shift is not recognized, the items can only be answered by guessing or by using the previous criterion. Once it is recognized, however, the question becomes fairly simple. Figure 2.7 shows an example of the shift. Box 4 is the answer that the testmaker marks as correct, since it is not linked together in a pair; but if the single principle were used, the correct answer could be box 5 since it is the only one not containing a curved figure, or box 2 since it is the only one containing shapes without a straight line. Whereas in the earlier questions one item is different in design or number from all of the others, in this question the one item is different from all of the others not in design, but in the fact that it is not a member of a pair. Either this problem results from carelessness in providing directions, or else it requires a peculiarly subtle *verbal* distinction for a test that is not supposed to depend on verbal skills.[57]

In this test, however, the way in which the directions are written renders any result questionable. Assuming that the misleading directions could be corrected, what the test seems to require is close observation and attention to detail in an abstract spatial arrangement, and perhaps the ability to move to a new level of abstraction when an older level proves no longer sufficient to the task at hand.

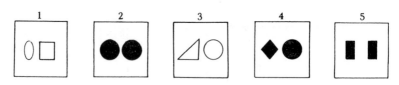

Figure 2.7.

The more general problem is not, however, restricted to the Cattell test, but applies to virtually all of the culture-free tests. Insofar as the test attempts to eliminate clutural interference by eliminating verbal content and by restricting performance to abstract spatial representation, it has rendered implausible any claim to being a test of general intelligence. This is because the very notion of general intelligence is meant to suggest a consistency of performance over a range of different kinds of phenomena, including verbal.

On another level however, the "culture-fair" tests are similar to the standard IQ tests. Although the range of phenomena on which performance is based is more restricted in the former test, many of the conceptual skills that it requires are the same as those required on the standard IQ test.

In summary, if we put aside the many particular problems that are to be found in both the standardized and the culture-fair tests, it is possible to identify a number of different kinds of activities that either illustrate the types of conceptual skills required or that can be said to contribute to the quality of conceptual performance. Some of these skills, such as the ability to pick out distinguishing characteristics of separate classes of things, to make inferences from given information, to group objects under a single abstract class, or to form compari-sons and to reason by analogy, describe some of the logical processes that are required by the test. Others, such as the ability to concentrate, to observe fine detail, to mentally manipulate abstract spatial objects, or to keep in mind a large amount of information, appear to describe certain psychological traits that can help contribute to conceptual performance. Still others, such as the tendency to break large problems into smaller, easier-to-solve pieces, or the tendency to hold some parts of a situation constant while considering variations in others, appear to describe the kinds of procedures that could aid conceptual performance in many types of cases. And finally there are a number of other modes of activity that, although complex and difficult to classify, nevertheless also contribute to performance. These involve such different types of things as planning ahead in order to see the consequences of possible courses of action, extrapolating a pattern, recognizing a trend or change in pattern, and of course being willing to actually work at the test. The list can of course be made longer or shorter than this depending upon how one wishes to break the various performances down and classify them.

The list is not intended to be exhaustive either of what the IQ exam tests or of the constitutive elements of intelligence. Moreover, the various activities probably play different roles with regard to our ideas about intelligent behavior. Some activities, like planning ahead or being able to draw inferences, seem to be entailed in the concept of intelligence itself. Others, such as concentrating or breaking up large problems into smaller units, seem to describe things that we sometimes do when we act intelligently. These kinds of distinctions remain to be worked out. Moreover, the many problems with the tests themselves, along with the fact that it often takes the most sympathetic examination of an item in order to extrapolate the kind of performance that it seems to require, make the claim that the test measures intelligence very questionable. For the present, however, it is most important to note just how straightforward such skills are and that at face value there is little about these skills themselves that should lead us to believe that the tests measure a level of conceptual development beyond which an individual cannot go.[58] To insinuate such an interpretation as fact and to then base a policy recommendation upon this interpretation as insinuated must thus be seen in terms of its effects – to deny a large group of youngsters the systematic opportunity to learn some very important skills. This can best be understood in terms of larger institutional values that block other possible interpretations and other possible choices.

Conclusion

The testing movement represents but one instance of the empirical tradition and its use in education. Recently a good deal of attention has been given to this movement because of the challenge that Jensen and other researchers have offered to the liberal, equalitarian concerns that were expressed during the 1960s and early 1970s. Much of the attention that was focused on this movement was concerned with addressing this challenge and providing solid scientific evidence to show that Jensen and his followers were wrong in their claims about racial variations in intelligence. For the most part, however, these challenges did not question the model of scientific understanding to which Jensen had implicitly appealed in making his case. In other words, it was felt that there was something wrong with Jensen, and perhaps also with the instruments that he used, but not with the scientific ideal of educational understanding to which he appealed. Although many people did fight the battle while objecting to the racist conclusions that they felt were drawn from Jensen's research, they largely fought it on Jensen's ground – by appealing to what they perceived to be a more adequate approximation of science. Thus, each side was implicitly willing to allow the empirical tradition, in its broadest terms, to settle the issue. To address the issue in this manner, however, was to overlook the way in which the empirical tradition functions in a practical setting like schools and to leave unexamined some basic normative issues. In the following chapter we return to the IQ debate in order to unravel some of these issues, and in the subsequent chapter we look at the way in which similar normative commitments inform a movement that is often taken within the empirical tradition as an alternative to IQ research.

3　Values and empirical research

The IQ debate tells us less about the distribution of human intelligence than it does about the limitation of the empirical tradition in the study of education. What is most interesting about Jensen's study is that it is an expression of a certain interpretive framework and set of values but that by itself it does not equip us to understand this fact. To put the matter differently, the study of education entails an examination of the dominant modes of consciousness that are transmitted across generations, and Jensen's work stands as an expression of such a mode. As such an expression it constitutes a part of the object of study for the educational scholar, and should not be confused with the study itself. This does not mean that educational scholars should ignore empirical findings. Rather, it means that empirical work, as important as it may be, does not tell us how it is to be taken. A critical analysis of Jensen's work is especially useful in helping to make this point. The fact that his findings are generated by stressing one side of the equivocal claim that ''IQ tests measure intelligence'' allows us to see more clearly than we might otherwise just how value commitments insert themselves into empirical work. By pursuing this issue we are also able to see that this insertion is not to be found in one particular study, but is rather a feature of the empirical approach itself.

In this chapter we look more closely at the values that are at the foundation of Jensen's empirical study, whereas in the next chapter we show that many of the same issues appear within a very different empirical model. In both of these chapters the major point is that the empirical tradition is severely limited in its ability to understand the process of education and that this limitation is rooted not just in its methodology, but in its truncated understanding of the domain of education itself. Once education is seen as the process of intergenerational continuity, then a large part of the study of education will involve an examination of the mode of consciousness that persists across generations. Since this consciousness includes the interpretive schemes and values that are transmitted across generations, a method that simply takes existing schemes as givens will fail to provide a clear view of education itself.

43

There are a number of responses to this argument that can be anticipated here and that will enable us to see the point in a different way. First it could be objected that Jensen is indeed aware of many of his own relevant values and does articulate them at various places in his writings. Second, even if Jensen were unaware of his own values and if other empirical studies were found with similar limitations, these should be seen as inadequacies of these specific studies, not of the empirical tradition as a whole. Third, there are many empirical studies that do indeed focus on the issue of values. Research on motivation would be one example, and much of survey research would be another. A close examination of these objections can help clarify the empiricist's approach to values and the precise limitations of that approach. Moreover, such an examination can help us to see just why these are limitations of the approach itself and not just of particular research projects.

In the first place, whether a value is seen as an attribute of the researcher (such as expressed in a decision made about the importance of a project) or as an attribute of the subject of the research, it is perceived first and foremost as something that attaches itself to an individual. Values, according to the empirical tradition, are to be understood as the preferences of individuals. We may, of course, speak of group values as long as we understand that in so doing we are speaking of a statistical aggregate of some sort. In the second place, although the subject of a research study may express his or her values at any time, the tradition imposes definite restrictions on the moments when the values of the researcher may be expressed. By formulating these restrictions as imperatives we can see something that is important in the empiricist's conception of value. Thus: Researchers *may* allow their values to determine the problems they study! Researchers *may not* allow their values to determine the methods that they will use to study the problem! Researchers *will not* allow their values to determine their findings! Researchers *may* allow their values to influence the activities that they engage in outside the research process! The point is that values are not only attributes of individuals but they are seen to be the kind of attributes that can be easily recognized and exercised at will. Thus, for example, Jensen quite readily reveals that his work has been guided by a desire to make selection fairer and more objective, and he does so without concern that values have entered into his study in any illegitimate way. Moreover, although it is possible that he may be mistaken about his own values and motives, his observation is perfectly compatible with the restrictions laid down by the empirical tradition. From the point of view of this tradition the only issue would be whether this, or some other, unstated set of values had imposed itself on his methodology or his findings.

Yet when we think about research within an institutional setting that is concerned with developing intergenerational continuity, such as a school, values must be understood in quite a different way. An institution is a systemized set of practices, expectations, and procedures, coordinated toward some specific social purpose, such as intergenerational continuity, in which values have already been crystallized. When we understand values in this way, then we can begin to see that they cannot be turned on and off at will because they do not belong simply to the single will of an individual or an aggregate of individuals. They are rather the taken-for-granted and shared features of social life that enable institutions to persist as they do. Because they are taken for granted they are most often perceived in their violation, in the uneasy feeling that we have when we sense that some fundamental boundary has been trespassed. Individual preferences are related to such boundaries and can be used to initiate an exploration of them and an ultimate decision about their merits. We should not, however, mistake such preferences for that which lies behind them.

Thus the values that are at work in an institutional setting do not belong simply to the subjective preferences of the researcher or to the researcher's subjects. Rather they are embedded in the very practices that constitute the institution that the researcher is investigating. As long as researchers continue to take these values for granted, they function, not as neutral external observers, but as important aspects of the institution itself, reflecting its basic assumptions in the alternatives that are projected and in the possibilities that are considered. Insofar as values are seen as but attributes of individuals, the basic assumptions of the institution will remain at the taken-for-granted level and will not become objects for rational deliberation.

To understand the nature of some of these assumptions as they function in education, and the way in which they are served by the empirical researcher, we return to look at the IQ issue in the context of some of the significant institutional and social values that are taken for granted by defenders of these tests.

The framework for understanding IQ tests

The preceding chapter only raises but does not answer the question whether there are conceptual limits beyond which some individuals cannot go; neither does it answer the question whether, if such limits exist, IQ tests measure them. These questions remain unanswered here, but they also remain unanswered by the existing literature defending IQ tests. While these issues (as well as the question of whether the tests measure anything at all) are still open ones, defenses of the tests and of their implications for educational policy are generally framed within a context that assumes that such limits do exist and that a score on an IQ test is an indication of them. This is not only the case with Jensen's discussion, but has often been built into many of the definitions of intelligence as measured by IQ tests. Thus, for example, Burt writes: ''The degree of intelligence with which any particular child is endowed is one of the most important factors determining his general efficiency all throughout life. In particular it sets an upper limit to what he can successfully perform, especially in the educational, vocational and intellectual fields.''[1] Moreover, even when test defenders have been forthright in suggesting that all that can definitely be said is that the tests "measure" speed of learning, their general discussions of IQ tests have tended to ignore the implications of this suggestion and have proceeded as if the tests were indeed measuring some kind of conceptual limit beyond which individuals could not go.[2]

That the problem of conceptual limits has not been recognized as significant by those who believe that IQ tests do measure intelligence does not mean that it is inherently unimportant. The importance of the issue can be seen in the following way. Assume, for the sake of the argument, that intellectual skills are arranged in a linear way, from lower to higher, and suppose that a score on an IQ test did indicate a conceptual limit beyond which some individuals could not go. Suppose too that there was a general field of knowledge, recognized as socially essential, that required skills at the higher end of the scale. Now, if IQ tests did measure the conceptual limits of individuals, then not to make the tests decisive in selecting people for training in these positions would be an inevitable waste of human talent and resources. If, however, IQ tests only measured the speed at which individuals learned such materials, then unless there were an overwhelming argument for selecting fast learners (say perhaps in a situation of severe scarcity of adequately trained persons and of persons to train them), the criterion for selection would be an open issue. It is important to note that there are limits to the extent to which IQ and other similar tests are able to predict proficiency within an occupation, but for now the important thing to see is just how much the present discussions about the validity of IQ tests deny the importance of other considerations by conceiving of the process of selection and (with Jensen) training as simply a natural extension of the fact that something called "intelligence" has been measured. In other words, although there is little scientific information that speaks to the question of whether IQ tests do indicate a conceptual limit, there is something within the framework in which such tests are discussed that allows testers to interpret them *as if* they were in fact measuring such a limit. In this chapter we examine the nature of the framework that allows the tests to be interpreted *as if* they were measuring a conceptual limit and thereby enables the test defender to put aside, as insignificant, the ambiguity involved in the claim that "IQ tests measure intelligence." It is in this framework that we will begin to see some of the ways in which, within the practical situation, normative assumptions guide empirical research and the way in which such research by itself inhibits these assumptions from becoming objects of rational consideration.

In order to bring this problem into sharper focus, return to the list of skills that seem to be called for by the "conceptual" items on the IQ test. What is so striking about Jensen's proposal to teach low-IQ children by associative methods is the fact that many children would be denied the opportunity to learn such conceptual skills through the deliberate instruction of a teacher. The very fact that some of these skills, such as learning to draw inferences or to break large problems into smaller pieces, are so important would appear to place a large burden of proof upon any pedagogical proposal that, for whatever reasons, would deny children the opportunity to learn them in a deliberate fashion. Jensen, however, avoids this burden by appealing to the scientific status of IQ exams. Yet even if one were to accept this appeal, the only conclusive *scientific* reason for adopting his proposal would involve showing that such tests do in fact measure conceptual limits, and that for children who score low on such tests, conceptual learning is usually impossible. In the absence of evidence that this is the case, then, the proposal can only be supported by a set of normative assumptions that would call for the same pedagogical treatment as *would be* called for if it were scientifically established that a score on an IQ test indicated a conceptual limit. The purpose of this chapter is to attempt to reconstruct those assumptions, to see the role that they play in the interpretation and social use of IQ examinations, and to sketch a criticism of them.

Before beginning this examination there are three observations that need to be made. First, IQ tests are only one form of selection mechanism that at higher levels of education is usually supplemented by other tests, such as the scholastic aptitude tests. In this section IQ tests will sometimes be discussed in the context of these other tests. Second, the kind of analysis that is involved here is not a scientific examination of these tests. Although one should perhaps not rule out the possibility that science could one day determine what, if anything, these tests measure, the issues that are involved in understanding why certain facets of a research program should be picked out as significant whereas others barely receive a nod is a question not for science, but for a close analysis of the narrative through which such research is reported. Third, this section is largely going to bypass one of the more penetrating criticisms that has been made of IQ tests, that of cultural bias. However, to look briefly at this criticism will provide an illustration of just how important the framework is for interpreting the IQ literature. The question of cultural bias will be used here as an introduction to the larger concern of this section.

A number of commentators have pointed out that many of the items on standard IQ tests have a built-in cultural bias, and that this bias likely not only affects the scores of children from minority groups, such as blacks, but also children from the lower social and economic levels of the society. For example, the Wechsler asks a number of questions such as "What are some of the reasons why we need policemen?" where the answers marked correct (such as to protect property) and incorrect (such as because of drugs) seem to have a clear socioeconomic bias.[3] Other questions, such as "Where is Chile?" seem to have a clear cultural bias. Yet the significance of these examples depends largely upon whether one generally accepts the idea of such tests to begin with. For example, in proposing revisions that would make the tests more adequate for children of Mexican-American origin, two researchers suggest that to the item "Where is

Chile?'' responses such as "in a can," "in a field," or "in a store" be allowable.[4] Thus, what might have signaled a much larger problem with the whole idea of IQ tests is looked upon here only as a problem with individual items, and as a problem which is thought to be correctable.

Yet in addressing the validity of specific items, we are restricting the examination of the test within the testmaker's framework. The frame can be shifted rapidly, however, by asking why these kinds of questions have appeared with such frequency on IQ tests and why the testmaker has generally failed to identify their culture-specific nature. To focus on this kind of question would immediately bring into relief the role of IQ tests in the larger culture and the function that the tests serve as political instruments, questions that need to be debated on political grounds.[5] In some instances the different frameworks can be explained by the kind of problem that is being addressed. In the case of revising the item about Chile, for example, the authors were confronting the immediate problem of finding a way to screen children for retarded classrooms while guarding against selecting youngsters who, otherwise normal, score low because certain test items are inappropriate in terms of their cultural background. Given the way the problem is set, the merely technical manner in which the tests are perceived is at least understandable. The problems of retarded children, however, represent a special case, and although the category is often abused, critics of tests are usually addressing broader concerns.[6] Of central importance here are issues concerning human rights and entitlements. The answers given to these issues largely determine the framework within which the significance of test scores is established.

Rights and entitlements

The way in which questions of rights and entitlements enter into the IQ controversy can be seen clearly by examining Antony Flew's philosophical defense of IQ tests and of Jensen's interpretation of them. In defending Jensen, Flew writes:

> The distinction between *ought* and *is* is fundamental here. This Jensen, unlike most of his critics, fully appreciates: "realization of the moral ideal of equality proclaimed by the Declaration of Independence . . . does not depend upon either phenotypic or genotypic equality of individuals' psychological characteristics". . . . Contrast with this clear statement the long executive resolution . . . adopted . . . by the New Orleans conference in 1970 in which it is said: "The American Anthropological Association repudiates statements now appearing in the United States that Negroes are biologically and in innate mental ability inferior to whites, and reaffirms the fact that there is no scientifically established evidence to justify the exclusion of any race from the rights guaranteed by the constitution of the United States." . . . The crux is that the signers were making claims about certain rights which all men *ought* to have, which claims neither entail nor presuppose that it *is* the case that all men are hereditarily equal in their talents or inclinations.[7]

Flew's objections to the AAA report represents a standard defense against the charge that Jensen's interpretation of IQ tests is racially biased. The defense is that there are certain *formal* political rights that belong to individuals regardless of their innate intelligence, and that the issues involved in the debate over IQ scores are strictly scientific questions having no bearing on these rights. Eysenck makes very much the same point when he writes:

All this is of course completely irrelevant . . . to the question of segregation. Human beings have human rights, irrespective of their IQ, and the fact that Negroes show some degree of genetic inferiority in respect to this particular measure . . . does not carry with it any implications whatever favoring differential schooling.[8]

While Eysenck's reference to differential schooling is meant to apply to segregation and not to Jensen's differential pedagogy, he also rejects discrimination in employment and other areas against qualified individuals because of racial considerations.[9] Yet the thrust of his entire argument is, like Jensen's, to support the claim that scientific studies of IQ show that there is also a smaller percentage of blacks who are qualified for such high-level positions. Given this thrust, Eysenck adds the following to his earlier statement:

This has one implication which may not appeal to American Negroes, namely the implication that no *inverted* racist policy should be allowed to operate, setting lower entrance requirements for Negroes, or introducing a quota system to make sure that blacks and whites attend universities in proportion to their numerical strength. . . . If accepted, such demands would mean that a well qualified, high IQ white student would be debarred from attending university in order to allow a less well qualified, lower IQ black student to take his place *on purely racial grounds*.[10]

The tone in which the above passage is cast makes it clear that Eysenck has already decided on the comparative intelligence of blacks and whites as groups, although some of his book is but a disarming plea that research into racial differences in intelligence should be allowed to continue and be encouraged without the added burden of political controversy.

However much defenders of tests, such as Eysenck and Flew, may wish such research to continue without the taint of political debate, it is clear from their own writings that the debate entails some fundamental assumptions about the nature of political and humans rights. What is presented is an argument that rests on the presumption that there are two different kinds of entitlements. The first has to do with "basic" political rights, such as voting, speech, assembly, and so forth. Here their argument is that these should be allocated univerally without regard to a score on an IQ exam. The second kind of entitlement has to do with educational and employment prospects, and here their argument is that these should be distributed in accord with an individual's intellectual capacity, as generally indicated by a score on an IQ test.

While the distinction between these two forms of entitlements has a certain amount of commonsense appeal, when it is *applied* to the role of intelligence in education, problems begin to surface. We begin with Flew. His defense of Jensen against the executive resolution of the American Anthropological Association rests upon an overly narrow application of the traditional philosophical distinction between facts and values. That someone has a certain IQ is a factual claim. That someone should or should not have certain rights is a value claim that, according to Flew, is not intended to rest upon any factual concerns about IQ.

One of the major difficulties with Flew's argument is that he uses the fact–value distinction selectively and fails to analyze the concept of human rights to which he applies it. In order to see this problem, return to the recommendation that Jensen makes for teaching low-IQ children by rote methods. We have seen that this recommendation can be supported in one of two possible ways. It could be supported without any additional normative assumptions if Jensen had also shown that a score on an IQ test is an indication of a conceptual limit beyond which an individual cannot go, and that for low-IQ children that limit is captured by what we call rote, or what he calls associative, learning. Since neither Jensen nor anyone else has established that the tests do measure a conceptual limit, however, we must assume that his recommendation is based on an unstipulated normative assumption that somehow renders the empirical question inconsequential. Flew, however, does not address himself to this kind of issue and instead focuses upon the more obvious (but not more important) problem contained in the AAA statement. Yet given the political nature of such a statement, it is not at all surprising that it did not take into account all of the subtleties involved in the fact–value distinction.

This does not mean, however, that the statement could not be reconstructed in such a way as to avoid, at least as much as Flew does, the problems inherent in moving from statements of fact to statements of value. This restatement would simply entail supplementing the merely formal concept of human rights upon which Flew's argument rests with a notion that takes into account the worth of those rights. Although Flew challenges what he perceives to be the implication of the AAA statement, that if taken seriously IQ scores should have some bearing on formal rights, he leaves unchallenged the more prevailing view that IQ and other indications of intelligence should be decisive in determining how people are to be treated with regard to educational and occupational opportunity. This view is clearly held by Jensen when he uses such scores to advocate differential pedagogy and by Eysenck when he argues against "preferential" college admissions on the grounds that IQ scores or some similar measure should be a decisive factor. Thus while Flew bases his defense of Jensen upon the belief that IQ scores should have nothing to do with formal rights, he leaves unchallenged the clear implications of Jensen's and Eysenck's proposals, that is, that IQ scores should have much to do with the actual worth of these rights (including the type and amount of education one is to receive) in contemporary society. More than likely it was to the worth of those rights that the AAA statement was intended to speak. Given Eysenck's view that higher-status positions should be open to those of higher intelligence, it is not at all difficult to see how abstract formal rights take on different values for different people under his recommendation. The implications of Jensen's proposal are even more severe in this respect. Insofar as the value of political rights is determined by a person's ability to make unmanipulated judgments and to evaluate different points of view on their own merits, according to the reasons that are provided, then Jensen's proposal for teaching low-IQ children by rote and avoiding methods that would involve conceptual processes would seem to be one step in the direction of assuring that such rights could not be exercised effectively. Given such severe implications, it is difficult to understand why anyone would propose simply on the basis of a score on an IQ test that such radically different methods be used. This is even more difficult to understand given the fact that Jensen, in a somewhat obscure and rarely cited passage, diminishes the force of his own argument. In commenting on the large difference that environmental factors can make on IQ scores (20 to 30 points) reported by Heber, Jensen writes:

The Heber results have recently been held up in the popular press as evidence that genetic factors are of negligible importance, and some writers have even pointed to the Heber experiment as a refutation of "Jensenism." Yet, interestingly enough, the results are within the range that would have been predicted from a genetic model assuming a heritability of 0.80.[11]

It is not clear how far beyond the subjects involved in the Heber study Jensen wishes to extend this remark: nevertheless, given all of the controversy that has surrounded his studies, there is something quite remarkable about it. For what Jensen seems to be saying is that even though the largest portion of an IQ score is determined by genetic factors, nevertheless that smaller portion that is influenced by environmental factors is in many instances sufficient to yield a 20- to 30-point increase in IQ scores. Yet when one realizes that in ordinary terms a 30-point difference can take an individual from borderline "normal" to "superior" or from "high average" to "genius," one might wonder, even granting Jensen his heritability level, why there should be much concern voiced at all.[12] To the extent that Jensen's remarks about the Heber subjects can be generalized to the larger population, the assumed connection between IQ scores and legitimate educational and occupational entitlements would appear to be significantly weakened. And at least for some people a low IQ score (again assuming a connection between IQ and intelligence) would appear to be, much like nearsightedness, a correctable "deficiency." The appropriate question would then seem to be whether there are good reasons to correct this "deficiency," or whether leaving it alone, it should be used as a strong guide in determining the allocation of educational and occupational benefits.

If the capacity of individuals is not fixed in the way that a large genetic factor usually suggests, then the weight that should be given to scores on a test in determining educational and occupational chances becomes a highly debatable issue. This would be so even if the genetic factor were quite large. Here the only initially decisive consideration would be whether the environmental component was sufficiently adjustable to overcome the initial genetic defect.[13] Any other consideration, such as whether resources should be committed to alter a deficiency, is a question to be decided by other than strictly scientific consideration.

Flew's defense of Jensen is but one illustration of the way in which the question of entitlement is both assumed and obscured by much of the writing in defense of tests. Another illustration is the way in which testers use a high correlation between test scores and success in other areas such as school or occupational status and income to verify the claim that IQ scores do measure intelligence. Now in many instances such correlations seem to be built into the very procedures by which the tests are developed whereby items that do not in fact correlate highly with success in these other areas are not included in the final test. Thus, for example, in selecting items for the Wechsler–Bellevue scale each test was checked against the judgments of teachers, army officers, and business executives.[14] If one is predisposed to believe that performances judged by these people do demand a high level of intelligence, one would accept the procedure of checking the items out with personnel in these different fields as an added safeguard. If, however, one rejected the idea that high intelligence was the most significant factor reflected in performance in these areas, then neither the procedure of checking the answers out nor the high correlation of tests with performance would add anything very convincing to support the claim that IQ tests measure intelligence. Thus one important question is whether success in the areas cited is best explained by high intelligence, and clearly there are many other factors that could be of significance here; factors such as motivation or willingness to conform could easily be offered as possible explanations.

Some testmakers have recognized the problem of separating out the different factors in a test that could account for high performance and have attempted to deal with the issue. For example, Wechsler, in trying to take account of some of the research that shows various personality factors to be of significance in determining scores on IQ exams, writes:

These factors . . . cover such items as the subject's interest in doing the tasks set, his persistence in attacking them and his zeal and desire to succeed – items which might more familiarly be described as personality factors, but which nevertheless must be recognized as important in all actual measures of intelligence. For this reason, one might appropriately refer to them as the non-intellectual factors, or more specifically, as the *non-intellective* factors in general intelligence.[15]

This awkward attempt to reconcile the problem is clearly inadequate. Note, for example, how Wechsler moves from the statement, probably quite correct, that such items must be recognized "as important in all actual *measures* of intelligence'' (emphasis mine) to the statement that these are to be appropriately referred to as the nonintellective factors in *general intelligence*. The first of these statements would appear to say something about IQ tests themselves, that is, that they entail certain impure factors that interfere with a true measurement of intelligence. The second statement, however, then takes what had been first described as an attribute of the *measuring instrument* and makes it an attribute of *that which is being measured*. The leap from one to the other is made without justification, and that should be problem enough. There is, however, an equally serious difficulty.

Assume for the moment that there really are two parts to general intelligence, an intellective part and a nonintellective one, and assume too that the intellective part is fixed in the way that many testers suggest. This tells us nothing about the extent to which the nonintellective part is or is not also fixed, and therefore it tells us little about the extent to which the cluster of qualities that we are measuring can be altered to meet the requirements of the tasks for which a high score on the test is thought relevant. Some researchers believe, for example, that many important personality traits such as initiative or passiveness can be explained largely in terms of the demands that different positions within a stratified division of labor make on individuals and their children and by the mutually reinforcing way in which these demands are transmitted by family, school, and work settings.[16] Yet when the testers argue for the validity of their tests on the grounds that there is a high correlation between test scores and occupational status, they have made the division of labor the measuring rod against which the validity of the test is checked. The approach, if successful, serves to place the division of labor itself outside the processes that are to be examined.

Presented in this way, what the correlational argument does is to make placement in high positions and status a natural process, with the implication that such status is *caused* by high intelligence, and is thereby a process that would be futile to challenge. Thus entitlement to longer and better education, to occupational status and higher wealth on the basis of high intelligence becomes equally as fixed as the formal political rights that are to be granted to everyone. In order to see how this ''argument'' works we turn to its employment on the concrete question of college admissions. Here we can see more clearly how the practical framework of institutions and the values embedded in them serve to generate a particular interpretation of tests.

The practical framework and the interpretation of tests

In a chapter of his book on educational differences, Jensen begins his discussion by *seeming* to admit what his earlier article had largely denied, that equality of opportunity does not exist in present-day American society.

The present demand that minority groups have equal opportunities throughout the educational ladder, from pre-school and kindergarten through college and graduate training, is one that, if realized, would benefit the whole society. No effort should be spared in pursuit of this goal.[17]

The impact of this remark is reduced, however, when he adds: "Indeed, vigorous efforts are already underway at all levels of education," and when he then goes on to argue that the barriers to equal performance are not to be found primarily in extrinsic factors such as discriminating laws, but more often in intrinsic ones having to do with psychological and intellectual characteristics.[18] Having made this point, Jensen then goes on to argue, on the basis of scores on scholastic aptitude tests (which he reports correlate well with IQ scores) that only a very small percentage "of Negro high school seniors" score sufficiently high on these tests to succeed in "the nation's most selective colleges,"[19] and notes that the percentage of blacks in selective institutions is reasonably consistent with the percentage that one might estimate falls within the acceptable IQ range (117 or above).

Now, these figures can and have been challenged on grounds relating to the cultural bias of the tests. What is equally interesting, however, is the fact that Jensen in a different passage provides a sufficient basis for puzzling about their significance, although he himself fails to do so. Not only does he leave enough room for a 20- to 30-point increase in IQ scores, as we have already seen, but in a passing explanation of the differential consequences that the same cutoff point has for blacks and whites in terms of college admissions he writes: "Thus, an average IQ difference of only 8 points can have quite impressive consequences in terms of population distributions, while a difference of 8 IQ points is trivial in comparing any two individuals."[20] And then clarifying, he writes:

Thus, these average differences of 15 IQ points between blacks and whites, which reduces to about 10 or 11 points when the racial means are compared within broad socio-economic classes, is of major consequence not because a difference of 15 IQ points between any two individuals is important in any significant social sense, but because *as populations* blacks and whites are so disproportionately represented in any selection procedure in which the cutoff is much above the white population mean.[21]

The reason this difference becomes important for Jensen on the group level, whereas its importance on the individual level is minimized, is because such scores are said to correlate well with established predictors of academic success. He writes:

The question concerning the *causes* of intelligence differences are, in fact, quite irrelevant when it comes to the use of tests for predicting performance in college. Doing well academically in college depends upon a conglomeration of developed abilities, skills, and thinking habits, which scholastic aptitude tests are designed to assess. The important question to the college admissions office is not why students differ on these tests, but whether the tests are valid for their intended purpose, namely, predicting college grades or probability of not flunking out before graduation.[22]

Having argued for the value of such tests on the grounds of their ability to predict college success, Jensen then observes that they are also one of the most effective ways to "protect the rights of qualified minority group members." He writes:

The use of objective tests is still the best safeguard that persons from a low-SES [socioeconomic status] background will be given a fair chance in the selection procedure. Wider use of tests in school, combined with wise counseling, would actually increase the pool of identified college-level candidates from economically disadvantaged backgrounds. Academically gifted children from poor families are much more likely to be identified by tests than by parents or teachers. Aptitude tests, properly used, tend to protect the rights of qualified minority group members.[23]

Now Jensen believes that such tests would protect the rights of minority members by increasing the pool of college-level candidates, even though he also believes that the pool would not be increased by a very large amount. The question then is: How is he able to view the tests as the protector of rightful entitlement for members of minority groups while at the same time denying the intuitive judgment that such groups are underrepresented in many select institutions of higher education? The point that needs to be seen is that Jensen does not confront the entitlement question head on by presenting a set of reasons for his point of view. Rather what he does is to link an argument about predictive validity to a causal category that is psychological in character, located within each individual and usually depicted as an unchangeable biological set for that individual.

In order to see this point more clearly, imagine that Jensen had made only an observation about the extent to which certain tests are able to predict academic success, but had not linked this observation to any causal claim. With the causal factor left open, a number of different possibilities could be considered of which native intelligence would be but one. Before considering native intelligence, however, one could inquire whether that for which people were being selected, that is, success in college, was itself governed by fair and reasonable goals. It would be quite possible for an unfair selection device to accurately select out otherwise acceptable candidates for a contest that will be decided by similarly unfair standards. If this were the case, then there would be little reason to examine the possibility that native intelligence was a causal factor before we first began to examine the standards. Presumably if the standards were then altered, the value of the tests for predicting success in college would also change. As this happened, then it could reasonably be said that the change in predictability was due to the change in the standards. And by way of hindsight, it could even be said that the cause of the former high predictability level was in fact the old, unfair standards. Shortly, we will see that this is more than simply an "academic" issue.

What the above remarks suggest is that because questions of entitlement are in fact bound up to arguments about test scores, the significance given to any causal factor (or to anything that is offered as a candidate for being a causal factor) will depend upon the reasonableness of purpose that tests are ultimately thought to serve. Furthermore, there can be little doubt that the critics of the tests have understood this fact much more clearly than the test defenders themselves. When charges of "racism" have been leveled against the use of the test on grounds of cultural bias, there has been an implicit recognition that the empirical claims of testers have become important enough to challenge in light of some added and hidden assumptions about entitlement. It is to the justification of these assumptions, articulated more often in images and offhand remarks, that we now turn.

The assumption that a score on a test should be related to entitlements comes most obviously into play in terms of access to selective educational institutions and professional training. Below that level there is also a relationship that is assumed such as when test scores are used to track youngsters into different curricula or to argue (as does Jensen) the need for differential pedagogy. Yet the relationship that is established on the lower level can best be understood in terms of its practical function of preselecting people out of the competition for the higher level. The general assumption is that because a score on an IQ test indicates intelligence, higher scores on these and similar tests justify greater claims on educational resources and professional training.

Before looking at the warrant given for this assumption, it is important to see that even among scholars who disagree with the claim that tests measure intelligence, there is often general agreement with the idea that higher intelligence should bring with it higher entitlement, thus restricting their challenge to a question of means. For example, after presenting a penetrating analysis of the way in which tests and other pedagogical instruments serve to legitimize and reproduce the class structure by, among other things, convincing people to "voluntarily" select themselves out of the competition, the French Marxists Bourdieu and Passeron write:

It is no accident that so many sociologists . . . are inclined to isolate dispositions and predispositions towards education – "hopes," "aspirations," "motivations," "will-power" – from their social conditions of production. . . . It is of little consequence to them that by social traditions, aptitude acquired by virtue of belonging to a certain background, etc., the intellectually brilliant son of a labourer would rather aim for the old practical schools . . . and . . . get a technician's or engineer's diploma . . . while a doctor's son prefers a classical education with a view to entering the faculties.[24]

Although their treatment of education emphasizes social factors and involves a penetrating criticism of testing as it is found in class societies, the passage cited above unwittingly shares some important ground with Jensen. The standpoint from which the critique of the social scientists is made is, at least at this juncture, the same standpoint from which Jensen defends the tests, that is, persons of high ability deserve particular entitlement regardless of social class.[25] The question still remains, however, as to how such an entitlement is to be justified.

From Jensen's standpoint the justification seems self-evident. He writes: "There is no getting around the fact that higher education is a highly competitive affair and given the values and needs of our technological society, this fact is not likely to change for the foreseeable future."[26] Unfortunately, Jensen is not very clear about the precise nature of these needs, and so it is not possible to examine his thoughts on this issue very closely. He does, however (in an example designed to explain how validity coefficients work), provide an idea of why he believes a higher test score should be related to a larger educational and occupational entitlement. Thus, citing Cronbach, he writes:

Suppose the 40 applicants out of 100 who score highs on a test are hired. We can consider the average production of randomly selected men as a baseline. An ideal test would be to pick the forty men who later earn the highest criterion score; the average production of these men is the maximum that any selection plan could yield. A test with validity 0.50, then, will yield an average production halfway between the base level and the ideal. To be concrete, suppose the average, randomly selected worker assembles 400 gadgets per day and the perfectly selected group of workers turn out 600. Then a test with validity .50 will choose a group whose average production is 500 gadgets, and a test of validity .20 will select workers with an average production of 440 gadgets.[27]

Jensen then goes on to comment: "The principle is essentially the same in educational selection except that instead of number of gadgets produced we would be speaking of the amount of knowledge and skills acquired."[28] Although the example is intended to explain the way in which the scholastic aptitude tests work to predict college success, its use here is instructive in a different way as well. For it reveals that the purpose of such selection is to provide a group of people who will be able to absorb, with maximum efficiency, the knowledge and skills taught in the college curriculum. However, given his previously cited concern about the needs and values of technological society, it would seem that Jensen's primary interest is not with all of the knowlege and skills that might be taught in the college curriculum. Jensen does not mention, for example, interpretative and normative skills, but seems mostly to be interested in knowledge that can most obviously be perceived as technologically exploitable.

Whereas Jensen is vague about the nature of the needs of a modern technological society, Richard Herrnstein does provide a rationale for larger entitlements based on higher test scores and in doing so speaks to the nature of these "needs." Herrnstein, viewing the problem in terms of society's need to husband its scarce resources, writes:

If virtually anyone is smart enough to be a ditch digger, and only half the people are smart enough to be engineers, then society is, in effect, husbanding its intellectual resources by holding engineers in greater esteem and paying them more. . . . By doing so, society expresses its recognition, however imprecise, of the importance and scarcity of intellectual ability.[29]

Herrnstein later goes on to observe that "there are simply fewer potentially competent physicians than barbers. The gradient of occupation is, then, a natural measure of value and scarcity."[30] Thus for Herrnstein the entitlement to certain kinds of rights, those associated with training into a profession, is justified as being an effective way for society to use its scarce resources. Although the argument has a certain commonsense appeal, it falters on a number of grounds that, when examined, reveal some of the serious problems that underlie the tester's views on entitlement and the institutional framework that generates them.

Whereas there may be little disagreement with Herrnstein's example that there are "fewer potentially competent physicians than barbers," the example is not nearly as instructive as he suggests. For equally important questions are how much fewer? and under what standard of competency? In other words, Herrnstein gives us no reason to believe that the potential pool of qualified physicians is nearly as small as the number of spaces available in medical school, and indeed there is little reason to believe that this is the case. Yet while he gives us no reason to believe that the size of the pool of talent corresponds to the number of positions available, his entire discussion of IQ tests, much like Jensen's, is framed in terms of just such a belief.

One can only speculate about why this belief remains below the surface of the argument and is not raised to the point where it can be rationally considered. If the pool of potential talent were significantly larger than the number of places available, the number of alternatives for using society's resources would expand beyond the narrow limits of Herrnstein's view. It could be decided, for example, to simply increase the number of positions available or, if this is thought unwise, the decision could be made to make intellectual competency a minimal requirement for entering the pool after which other considerations, such as a demonstrated commitment to service areas of greatest need, could come into play in making a final selection. By not entertaining these possibilities Herrnstein's argument allows the structure of occupations to appear as a strictly natural event, and thereby his argument, like Jensen's, becomes a justification for not challenging the existing state of affairs. Yet this justification rests on the very fragile belief that there is a reasonable match between the number of positions available and the pool of competent people. To question this unsupported belief is also to question the assumptions about entitlement that underwrite the defense of tests. Although the idea that there is such a match seems intuitively unsupportable, and although professional schools of medicine, law, and engineering have never attempted to create spaces while giving serious consideration to the number of potentially competent people that could in fact comprise such a pool, the belief in such a match provides the only plausible justification for the entitlement assumption. What does seem to happen in these areas is that spaces are created or eliminated according to many considerations, including the desire to control competition within a profession. Given the available pool, whatever its size, professional schools generally define the most desirable candidates in terms of how well they do on tests and other similar "indices" in comparison to the rest of the pool. In other words, if there were five hundred positions, and five thousand people took the test and all showed sufficient competency to successfully train in the profession, the five hundred positions would generally go to those who scored highest. The number of people selected speaks (of course) to the number of positions available, not to the size of the talent pool. Now this point is obvious, and the question that needs to be asked is why it has been so often overlooked.

Jensen, in a citation noted earlier, provides much of the answer when he writes: "The principle is essentially the same in educational selection except that instead of the number of gadgets produced we would be speaking of the amount of knowledge and skills acquired."[31] The general idea (whether the tests are adequate in meeting it or not) is, given the total pool, to select that group of people who are the most likely to "absorb" the technologically exploitable knowlege at the fastest pace. In other words, whatever the size of the potentially competent pool may be (and tests are not generally engineered to determine this), the important consideration is the speed at which a candidate is likely to learn the material. What may be for some *at best* only an indication of learning speed is then treated as an indication of a conceptual limit. This then not only determines who is to be accepted, but also has a strong influence on the size of the pool. As Bourdieu and Passeron rightly point out, the nature of the selection process strongly influences the decision of whether or not to compete in the first place.[32] From the point of view of the test defenders, this confusion is insignificant, however, because the institutional goal under which their interpretation of tests has been developed is to provide the conditions for the maximum development and exploitation of technical knowledge, as this is understood within the existing social and political framework. In other words, given this goal, lack of speed would entail the same difficulty as would the presence of inadequate conceptual ability. Moreover, given this goal, one can also understand why testers have often been insensitive to charges of cultural bias. Insofar as the knowledge structure required for successful performance on a test reflects the knowledge structure required for fast and successful performance in a given curriculum and field, the cause of that performance is insignificant. In other words, for these purposes a cultural difference can be treated in the same way as an intellectual one. What is important is that the conditions be established for the growth of technical knowledge at the most rapid pace feasible, such that increasingly larger number and kinds of contingencies can be managed. One of these conditions is the ability to select for training those individuals whose test scores and past record indicate that they will be likely to absorb a given segment of that knowledge at a quicker pace than their competitors. Once selection takes place, then market conditions can determine which contingencies will receive priority, and this is largely a function of who has the means to enter the market to begin with and control it.

Whether as a matter of fact various forms of tests have been successful in such selection will remain largely a matter of conjecture, and there is reasonable evidence to believe that beyond a certain level of competency such tests do little to indicate the level at which individuals will perform in their profession.[33] Although this is but a question of means, it is quite clear that such a goal has in fact governed the defense of IQ and other tests as selection devices.

Yet there is a more important consideration here than the issue of means. Herrnstein is correct in the sense that if higher test scores are to bring about larger entitlements, the relationship can be justified only in terms of some form of social benefits. Unfortunately, Herrnstein speaks of society only in the abstract and fails to address the question of how different segments of it are to benefit by selecting talent in the way that he approves. Even if there were established a direct relationship between a high score on a test and high proficiency in a field, that relationship does not establish a direct connection between high proficiency in a field and some set of defensible social benefits. Indeed, in some fields, such as medicine, the selection, training, and socialization process seems to have contributed to an overly specialized profession at the expense of the availability of basic health services to many areas of the population. Although selection on the basis of intelligence alone, whether or not such intelligence is adequately identified by test scores, may facilitate the accelerated growth of knowledge through the development of specialization, there is little reason to think that such a policy will best serve the social needs of groups that are deprived of material resources.[34] Nowhere is the difficulty illustrated more clearly than in a proposal by Jensen intended to show how tests could be helpful to qualified students from minority groups. He writes:

Therefore, if we are to increase the number of minority and disadvantaged students who can go to college profitably, I would urge that we seek adademic talent in these groups as early in their schooling as possible, and then make very certain that it is properly encouraged, stimulated, and cultivated. . . . Such children, when they are from a disadvantaged background, should be given special attention. They should not be forced to languish in classes with a high percentage of slow learners who demand most of the teacher's attention. The able children especially need the stimulation of smaller classes, better teachers, and tutorial attention from teacher's aids and volunteer college students. The tutorial attention is not so much for purely scholastic reasons as for giving the child intellectually and academically orientated persons with whom he can feel some identification. . . . Greater efforts can be made to prevent the loss of academic potential resulting from unstimulating and discouraging home and school environments.[35]

The passage is not without some initial appeal, but its appeal is established precisely because we have an idea about what life would be like for these children if they were not singled out for special treatment. That is, their situation would be similar to those who in fact must "languish" behind without special attention. Yet Jensen's proposal when placed in the context of contemporary American society would likely lead to alienating the brightest youngsters from their community and its concerns. Moreover, given his earlier proposal for educating those who score low on IQ tests by methods that would stress rote learning, there is little reason to believe that the school system would be able to help those who remain behind to develop the skills required to articulate or address those concerns by themselves.

The above problem is not one that test defenders have felt to be significant enough to address, but their proposals would, if successful, have the impact of increasing the distance between the most and least advantaged members, both within and between communities. Fortunately, the fact that there are so many problematic features to the arguments for the validity of IQ tests means that the picture is not as bleak as might otherwise be the case. Whatever may or may not be the accuracy of IQ examinations, the test defenders' use of them serves to conceal the many critical decisions that remain open even if it is granted that in a general way some people are more intelligent than others. By raising to the level of choice issues that testers have rarely acknowledged as important, such as whether tests measure conceptual limits or speed of learning, this framework can be brought to the surface. Once this is accomplished, then these decisions, previously treated as but a "natural" extension of the data, can be raised to the level of political discussion, where they largely belong. Yet this requires that institutional assumptions not be taken for granted and that the study of education be viewed as more than simply an applied discipline.

Conclusion

The defense of IQ tests can be viewed from two different critical standpoints. The first provides a challenge to the actual empirical claims that the testers raise considering such questions as the relationship between genetic and environmental factors, the merits of IQ tests as a scientific instrument, and the claims about individual and racial variations in intelligence. All of these challenges, however, arise within the framework of understanding provided by the empirical tradition. Here the problem with IQ testing is that the researcher has not been empirical enough and has allowed his or her own values to influence the findings. To a certain extent the examination provided here supports this challenge, for we have indeed found that values have guided the presentation of IQ research at a number of different levels. The difference, however, is that whereas the critic from within the empirical tradition understands these values as belonging simply to the subjective preferences of the tester, many of the values we have identified are located at a much deeper level than that. Many of them represent the shared values and taken-for-granted meanings that have constituted the institution of schooling. These values cannot be expressed in simple terms, such as racist or elitist, but they are found in a network of ideas that tell us what schools, as we understand them, are supposed to do. They include notions about the rights and entitlements of individuals, about the reality of the individual as opposed to the presumed artificial status of the group, and about rules of "fair" selection. They also include ideas about the relative worth of different kinds of knowledge and about the role of the school in furthering such knowledge. The IQ debate comprises a very small and rather surface issue within this entire network. It is basically a debate over what the most effective means are for selecting individuals for certain roles within this framework.

Both the defenders and the critics of IQ tests have missed this point because both have assumed that values belong only to the subjective preferences of the researcher. Thus they simply disagree about what such values are. Jensen sees his work as guided by a desire to further equality of opportunity by providing fairer, more efficient means of selection. His critics view his work as racist in intent and consequence. Both may be correct. However, without understanding the much more complex network of shared values that comprise our understanding of schools as a whole, each furthers an image of the ideal researcher as separate and external from the enterprise that is being studied. Once we understand the way in which researchers carry many of these values with them into their study, then we can begin to examine them and the implications that they hold for our understanding of education. Without such an examination, as we will see in the next two chapters, many seemingly conflicting research programs serve strikingly similar ends.

4 Educational research and classroom knowledge: The case of behavioral theory

The empirical mode of educational understanding has implications for what is considered to be acceptable knowledge both in the classroom and in the society at large. It is not that such research *causes* an emphasis on one kind of knowledge and a deemphasis on another, but rather it focuses our attention more acutely on forms that have already gained ascendency and thereby enhances their value even more. In this chapter we will look at the role that such research plays in the classroom and the school whereas in the next chapter we will examine some of the implications of the empirical tradition for the society at large. Here we will look at the role that behavioral theory plays in defining classroom knowledge and in limiting the development of alternative modes of knowing within the school setting.

At first glance behavioral research, with its emphasis on environmental causation, and research on intelligence or IQ, with its emphasis on hereditary causation, may seem like an odd pairing. Indeed, some of the harshest criticisms of Jensen have been developed by behaviorally oriented theorists.[1] Yet these differences are largely about the causal factors involved in different scores on IQ tests. Although these differences are important and should not be minimized, there is an important feature that is shared by the two camps. There is in each a generally accepted idea about the nature of reliable knowledge. Each accepts the view that science as traditionally understood provides the basis of such knowledge and that scientific explanation deals with observable, public, measurable, and verifiable entities. Each believes too that there is little difference in principle between the natural and human science, although they grant that the human sciences must deal with more complex variables.[2] Moreover, while Jensen minimizes the influence of environmental factors in the development of intelligence, he is, in his advocacy of associative teaching, quite willing to incorporate certain features of behaviorism in his treatment of low-IQ youngsters. Hence the pairing may not be as odd as it initially appears to be.

Sections of this chapter appeared in an earlier version in *Philosophical Forum*, Vol. 6(1), Fall 1974.

Although the use of IQ tests is under attack and has perhaps declined somewhat, the influence of behavioral techniques still has a good deal of support, especially within the school system. Indeed, one of the programs that Jensen cites as a model for teaching low-IQ children, that developed by Bereiter and Engelmann, is a paradigm of the application of behavioral theory to education. This program has been adopted in several areas of the country and has attracted both state and federal funding. Behavioral techniques have advanced on other fronts as well. Serious attention has been given in many states to mandates that the competency of prospective teachers be measured against a prescribed set of behavioral norms; the old lesson plan is giving way to a seemingly more "scientific" list of behavioral objectives, and terms like "positive" or "negative reinforcement" are heard almost as frequently as their colloquial counterparts – "rewards" and "punishment."

Some of the behavioral programs that have been designed to develop or improve specific skills work quite well, although one may question whether in many of these cases behavioral theory is any more than a new costume for some very old pedagogical techniques such as drill, memorization, and praise. Other behavioral "innovations" involve little more than substituting new terms for older ones, appearing thereby to replace common sense with science. Yet behavioral theory is more than simply a new way to speak about old techniques. It also claims to better explain human learning and as such it provides us with a certain picture of human beings.

As a theory of learning, behaviorism, as we will see, is inadequate. However, it must not be thought that all aspects of behaviorism are inappropriate for teaching. For example, to the extent that behaviorism directs teachers to be more aware of the component steps in teaching a complex task, it can be useful despite its theoretical limitations. This, however, is the kind of insight that most good teachers would be aware of even without the aid of a theory of learning such as behaviorism.

Yet behaviorism does more than simply propose a series of classroom techniques; it also expresses a particular view of human nature and defines what is to count as appropriate knowledge. Although this chapter will concentrate on the latter issue, a brief look at the question of human nature will help to set the stage for the more detailed study that follows. The general concern here is that whereas behaviorism puts itself forward as a theory of learning, more important is that it implicitly provides an established way in which to "understand" human consciousness and the kind of knowledge appropriate to it. By so doing it has has more than a small influence in legitimating the forms of knowledge defined as appropriate for schools, and especially for students who come from minority and low-socioeconomic groups.

The above point is similar to the one made in an earlier chapter about Jensen. There is, however, a surface difference between Jensen's claim that there are two different kinds of learning and the view of learning put forward by behaviorists. In contrast to Jensen, behaviorists argue that their concept of learning is universal, that it applies, without exception, to all human beings. Thus is would seem to avoid the duality between associative and conceptual learning expressed by Jensen. Yet this avoidance is only on the surface level.

Behavioral theory emphasizes the view that all human nature is explainable in terms of fixed laws and that human beings are thus subject to the same degree of manipulation, control, and predictability as any other natural object. Behaviorists have been quick to note that one implication of this view is that notions such as "free will" or "human insight" are simply ways to express the fact that in any given instance we may not be aware of all the variables that would be needed to explain or predict a given behavior. Another implication, one that has received much less emphasis, however, is that this view implies two fundamentally different levels of human activity. First, there is the behavior that is governed by universal laws, controlled by environmental stimulation, and thereby subject to change and prediction through environmental manipulation. And second, there is that form of human activity that knows the laws that control behavior and that is able thereby, through manipulating the environment, to predict, control, and change that behavior. Hence, the duality that was noted earlier in the work of Jensen reappears in a different form in behavioral theory.

The examination that follows is intended to illustrate the way in which behavioral theory attempts to define what is to count as appropriate knowledge for schools and to show some of the equally legitimate modes of knowing that are left out of consideration by the behaviorst approach. To make this case, it is necessary to show that behavioral theory, and its assumptions about human nature and human learning, inadequately and arbitrarily limit our conception of knowledge.

Behavioral theory and its deficiencies

Current educational practice reflects behavioral theory in two distinct but related ways: First in official edicts that require learning goals to be stipulated in terms of behavioral objectives, or in terms of the observable behavior that will count as an indication that a student has achieved the desired learning; and second in its use as a method for bringing about learning (behavior modification), a use that stresses "appropriate" reinforcement schedules. The assumption behind both of these expressions is that human action can be described in causal terms, that thought and feelings, which we so often conceive of as private, are basically public and observable, and that behavior can be altered by manipulating the causal factors involved. All of these assumptions are to be found in arguments supporting the current popularity of behavioral objectives, and it is to these arguments that we turn.

Given a limited application of behavioral objectives, they present no great cause for alarm. If, for example, when asked why he is listing all of his goals in behavior terms, an individual teacher were to respond that he has found such practice to be useful for assessing student progress, it would not be unreasonable to accept his point of view and to then evaluate his teaching in terms of the interactions occurring in his classroom. If, however, we were to ask a state superintendent of public instruction why she required all of her teachers to state their goals in behavioral terms, and she replied that there is no other way to evaluate successful teaching, then it would be reasonable to ask for some justification of this point of view.

Advocates of behavioral objectives frequently reject the usefulness of such nonbehavioral aims as "to know," "to understand," and "to appreciate"[3] on the grounds that these refer to mystical inner states rather than to objective behavior. Yet such a view presents an initial difficulty. The implication of this rejection is that when we use such terms as "know" or "understand" as indicative of learning we have mislocated the learned event by placing it inside a person rather than in his overt behavior. This response is typical of the behaviorist view that all human events are, in principle, public and thus subject to observation and scientific scrutiny. It is because of this that it is thought that all learning is properly expressible in terms of observable changes in behavior. In the last section, we will see that by framing the issue in terms that insist upon a dualism between the public and private nature of behavior, behaviorism has missed the most important reason why learning cannot be summed up by a list of observable behaviors. For now, however, it will be useful to accept the dichotomy proposed by behaviorism and to see just how difficult it is to support the view that all important human activity, learning included, is ultimately public and observable.

As we look at this issue it is important to keep in mind the dual nature of consciousness that behavioral theory rests upon. As a person becomes the object of behavioral research, certain seemingly unique features of consciousness, such as intentionality and the ability to perceive relations between different events are, in principle, no longer ascribable to that individual. This is because such features are not believed to be observable in the way that behavior is. Yet, as we will see, the continuation of the behaviorist's own research program depends both upon the fact that some ascription of intentionality is made, even if only implicitly, and upon the ability of someone to perceive relationships between separate events. As these attributes are removed from the consciousness of the subject, they remain, of course, as attributes that the researcher can and does implicitly ascribe to him, but without the need for consultation or dialog. We can see this issue more clearly be returning to the view of the public nature of learning upon which the appeal to behavioral objectives rests.

By entering the dispute about whether learning resides in some form of publicly accessible behavior, we have already circumscribed the debate by agreeing to view learning, in the most general sense, as locatable in some specific way. Although this is not the most productive way to think about learning, it is useful to push the question of location in order to see just how well the behaviorist's view can hold up.

If we were to agree that learning is in part describable in terms of behavior, the question could still be reasonably asked: Where does that which has been learned reside when it is not being expressed? One way out of this problem would be for the behaviorist to review his claim about location and to argue instead that "learning" and the "exhibition of learning" are synonymous terms, and that to call a certain behavior "learned" would simply refer to the fact that it is of such a complexity as to require a deliberate reinforcement schedule in order to assure its eventual and continued performance. In this instance, "learned behavior" would involve a relationship between a complicated (as opposed to a simple) response and a stimulus that evokes that response or a reinforcement that develops and sustains it. This position is difficult to maintain, however, without undercutting the very research programs for which behavioral theory has become known. We can see this in the following way. Even in the attempt to strip language of references to internal mental events, the behaviorist still has occasion to speak in terms of problem-solving behavior, but to speak in terms of a problem is to place all behavior in the context of a non-yet-present response. The here-and-now act takes on significance only by virtue of the end toward which the organism is moving. The rat does not simply run the maze: he runs it *in order to* get food. And if he is seen as simply running it with no determinable end in view, then the term "maze" is a misnomer. And even though it would be possible to look upon the running and the eating as two distinct acts having no connection to one another, the behaviorist's research program and his concern for problem-solving behavior must assume that there is a connection. The connection itself, however, cannot be discovered by the observation of behavior. We can imagine a machine that was constructed to do two things, navigate a "maze" and consume "food." If we were to describe the behavior of such a machine, it would be more appropriate to say that it moved along the "maze" *and* it consumed the "food" rather than it traveled it *in order to* consume the food. The phrase "in order to" suggests a notion of intent or final cause that in the case of the machine is inappropriate, but that is in fact essential to the behaviorist's research program on animal and human learning. However, the behaviorist research program must be distinguished from behaviorist theory itself.

A strict behaviorist who wished to be true to his own theory would do better to describe the animal's behavior as we just described the machines' movements. Hence he would say that the rat ran the "maze" *and* he ate the "food" and would remove from his language terms such as "problems" or phrases that point to intentional connections. If he were to do this, however, he would have no criterion by which to decide which acts to describe in his sequence. Thus he might just as well say that the rat wagged his tail and he ate the food. The very fact that he chooses to observe some acts and to ignore others, and then to describe, on the basis of his observations, a sequence of acts, means that the behaviorist has assumed, as the condition of his own research program, a connection between certain acts that remains as mysterious as the internal states whose existence he wished to deny. Thus, if the behaviorist wishes to hold on to his theory by denying the significance of the questions about location, he can do so only by rejecting his own research program. If, instead, he decides to maintain his research program, he must find a way to address the issue of location.

Some behaviorists, such as Skinner, have attempted to redefine "problem-solving behavior" in order to take into account difficulties like those raised above. These, however, do little more than beg the question. Skinner has argued, for example, that a situation can be identified as problematic when it is shown that a response exists in strength that cannot be emitted. To the question "What would it mean for a person to have a strong unemitted response?" He answers that the strength of the response can be demonstrated by showing that it occurs as soon as "the occasion is suitable."[4] Assume, for example, a man fumbling with his keys and then, after locating the proper one, opening the door. Skinner would say that the response required to open the door existed prior to the occasion of the key being found. But where was the response before the door was opened? Why not simply assume that "fumbling" with keys and opening doors are two discrete acts and thus rid the language of such mysterious entities as "unemitted responses?" Nor does the phrase "suitable occasion" really help, for it merely says that when the occasion arises, it arises. What Chomsky has said about the use of the term "reinforcement" can also be said of a term like "unemitted response": It is a cover for terms like "wants," "intends," and "desires"[5] Despite the behaviorist's denial, the fact is that without such invisible entities the possibility for behavioral research would crumble, and thus what the behaviorist must take away with one hand must be given back with the other.

If we turn now from states of knowing to states of feeling, we can again see how behaviorist theory can address its critics only by denying the validity of key aspects of its own program. Here the problem is not that of the location of an event, but the extent to which a feeling can be known by someone other than the person experiencing it. In this case the behaviorists' argument is not that we are using the wrong terms in describing a feeling event (as we were when describing learning in terms such as "understanding," "appreciation," etc.) but that we are misled in believing that such terms have reference to strictly private occurrences. The general point is that in principle there is no difference between knowing the "sensations" that another person is feeling and knowing any other aspect of his situation. However, this general point is interpreted somewhat differently by different behavioral theorists, and provides an illustration of how the program is forced to reduce its claim when confronted with serious criticism. In what follows, I will deal briefly with the views of Skinner and Norman Malcolm, showing first the different interpretations that are given to this central plank of behavioral theory and how each of these interpretations again requires the relinquishing of a central aspect of the behavioral research program. After this, we will be ready to suggest the range of educational activities that is neglected by the wide-scale commitment to behavioral practice.

The first interpretation that is given to the view that there is no difference in kind between knowledge of a person's sensations and knowledge about other aspects of that person's life is best expressed by Skinner. He holds that there is no sensation to which language refers that is, in principle, private. What we think of as private sensations is thought of in that way not because of the peculiar properties of those events, but simply because other people have limited access to them. If, for example, my decayed tooth were transplanted into your mouth, then under Skinner's view there is every reason to believe that you would feel what was previously my pain. Skinner writes that "we have no reason to suppose that the stimulating effect of an inflamed tooth is essentially different from that . . . of a hot stove. The stove, however, is capable of affecting more than one person in the same way. In studying behavior we may have to deal with the stimulation from a tooth as an inference rather than as a directly observable fact."[6]

In assessing Skinner's argument, it is important to note how he treats events such as the toothache in the above quotation. The nature of the event is determined not by the event itself, the pain involved in having a toothache or in touching a hot stove, but rather in an understanding of the nature of the stimulus that produces the event – the decayed tooth or the hot stove. Indeed, his argument has nothing to do with the privacy of the event, but rather with the degree to which the stimulus producing the event can affect more than one organism. Knowledge of the event is always, at least in principle, public only because such knowledge is for Skinner really a knowing of the stimulus that is located in an environment that is essentially public in character. Events sometimes have a private appearance because the environment, which Skinner defines as "any event in the universe capable of affecting the organism,"[7] is sometimes, as he says, located "within the organism's own skin" and thus in practice others have limited access to it (the decayed tooth differs from the hot stove in terms of the number of people who can, in practice, experience it).

When Skinner decides to include as part of the environment events that take place within the organism's own skin, by implication he unwittingly rejected one of the critical distinctions upon which behavioral practice rests, thus again threatening to destroy behavioral practice by the tensions in behavioral theory. Behaviorism as a practical science rests upon a clear-cut distinction between an environment that, as an independent variable, conditions behavior and the behavior itself. Stimulation, reinforcement, and so forth are part of the environment and are to be distinguished from the organism that is reinforced and that behaves. However, when Skinner extends the meaning of "environment" to include some events enclosed within the organism's own skin, he has obscured this seemingly necessary distinction and has failed to explain what we should now take to be the organism that behaves.

This difficulty becomes even more acute when, in trying to protect his theory against its critics, Skinner writes in *Behaviorism at Fifty* that "many contingencies involving private stimuli . . . follow from simple mechanical relations among stimuli, responses, and reinforcing consequences. The various motions which comprise turning a handspring . . . are under the control of external and internal stimuli and subject to external and internal reinforcing consequences."[8] Unhappily for Skinner, it is difficult to say what an "internal reinforcing consequence" could be other than a general feeling of satisfaction or rightness that Skinner does not wish to acknowledge and which is indeed difficult to manipulate. Thus for Skinner to admit the reality of such private events as satisfactions would be to reduce the effectiveness of external reinforcement mechanisms. To call such seemingly private events "internally reinforcing" doesn't help very much, for it is simply to admit that part of the reinforcement mechanism remains outside the control of the behavioral technician.

One might think, given this theoretical backtracking, that behaviorism would have experienced similar setbacks in the area of educational policy. One of the major reasons for the appeal that behavioral theory has for educational policy-makers is the promise that it is supposed to hold for manipulating learning in desired directions. The more the theory is able to identify aspects of the environment that can be used to control behavior in predictable ways, the more appeal it holds for contemporary educational practice. Conversely, one might think that the more the distinction between the environment as the initiator and the behavior as the result is obscured, the smaller the appeal of behavioral theory for school policy. Such a retreat has generally not taken place because behaviorism, as a theory, is more than simply a guide for specific programs. As we have seen, it also provides a way in which consciousness is to be understood, and the various and subtle distinctions that have been raised above have not penetrated this understanding. Such theoretical problems are viewed not as an occasion to retreat from practices that are described as behavioral (and that often work within a circumscribed set of aims), but rather to continue to patch up the theoretical difficulties that have been revealed. Thus a number of philosophers who, with reservations, have been sympathetic to the general behaviorist point of view, have attempted to patch the theory up by amending the treatment of private entities. Yet even the most sophisticated of these attempts have been able to succeed only by abandoning some of the basic assumptions of behaviorist theory. Norman Malcolm, as a case in point, has proposed some adjustments in the behaviorist's notion of language that he believes will keep the theory intact.

Recognizing that there are many problems with the claim that a language that purports to refer to sensations can be strictly public, Malcolm finds the source of these problems in two underlying assumptions. First is the assumption that statements about such things as pain are really statements about sensations, and second is the assumption that the two grammatically similar types of statements illustrated by "I have a pain" and "he has a pain" require the same procedures of verification and are both verifiable.

Malcolm rejects both of these assumptions. Taking his cue from Wittgenstein, he suggests that statements such as "he has a pain" do not refer to sensations at all and that they are not to be verified on the basis of a shared sensation (such as that resulting from touching a hot stove) but on the basis of an observation of behavior. A statement such as "I have a pain" is not verifiable at all for there is no criterion to which the person who utters it would refer in order to ascertain its truth. Rather, like a grimace or a groan, this kind of statement constitutes part of the criteria that an observer would use to assess the truth of "he has a pain."[9]

For Malcolm a statement such as "I am in pain" has the same quality as a series of yelps. It is not an expression that I am meant to verify, for "being in pain" is not meant to qualify the I who makes the statement. His point is that when I say "I am in pain," few people would think of asking how I know that, and if I were asked such a question, I would not answer by saying "because I am jumping up and down holding a hammer in one hand and shaking my other hand."

However intent Malcolm may be on saving behaviorism, if his position is accepted, it undercuts Skinner's understanding of behaviorism as a science. Recall that part of the behaviorist's concern was to erase the distinction between "mental" and "physical" aspects of behavior. By eliminating events that supposedly could not be subjected to public verification, if was believed that a true science of behavior could be established. Skinner had said, for example, "We cannot apply the methods of science to a subject matter which is assumed to move about capriciously. . . . If we are to use the methods of science in the field of human affairs, we must assume that behavior is lawful and determined."[10] Skinner believes that behavior can only be lawful if the conditions governing it can, in principle, he observed. That we cannot observe "internal" states provides reason for dismissing them.

Returning to Malcolm, his observations about the different nature of first- and third-person statements leads him to conclude:

People tell us things about themselves which take us by surprise, things which we should not have guessed from our knowledge of their circumstances and behavior. A behaviorist philosopher will say that if we had known more about their history, environment, and behavior we should have been able to infer this same information. I do not believe there are any grounds for thinking so. The testimony that people give us about their intentions, plans, hopes, worries, thoughts, and feelings is by far the most important source of information we have about them. This self-testimony has, one could say, an autonomous status. To a great extent we cannot check it against anything else, and yet to a great extent we credit it. I believe we have no reason to think it is even a theoretical possibility that this self-testimony could be supplanted by inferences from external and/or internal physical variables.[11]

Malcolm implies that there are two sources from which we draw our knowledge of human beings. One is the conditions (public and observable) that allow some accurate predictions about behavior to be made. The other is the testimony that people *choose* to make public about themselves. Yet it is precisely this kind of conclusion that Skinner was hoping to avoid. If it is the case that we cannot in principle predict behavior from a full-scale knowledge of the past and present conditions surrounding a person, then it is also the case that all the determinants of behavior are not, even in principle, observable. Malcolm's amendment raises the very problem that the behaviorist had hoped to avoid. In giving special status to the first-person statement, it has undermined the behaviorist's concept of evidence.

Malcolm's own view is not without its faults, however, and it is worth mentioning one of these before examining the practical limits of behavioral techniques. In its effect, the impact of Malcolm's point of view is to avoid dealing with the question of the private or public character of such things as sensations and to look instead at the structure of language. Yet if first-person statements such as "I have a pain" are to be distinguished from third-person statements such as "he has a pain," what status should be assigned to first-person statements that are uttered in the past tense? The statement "I *had* a pain" does not appear to be simply an expression of behavior, a sophisticated grunt or groan. Yet if the intent is to avoid dealing with the status of sensations, then the meaning of such a statement is problematic. It does not seem correct to suggest that when I say "I had a pain" I am referring to a set of past *behaviors* that I now recall exhibiting, but it would seem equally peculiar to say that I am simply exhibiting pain behavior once removed.

In the next section we will look at some of the implications that are entailed for pedagogy by different views about the nature of knowing and the location of knowledge. Here, however, it will be useful to conclude this section by sketching another point of view.

Peter Strawson, in his critique of Wittgenstein's *Philosophical Investigations,* suggests that only if sensations are accepted as real can Wittgenstein's view of language (which Strawson interprets similarly to Malcolm) make sense. Strawson's argument focuses upon the different status ascribed to such things as colors (generally said to have a public quality) as opposed to that which we ascribe to pain. Strawson summarizes Wittgenstein's position in the following way:

Let us suppose first that we feel pain only and always under the condition that our skin is in contact with the surfaces of certain bodies. . . . The pain begins and ends with that contact. This is generally the condition under which color is experienced. Then our pain language might have a logic wholly different from that which it does have. Instead of ascribing pains to sufferers, we might ascribe painfulness to surfaces, much as we at present call them rough, smooth, hard, soft, etc. Another possibility is this. . . . Let us suppose that any person felt pain if and only if every other normal person in the same region . . . at the same time also felt pain. Then we might ascribe painfulness to regions instead of pain to persons; saying, e.g., "It's painful today," or "It's painful in here." The point of both examples is that in each case we should have as impersonal a way of describing pain-phenomena as we have of describing color-phenomena. But of course the incident of physical pain is not like this. The causes of pain are often internal and organic. . . . A set of people together in certain surroundings will be in general agreement on "what it looks like here, what it feels like (to the touch) here, and what it sounds like here." In this possibility of a general agreement in judgment lies the possibility of a common impersonal language for describing what we see and hear and touch. But there is no such general agreement as to whether or not "it's painful here," as to what it feels like (as we misleadingly say) *within*. . . . Because of certain general facts of nature, therefore, the only possible common pain-language is the language ascribed to those, who talk the language, the criteria for its ascription being (mainly) pain behavior.[12]

Strawson then concludes:

It is the above points which I take Wittgenstein essentially to be making. . . . But the way in which he makes them is, in part, at least misleading. For from none of these facts does it follow that "pain" is not the name of a sensation. On the contrary. It is only in the light of the fact that "pain" is the name of a sensation that *these* facts are intelligible.[13]

Although Strawson's interpretation of Wittgenstein is unclear in terms of whether he believes Wittgenstein intended or not to deny the existence of sensations, his general point can be taken as a guide for the discussion that is to follow: The very fact that we do not ascribe pain to areas, that we do not talk in terms of it being "painful today," suggests that although pain language need not be taken as referring to private sensations, the privacy of sensations seems to be a necessary presupposition of all pain language. An analogous point might then be made about knowledge: That while language that refers to states of knowledge need not be referring to private states, nevertheless such private (or subjective states) may be taken as a precondition of all language about knowledge. I will not try to develop this point here, but will suggest some of its implications for understanding education in the following section.

Schooling and behavioral techniques

The difficulties with both Skinner's and Malcolm's views regarding sensations lend credence to the possibility of private entities that are presupposed by the very grammar of the language, a grammar that is itself public, but in a very different way than the behavior described by Skinner. If this is the case with pain language, then it may also be the case that the very fact of language itself presupposes shared procedures for making sense out of the world. A detailed argument for such internal, sense-making procedures on the species level would not be too difficult to support given the psychological theory of Piaget or the linguistic theory of Chomsky. For now, however, it will be sufficient to contrast the pedagogical implications of a model of this kind with more behaviorally oriented practice. First, a few preliminary remarks are in order.

Much of behavioral technology when practiced by a good teacher sounds like simple common sense. After all, it is not unreasonable in some situations to reward children for certain behavior or to state one's goals as clearly and precisely as possible. Further, if those goals happen to be behavioral in some sense, then a language that describes the projected behavior is appropriate. However, such commonsense rules of thumb do not constitute science, and do not by implication rule out other activities. The problem with behavioral theory is that it raises commonsense practice to the level of an exclusive science and thereby rules out the value of activity that does not conform to its rules and its narrow view of consciousness. The advocates of behavioral techniques model all learning upon a notion of simple skill acquisition, and they build around this some questionable assumptions about the nature of human consciousness and learning.

Implicit in behavioral education theory are two assumptions. The first is that the object of learning is initially to be found outside the child existing in the form of some well-defined model of appropriate behavior. It is this model that is to be described by the teacher in her statement of objectives. The second assumption is related to the first. Because it is believed that the model exists externally to and independently of the learner, it is also assumed that it can be stated prior to and independently of the act of learning. Behavioral objectives tell us what is to be learned and how we are to know that learning has occurred.

The claim is that there is an external structure to knowledge and that it is the school's responsibility to articulate this structure, to select a program for teaching it, and then to devise a test to measure whether it has been taught. The individuality of the child is considered only in terms of diagnostic procedures. The process of diagnosis, however, is seen to have nothing to do with *what* is to be taught but is relevant only to how it might be learned. For example, a teacher has set up a procedure for teaching the 5's tables and upon implementing the procedure discovers that some children are having difficulty with it. He then diagnoses the problem and finds that some youngsters have not yet caught on to multiplying. Because the logical structure of knowledge is presumed external to the child, the teacher puts aside the 5's tables for few weeks and returns to the drills of addition. In other words, he believes that his students do not know the prerequisite of multiplication and pauses in the week's activity to teach it to them.

However, the diagnostic procedures do not lend themselves to an understand-

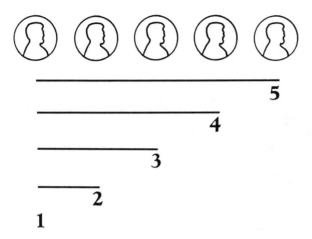

Figure 4.1.

ing of the *sense in which* the children do not know multiplication. Rather, accommodating the child to the external structure of knowledge remains the sole priority. Consider as an example of a different procedure the following incident involving a preschool child 4 years old:

The teacher holds out a handful of pennies and asks the child, "How many pennies do I have in my hand?" The child quickly responds, "five," The teacher, concerned about the possibility of a correct guess asks again, "How many?" The child responds, "four." "How many?" "Three." The teacher becomes frustrated, "How many!" "Two." The child has uttered each succeeding number with the same sense of definiteness as she had uttered "five." Just before the teacher is about to tell the child she is wrong, the supervisor steps in and supports the youngster. "That is right and she also has one penny in her hand." The child nods her approval. "How many different ways can you make five?" the supervisor then asks.[14] [See Figure 4.1.]

In this case the imposition of behavioral objectives would have destroyed the opportunity the child had to articulate the way in which she in fact does make sense out of her world, and would have forced the teacher to insist that there was only one way to see it correctly. As another example, imagine the following teaching episode:

The teacher rolls one ball against another and asks, "Why did the second ball move?" "Because the first one pushed it." "How does one thing push another?" "By putting its force into it?" "How could you demonstrate that that is the way it works?" "If you pushed that heavy table you would soon get tired, which would mean that you would have lost your energy. Since energy is like force, that would demonstrate that you had given your energy to the table." "Can you lose energy without giving it away to something else?" "Well, maybe, but I think in this case we can see that you gave it to the table."

"How? Can you see energy?" "No, but you can see what it does." "Is there any other way it can be explained?" I don't think so."[15]

This youngster has failed to provide what would be considered an accepted physical explanation by contemporary classroom standards. However, even though his ideas may have more kinship to Aristotle than to Newton, he has been allowed to elaborate his own sense-making procedure by demonstrating its application. Moreover, he has begun to distinguish what he actually "sees" from the concepts that he uses to explain what he sees.

Although it would be perfectly appropriate in the above situation for the teacher to have described the objectives in terms of helping the student to articulate and elaborate his own thought and to generate concepts that would help to explain the observed phenomena, there is no way in which he could state prior to the lesson what specific behavior would indicate that the student had achieved his objective. Of course, upon completing the lesson he might be able to justify its value by describing the verbal transaction that took place, indicating the acts of articulation, elaboration, and concept formation. However, this "afterthought" would in no way meet the misplaced demand for precision that is made by the advocates of behavioral objectives.

Once we move beyond the level of seemingly simple "skill" acquisition, it is difficult to say from a *purely pedagogical* point of view what function behavioral objectives have in education. As we move away from such simple acquisition, we move into areas where the right answer is not always obvious (and where it is perhaps not available) and hence where it becomes increasingly difficult to describe beforehand what the "appropriate" behavior might look like.

If there is reason for concern about the constricting effect that the adherence to behavioral objectives can have on education, then there must be similar reason for concern about behavior modification techniques, for such techniques require that appropriate behavior be reinforced in a positive way. As soon as the range of appropriate behavior is expanded beyond the narrow limit set by behavioral objectives, then it becomes problematic what manifestations of that range to reinforce.

Much of the persuasiveness of the idea of behavioral objectives is found in the simple fact that many kinds of learning, for example, learning to ride a bicycle, repair a radio, drive a car, solve an equation, are clearly expressable in some rather specific behavioral terms. Yet the fact that these examples are expressable in behavioral terms should not blind us to the fact that there are more complicated issues at stake here. Consider, as a counterexample, learning to vote. I do not mean here the problem of learning to vote wisely, or for the best candidate, activities that are obviously complicated to understand. Rather, I mean the seemingly simple act of learning how to vote and the question of what behavior is to count as having learned to do so. Clearly, there are many behaviors that can be taken to count as voting, and there is no vote that is not accompanied by some form of behavior. However, just which behavior is to be singled out as indicating that a vote has been cast or that a person has learned to vote? Shall we prescribe, as our objective, entering a curtained booth and pulling a lever? If so, then will it count even when there is no ballot in the machine? Is marking a ballot then to count as voting? If so, then will it be counted even if the names on the "ballot" do not refer to real people? Is voting raising a hand? Saying "Aye"? Grunting approval in a meeting? Or saying nothing when objections are called for? The point is that any and all of these behaviors and nonbehaviors may count as voting and any and all of them may not count as voting depending upon factors in the situation and upon how those factors are understood by the person whose behavior is being counted. Certainly voting is a public, observable act. Yet what makes that act an act of voting, rather than something else, is not the behavior itself but the fact that the behavior takes place in the context of a shared set of rules and institutions that makes the raising of a hand, the entering of a booth, the grunting of approval, or the maintaining of silence carry a meaning of a vote. And when one learns how to vote, what is learned is not primarily voting behavior (that is incidental), but rather the institutional relations and rules that give meaning to that behavior as voting. Moreover, what makes any particular act an act of voting is first that the voter has some general understanding of these relations and rules and second that she understands this particular act as an act of voting. That is, the individual who has learned how to vote has learned to participate in the meaning system of which voting behavior is a part and she has learned to interpret the contextual codes that call for that behavior. Yet the meaning system itself is rooted in concepts that go far beyond the immediate behavior. As Charles Taylor has observed:

If there is not some significance attached to our behavior, no amount of marking and counting pieces of paper, raising hands, walking out into lobbies amounts to voting. From this it follows that the institution of voting must be such that certain distinctions have application: e.g., . . . that between a valid vote and an invalid one which in turn requires a distinction between a real choice and one which is forced or counterfeited. . . . For there to be voting in a sense recognizably like ours, there must be a distinction in men's self-interpretation between autonomy and forced choice."[16]

The problem with an overemphasis on behavioral theory is not only that it denies the very possibility of autonomy, although that is certainly a problem. The real problem is rather that it ascribes a form of consciousness to human beings that would deny the very possibility of exploring the meaning systems that give any behavioral event its significance. Yet the emphasis given to behaviorism has been a strong weight in favor of such a view of consciousness and its implications for schooling.

There is another issue that these examples raise, and that is the significance of interpretation in understanding educational activity. Education is a human activity and as such we never perceive a sample of behavior pure and simple. The perception of behavior in education involves an interpretative network that gives that behavior meaning. We will examine this issue somewhat in the next chapter when we examine the taken-for-granted framework of empirical research, and then more systematically in Chapter 7 when we look at historical scholarship in education. For now, however, it is important to see that just like the IQ researcher, the behavioral researcher presents himself as standing outside the object of study as a neutral, impartial observer. Yet insofar as the researcher must render an interpretation of that behavior, as he must, then he too is bound within a meaning system. This means that he cannot stand outside the object of study, but must in some sense understand and participate in the framework through which that object takes on meaning.

It is the concern with meaning that has occupied the attention of educational philosophers, but as we will see shortly, their treatment of this issue has vested meaning with the same object status that other researchers have given to behavior. In other words, this meaning resides in words and their use, and the philosophers perceive their role as but rendering such meaning clear. Before we look at this tradition, however, it will be useful to examine the way in which empirical research functions in the context of the educational system as a whole.

5   Empirical research and the goals of the educational system

It is supposedly a truism that educational institutions and practices cannot be understood in isolation from the societies in which they are found. For much of the history of educational thought, scholars have been guided in their deliberations about the role and limit of education by their awareness of this essential relationship. Educational theorists spanning the centuries from Plato to Dewey saw that the first and most important limitation on education was the values projected and manifested in the day-to-day activities of the people in the society. The perennial debate about whether schools can change the values and structure of the society, or whether they must simply follow changes initiated in other quarters, cannot of course be answered in any absolute way, but the debate is nevertheless a reflection of the recognition of this relationship.

However important this relationship may have been in guiding the thought of educators of the past, it has been largely ignored with the recent emphasis placed on empirical research. To take but three recent examples which illustrate this oversight, Arthur Jensen believes, as we have seen, that the limits of reform are to be found in the intellectual capacities of children in school. Given this view, the reason many children are not able to learn how to read, write, or do arithmetic can be explained primarily by a score on an IQ examination and by attempts to teach them in a cognitively stimulating way. For Jensen, as we have seen, they are also to be explained by the dysfunctionality between certain teaching and learning styles.[1] Edward Banfield,[2] who sharply criticizes Jensen and rejects the significance of IQ scores as indicating any significant limit to schooling, nevertheless argues that educational reform is limited by the class composition of the children in school, and further that important class characteristics are transmitted from generation to generation by the various child-rearing practices of different families. In elaborating this point, he proposes that the most important charac-

Sections of this chapter appeared in an earlier version in R. H. Weller, *Humanistic Education: Visions & Realities; Proceedings,* Berkeley: McCutcheon, 1977, and appear here with permission of the publisher.

teristic of class is not a person's social or economic status, but rather a person's ability to project himself into a future time and place and to delay the gratification of present impulses for more satisfying and worthwhile goals later on. Periodically, however, a more promising note is sounded. Charles Silberman,[3] in synthesizing various research, much of it based on the cognitive psychology of Jean Piaget, locates the limits of schooling in the mindless practices of teachers and administrators who foster needless routine and impose harsh, external discipline upon the child. He proposes that these accidental features of schooling could be changed by a more open approach to education.

Although there are many differences that exist among these three points of view, it is important to see how each one of them has circumscribed the factors of schooling so as to allow the relationship between school and society to be ignored. Jensen does this by locating the major limiting factor inside the skin of the child, perhaps in the electrical charges that carry impulses from the senses to the brain, or perhaps in the structure and complexity of the brain itself, or in some other physiological correspondent to a score on an IQ examination. Banfield does it by locating the limiting factor in the transaction between a parent and a child and by defining class in such a way that psychological characteristics are highlighted and the social and economic conditions that might influence those conditions are deemphasized. And Silberman does the same by isolating as the essential relationship the transaction between a teacher and a child. Here the term "mindlessness," which he often uses to describe the behavior of teachers and administrators, can best be seen simply as a way to dismiss, as not worthy of examination, the social forces and values that influence the practices he objects to.

In order to see the similarities between most contemporary theories of educational reform, we need only to look at the accompanying chart (Table 5.1). Here there are two primary variables each one of which is divided into three subsections, making a nine-box matrix. The first primary variable simply indicates where a person locates the major limit to educational reform. Here the limit can be located either in something about the individual himself, such as his personality structure or IQ, or in the individual's culture as Banfield does in his stress on present orientation that is transmitted presumably through child-rearing practices from generation to generation. Or finally, the limit can be located within the institution of schooling itself, as is the case with Silberman's attribution of "mindlessness," or with others who, like Skinner, believe, for example, that the major problem with school results from the inadequate training of teachers in behavioral techniques. Once the limit is identified, then the extent to which a particular viewpoint is associated with change depends largely upon the extent to which it is believed that the limit can be overcome.

Out of the various boxes in this chart, we could probably generate many of the most recent positions on educational reform and the limits of schooling, but the

Table 5.1. *Types of theories of educational reform according to two variables*

Extent to which limit can be changed	Location of limit		
	Individual	Family–culture	Institution of schooling
Impossible	1 IQ genetically determined capacity to learn. (Jensen)	2 Every society has a top and a bottom group. There is a culture of poverty that is transmitted from generation to generation and cannot be dislodged by state intervention.	3 Every society has an agency for sorting the top from the bottom group. Our agency is the school.
Possible, but too costly	4 Cultural and psychological orientation. To try to improve the education of the bottom will eventually take away resources from most talented members of society. (Banfield)	5 Eliminating the culture of poverty could only be done by denying the right of parents to govern their children or by taking away opportunities from the top and destroying initiative.	6 If schools try directly to bring up the bottom at expense of the top, there is backlash and everyone is worse off.
Possible and desirable	7 Environment that can be altered through enrichment. (Skinner, Silberman)	8 The major defects attributed to culture such as restricted language code, deficient conceptualization, low motivation, etc. can be improved through government programs, by community action, etc.	9 The problem with schools is the attitude of teachers and their poor preparation, or school boards, etc.

important point to see is the way in which these factors circumscribe and limit the examination of educational reform. For whichever box or group of boxes that we choose, it will have circumscribed the problem as resulting from the transmission between the school and the child, and then the only thing that needs explaining is whether the interference in this transmission occurs on the side of the child or on the side of the school. With the problem circumscribed in this way, the truism that the school cannot be understood in isolation from the society has been forgotten. The purpose of this chapter is to recall that truism, to take it seriously, and to see what light it can shed on the question of educational reform. I will begin by first saying something about the nature of a limit in order to show that there is a conceptual error in speaking of schooling as if it just involved the transmission between a teacher and a child, and then I will relate this discussion to questions about the goals of schooling in general. After this I will specify what I take to be the essential relationship between schooling and society and how this relationship influences both the goals and limits of schooling. Finally I will conclude by saying a few words about how the more prominent empirical approaches to education serve this relationship, by taking for granted the social goals of the enterprise of schooling.

The relation between goals and limits

One of the characteristic inadequacies of empirical work in education is the failure to analyze the goals of the educational system. Instead, one or another ideal is usually accepted as the proper one, and then the limits of schooling are addressed in light of that assumed goal. One of the problems with this approach is that it fails to recognize that the very concept of a limit takes on meaning only in the context of some particular goal. If, for example, my goal is to run a mile in under four minutes, then the limiting factors are such things as the shortness of my legs and the capacity of my lungs. For a well-trained athlete who actually has the capacity to run a mile in four minutes, the limiting factors will be of a different nature – the state of the track or perhaps the quality of the competition. If, however, my goal is to type this chapter at fifty words a minute, then the limiting factors will be found elsewhere. Or, to return to the field of education, if one characterizes the goal of education as allowing each person to achieve according to his or her maximum potential, then IQ scores cannot, even if they do indicate intelligence, serve as a limiting factor. The reason is simply that the development of a person's intelligence in this case characterizes the goal itself, not the limited means to achieve it. What might constitute a limit in this case is the availability of financial resources, motivational techniques, or adequate teaching strategies. If, on the other hand, the goal is to fill a certain number of positions in the labor market as quickly as possible, then, depending upon such factors as the nature of the positions, IQ scores can indicate the presence of certain limitations.

The point of this discussion can help us to see some of the problems that result when there is a failure to adequately characterize and evaluate the goal of education. The goal itself circumscribes what is appropriate to seek as a limit. Without such an evaluation, the likelihood is that seemingly conflicting educational theories will simply be speaking past one another. The result, more often then not, is a simplistic theory of the possibility for educational reform. And by simplistic I mean either theories that project easy changes, such as that found in Silberman's book where the idea is just to get teachers to *think* about what they are doing, or else theories that can be used to justify any social order no matter how discriminatory or oppressive it may be. The latter characterizes the likely use of theories like those put forth by Jensen and Banfield.

One other preliminary point needs to be made. In addition to understanding the goal that is being stipulated before we can make a judgment about the appropriateness of the limit that is being projected, there is also a need to make explicit the subject for whom it is a goal. That is, we need to make a judgment about who or what is supposed to have this goal. In the case of running a four-minute mile, it makes a difference in terms of what is identified as a limit whether the goal belongs to a well-trained athlete or to someone else. If, for example, someone were to say that what limited Tubby's running the mile in four minutes was the quality of the track and the pace of the competition, we would find this puzzling. Here, we would find his natural endowments and perhaps his sedentary habits to be much more appropriate limits. In his case, the quality of the track and the nature of the competition would be quite irrelevant, but not so in the case of a well-trained athlete. Given these preliminary remarks, we can now return again to the question of schooling.

The system of schooling and the division of labor

When we speak of schooling, we are not just talking about a single building with its classrooms, teachers, and students, where the essential transaction is indeed the one that occurs between a teacher and the students. Rather, we are also speaking of a system that is defined in terms of a series of internal and ongoing relationships of the different parts to each other and to the whole. We are speaking, for example, of the degree of congruence that exists between grade school and high school, and between these and the university. We are speaking too of the selection procedures, both formal and informal, by which it is determined whether an individual moves from one part of the system to another. We are speaking of the curriculum, the teaching strategies, and the materials that are used, the textbooks, the *Weekly Readers* put out by Xerox Corporation, the health brochures printed and distributed by candy manufacturers, and a host of other characteristics that comprise the school system as a whole. We can summarize these characteristics by saying that the school system consists of those procedures used to transmit a selected portion of the cultural tradition from one generation to the next, in a more or less formal manner and sanctioned by some state body for the purpose of establishing ideological congruence and reproducing skills and labor. This definition is somewhat open-textured, leaving a number of questions unanswered. It would have to be argued, for example, whether private or parochial schools are part of the school system since they are sanctioned by the state in a very different way than public schools. Moreover, "skills" needs to be taken in a broad sense and include not just rote learning, but the development of scientific talent as well. Nevertheless, for our purposes the definition is adequate because it highlights the fact that when we speak about the goals of schooling we need to distinguish whether we are speaking about the goals of the system as a whole or about a particular part of that system. Once this distinction is made, then it is easy to see that some particular part of the system could be unsuccessful in achieving its goal while the system as a whole is reasonably successful in affecting its end. Think, for example, of the different clubs in a professional baseball league, each one of which has the goal of winning the pennant, a goal that only one of them can achieve. The failure of all but one of the clubs to achieve this ultimate goal does not mean, however, that the management of the league must be unsuccessful in their goal of keeping public interest and gate receipts high. Although I am sure that this analogy would break down if carried too far, the point is a rather simple one and it can help us to see some things that are often overlooked in discussions of educational reform. The failure to distinguish between the goals of schooling as related to a particular transaction between a teacher and a child in an individual school and the general goals of the school system itself functions to shield from examination the interrelationship between school and society. Yet it is important to realize that the goals that are established by individual members of the school system are done so in terms of their congruence with some aspect of the goals of the system as a whole. Whether it could in fact be otherwise is a difficult question to answer, but the recognition of this attempt to establish congruence should lead to an examination and evaluation of the systemic goal of schooling.

In order to understand the goals of the American system of schooling we need to return to the definition offered above. Although the definition itself does not spell out what these goals are, it does tell us where to look. The definition itself tells us that the procedures used in schools are designed to reproduce labor, skills, and ideology, and that to understand the nature of schooling we need to be able to characterize in a general way the kind of skills and ideologies that are being reproduced.

The system of schooling as we know it today, with its age-specific classrooms, compulsory attendance laws, and emphasis on mass testing, had its roots in the developing urban life of contemporary society and in the new processes of production that, as Cremin reports,[4] seemed to render apprenticeship programs obsolete and to disrupt the traditional modes of socialization, such as could be found in the family and the external community. It is to these roots that we must return in order to understand the direction and function of the American school system today.

Before we return to look briefly at the origins of public education, a brief word of caution needs to be voiced. There are many scholars who would object to the attempt to characterize the goal of schooling in any general way, and there are many others who would object to looking for that goal in the origins of the school system. Both groups have a point. After all, it may be said, *people,* not *systems,* have goals, and further, different people have different goals. Moreover, whatever the goals of those in the past may have been, they are clearly not the same as those of people today. These observations seem to have the weight of common sense behind them. After all, goals do belong to persons, and systems may be seen as simply the impersonal bonds that bind people functionally together in institutions. Moreover, the difference between, say, the 1850s or '60s and the 1970s and '80s is so obvious that no comment need be made. Yet however much these observations may be supported by common sense, they are somewhat beside the point. To say that an individual has such and such a goal is to say that his or her behavior can be understood as a continuous series of acts that are designed, usually consciously, to bring about a certain end. To identify the goal tells us what to count as relevant behavior and what to identify as important. Personal behavior is itself multifaceted. People wake up in the morning, brush their teeth, eat breakfast, rush to work, and so on. Many of these activities are not usually identified as goals, but rather as functions because they are usually the taken-for-granted and general conditions that enable us to carry out more distinctive activities. When such functions cannot be performed, however, and relearning them becomes the focal point of our behavior, then we quite properly identify them as goals. Because human beings are conscious agents, we often take their own statement of their goals as definitive, as Norman Malcolm observed in the preceding chapter. This is why some people believe that only individuals can have goals. However, even in the case of individuals the actor's understanding is not always taken as definitive. People are capable of understanding their own goals, but they are also capable of self-deception, or *misunderstanding* their own goals. This means that the understanding of a goal requires an interpretation, and the interpretation that best represents the goals of the actor is determined by the extent to which coherence can be found in seemingly discrete acts. The observer, of course, has the added burden of having to include in his understanding the way in which the agent understands his own action. What is most important, however, is not where the interpretation issues from but the fact that it is able to provide an account of the organizing principle that lends coherence to otherwise discrete acts.

Once we understand that a goal is identified in terms of something that is reasonably distinctive and that establishes relevance by postulating a continuity to otherwise discrete acts, then we can see that goals may belong to individuals, but they may also belong to individuals as they are related to each other in acts or institutions. When, for example, people moved westward, they did so for many different reasons. Some went to escape debt, others to make a fortune; some went to farm, others to pan gold, or to sell merchandise; some went as soldiers, others as trappers and hunters. Whereas it is perfectly proper to speak about the continuity of any series of acts performed by an individual in terms of a goal, it is equally appropriate to speak of the whole series of acts performed by different individuals, along with the acts of the government that supported them, such as the Homestead Act and the building of railroads, in terms of the *general* goal of settling the West. It is this way of speaking that allows us to make sense out of all of these acts and to see them as forming some kind of continuous, meaningful event. Moreover, it is equally appropriate to speak of the goal as beginning with the movement of the first settlers West, even though these people may not have had a whisper of an idea about the overall historical significance of their act. In the very same way, it is appropriate to speak of the goals of the school system as a whole. To begin to characterize those goals by looking back to the origins of the school system itself is not necessarily to claim that the goals were fully understood at that time. It is simply to say that in light of these goals we can understand some of the major lines of continuity between the activity of the past and the activity of the present, as they involve the establishment and development of schools. With this word of caution behind us, we can now return to look briefly at the origins of schooling.

The initial relationship between schooling and industrialization meant not only that schools were to assume many of the functions previously located in the family, but also that they were expected to be a major source of manpower supply. Initially, this latter expectation meant that schools were to provide the low-level skills and socialization needed to ease the transition from the farm to the factory. In the beginning many professional skills such as law and medicine did not require university training, and most of the knowledge needed for managerial assignments was transmitted through work in the family enterprise, or in some form of "on-the-job training" – a term that only makes sense against the background of a well-developed school system. Eventually the training for these jobs became more and more restricted to the higher units in the school system. Thus, on the higher levels schools were judged more and more by their ability to match the prerequisites needed for market demands in specific fields, whereas on the lower level and in a less formal way, they were judged by the congruence between their curriculum or methods and the occupational possibilities for a given child or group of children. The impulse behind this development came as part of a more general desire on the part of many people to control the contingencies of human life, a desire that, although not unique to modern times, was strengthened by the hope that some people placed in the development of new technology. The impulse guiding the development of schooling at both the higher and the lower levels was the impulse to control an ever-widening sphere of activity by controlling the knowledge that those who practice the activity would possess. For those at the highest levels, part of this knowledge included a general understanding of the kinds of skills needed for performing a task at the lower levels of employment, and the way to assure the possession of this knowledge by constantly rendering those lower-level skills less complex and increasingly inter-changeable with other skills. For those at the lowest levels, it required a degree of passivity[5] that hopefully would enable them to become tractable members of the labor market. Both of these impulses were expressed in the late 1800s by a United States commissioner of education when he warned that the children of the common laborers must be educated to protect property from the threat of commu-nism, and then again when he cautioned that without a highly developed public education system the nation's industrial development would take a back seat to that of other countries.[6]

While the mechanisms for matching the program of a child to his or her future possibilities are much more informal on the lower levels of education than on the higher ones, they are no less important, and this very informality makes these mechanisms more difficult to change. For example, even though many poorer parents will look upon the schools as a possible vehicle of upward mobility for their children, they will also look upon them as an insurance policy that, if everything else fails, will at least allow their youngsters to assume the kind of work routine that parents themselves are used to. If the parent's job is dull and routine, if it demands passivity rather than initiative, and requires that orders be followed rather than discussed and evaluated, then it is unlikely that parents will demand otherwise from their children's schools, and it cannot be unambiguously argued, given the present division of labor, that teachers should try to subvert the parents' inclinations. Yet to go along with these inclinations means to give up the educator's essential role of introducing youngsters to the elements of rational thinking, of opening their minds to different alternatives, and of developing their aesthetic and humanistic sensitivities. Given some research that shows a strong correlation between lower, working-class states and conformity, and given other research that suggests that the percentage of working-class mothers who prepare their youngsters for a passive role in school is significantly higher than that of middle-class mothers, and given too studies that show the direction of work on many different levels has been toward more routine and less discretionary roles, it is suprising how little attention has been given to the relationship between the work requirements of the parents and the desired education for the child.[7] The way that schools handle this dilemma may differ according to the overall com-position of the student body. One observational study has shown that teachers assign children to different groups on the basis of nonintellectual criteria, such as appearance, and then encourage active behavior from the higher-status group and passive behavior from the lower-status one;[8] but the details of the ways in which the structure of work is reflected in the structure of pedagogy and in the desires and practices of parents have yet to become a significant element in the empirical research program.

The point of the above discussion is simply that if we are to understand the limits of educational reform, we cannot do so by focusing our attention solely on the transaction between a student and a teacher, or by examining the intellectual and cultural interference that is said to distort the transaction. What is seen as interference from the point of view of an individual school may be reasonably compatible with the demand that the system as a whole service the division of labor. It seems perfectly reasonable to suggest that if there is to be a significant, lasting, and positive change in the school system, it can only be accomplished in the light of a projected and concomitant change in the division of labor. Moreover, in a society such as our own that judges progress by the size of the gross national product and strives thereby to maximize production, it is unlikely that the desired changes will take place by substituting the labor of machines for the labor of men. Machines can eliminate some of the backbreaking toil, but they are also developed so as to make complex human operations into simpler mechanical ones performed by human beings. If machines have helped to make hard physical labor easier, they have also helped to make some reasonably interesting jobs more routine. Although I am not so pessimistic to believe that machines must be used in this way, it is not too difficult to see why they have been so developed. Given the impulse to control production and to minimize costs, the more routine the labor, the larger will be the size of the population who can perform it, and the less dependent is management on any single individual. The more know-how required to perform a human activity, the greater is the manager's dependence on the individual operator, and the smaller is the area of control. This observation does not seem to be mitigated by the so-called growth in skilled labor and the reported decline in the unskilled sector. As Braverman points out, much of the classification of skilled and unskilled labor is rooted in simple views about white- and blue-collar work. However, as he also points out, the trend has been toward the routinization of much white-collar as well as blue-collar work. A more accurate way to measure the routine of a job might be the length of time needed for training.[9]

Given the pressures that the division of labor exerts on the schools, it is not difficult to see how the education system as a whole can be reasonably successful in meeting its purpose even while many parts of that system are struggling, perhaps unsuccessfully, to avoid failure. The division of labor sets limits to what the schools can do, but it does so for the system as a whole in a way that is different for any of its particular parts. For any particular school, or group of children, the division of labor strongly influences the goal that it is reasonable to strive for, given the likely prospects for its students. If, for example, the school is in a poorer area, perhaps populated by children from minority groups, it will seem perfectly reasonable, especially under conditions of slow economic growth, to direct the industrial process in such a way that each student will acquire the habits needed for work in an industrial complex. If the school is located in a largely middle-class, professional area, these habits alone will not be sufficient, and the school will be more likely judged by the ability of its academic program to prepare students for high-ranking colleges. Yet even if a large number of schools happened to be unsuccessful in achieving a selected goal, it does not necessarily mean that this failure will be reflected in the results of the school system. The success or failure of the system is not judged by the success or failure of its parts alone. The reason for this is simply that the division of labor stands to the school system in a way that is different than the way that it stands to any of its parts. The division of labor together with the specific characteristics of a group of children determine what it is reasonable for a given school to strive for. With the system as a whole, the division of labor stands not as a guide, influencing what are reasonable aims; rather it stands as an essential part of its overall goal, of reproducing labor. It fails if too many people are prepared for high-level professions as well as if too few people are prepared for them.

The school is not the only institution that serves the function of reproducing labor in general. Depending upon its characteristics, the family and other institutions in the society serve this function through their general socializing role, and as more and more families become adjusted to the industrial age, it is possible that the school's lower-level socializing roles will decrease in importance. When we survey some of the functions that the school system performs in serving the industrial division of labor, we can see that a number of them can possibly be assumed by other agencies as a society completes its transition from a preindustrial to an industrial era. Many of these functions are general in nature, and were assumed by the school simply to balance and counter the socializing influence of the preindustrial family. For example, in industrial settings individuals need to learn to distinguish between the agent who performs an activity and the people who hold ultimate responsibility for that activity. Prices are set by an enterprise, not by the person who sells the item. Labor time is determined by a contract between a union and management, not by the individual performing the task. And no matter how pressing the concerns of the client may be, rules rather than sentiment generally must guide the conduct of welfare workers.[10] Regarding these functions, schools are especially important where families are organized around preindustrial personalistic norms and where the society is in a state of transition from informal, communal structures to impersonal bureaucratic and contractual ones. Once the transition has been made, however, schools may be less important in this regard, and it is quite understandable to find more conservative scholars, such as Banfield, joining with some of the more radical critics of schooling in calling for a reduction of the school-leaving age.

Although it is conceivable that the time may come when schools are no longer required to perform many of their present socializing functions, there is another way in which the school system has served the division of labor, and to challenge this function would mean a much more radical examination of American schools and institutions. The drive to expand the human capacity to control nature has led not only to new techniques for directing men and machines, it has also generated institutions that, within the limits of existing resources, are designed to maximize the growth of technological knowledge. The school system has been the central institution in this development.

Schooling and technological knowledge

Although the goal of maximizing the growth of technological knowledge is not the only goal of the school system, it is one of the few that has not arisen from its assumption of the responsibilities of other institutions, such as the socializing functions once performed by families and communities, and it is therefore reasonable to speak of this as a major, if not essential aspect of school systems in the advanced technological societies of the Western world. In order to understand the school's role in maximizing technological knowledge, we need to think of schooling in terms of a longitudinal structure starting at kindergarden and ending at the graduate and professional level, and we need too to think of technological knowledge as a generalized scheme that outlines various routes to a given goal together with all of the possible contingencies that could arise to direct that one route, rather than another, be chosen as the most effective and least costly way to achieve a stipulated goal. Thus the totality of technological knowledge can be conceived in terms of an ideal scheme of all possible routes and all possible contingencies.

The ideal of maximizing technological knowledge is one that directs society to invest its educational resources toward the future provision of the most detailed and comprehensive scheme of possible routes and contingencies. The idea is to invest existing knowledge so as to maximize the store of future knowledge. Given whatever minimum amount of education is deemed appropriate for the general student population, the most effective way to proceed is to use the initial years of education to select for subsequent training those individuals who, because of intelligence, cultural background, or the appropriate value structure, are able to absorb existing knowledge at an accelerated pace and then exercise that knowledge in existing bureaucratic structures. The financial resources of the society and the ability of its material base to release individuals from immediately productive activity and then to absorb them later at a higher level serve as limiting factors.

Among the important features of the goal of maximizing technological knowledge is that it is largely indifferent to the distribution of knowledge among the members of a society. In other words, if the growth of knowledge can best be served by selecting out a few individuals for extra training, the size of the gap that develops between these and the remaining members of the society is not a matter of major concern. That the development of a large gap under the principle has normally been the case is strongly suggested by a study conducted for UNESCO by Johan Galtung and his associates. They found that the greatest educational disparity existed among those countries with the highest educational growth.[11]

When we speak here of the distribution of technological knowledge we are addressing the question of the way in which institutions are ordered and the purposes they serve. The distribution of knowledge, for example, is to be distinguished from the distribution of income in the sense that there is no single unified measure, such as dollars per year, which can be used to determine different allocations. However, there are looser measures that can be used, such as the number of years and the kind of education available to different people, the selection criteria used for entrance into higher-level programs, the kind of socializing influence that can be attributed to curriculum knowledge, and the extent to which different people benefit from the kind of knowledge that is developed. Undoubtedly, some of these measures are more closely tied to the concept of the growth and distribution of knowledge itself, and others to the likely consequences of a given system of distribution. The general impact, however, is to focus our attention on certain areas of educational research that have often been neglected.

For example, given the goal of maximizing the growth of technological knowledge, it is fairly easy to see that another, related kind of discrepancy will likely develop. This discrepancy involves the question of the extent to which different classes will likely benefit from the growth in technological knowledge that does occur. A commitment to a high rate of technological growth is generally indifferent to questions of moral priority. Thus it is of no major concern, for example, whether people trained for food research concentrate on developing potato chips that can be of uniform size and shape, allowing them to be stacked in a can, or whether they will concentrate on making basic grain and protein sources more palatable to human taste, thereby reducing the amount of protein loss that occurs when grain is fed to cattle. These concerns are settled largely by market considerations, and in this case there is little doubt that the race goes to the swift, to those individuals who are the repositories of existing technological knowledge.

The discrepancy is understandable once we recognize the generally accepted goal of maximizing the growth of technological knowledge. Without regard to the gap that develops, knowledge becomes the supreme commodity, and one pays for the fruits of one kind of knowledge with those of another. Moreover, the fewer those who share in a given knowledge system, the more valuable is the knowledge that they process and the greater the access of those who do possess it to the fruits of other knowledge systems. Medical and other research thereby is directed to minimizing the hazards of everyday life by managing all possible contingencies for those whose position allows them to take advantage of the progress that is made. In advanced societies such as our own where the benefits of such research are relatively large and where the level of capital development allows a reasonably high percentage of people to take advantage of them, the threat to social stability is reduced, but as we will see later this does not mean that the gap has been narrowed. The need for health care in many areas of the country and the reduced but still high infant mortality rate among certain groups speak to the fact that the gap is large and that many people suffer its consequences. However, in developing societies that adhere to the Western model of educational and technological growth, the gap between the least and the most educated and the lopsided development that occurs between rural and urban, educated and noneducated, can go a long way toward explaining the revolutionary fervor experienced today throughout the world. And even in our own country these considerations would probably be worth considering when one tries to understand the hostility expressed in many impoverished areas toward public schools.

The social implications of the present direction in education

Given these observations, we can begin to see the way in which the maximum growth principle directs empirical educational research. The educational research industry has directed much of its funds and energy to developing empirical instruments that will match an individual student to the requirements of a given curriculum. The medical aptitude tests, for example, are intended to identify those students who will be most able to conform to the routines of medical training. Very little research has been done, however, on the extent to which the selection criteria and the curriculum itself matches the health needs of the population as a whole, or on the selection criteria that would be needed for training competent general practitioners who would meet the health needs of a large number of people with limited access to health care facilities. Rather, the ideal is otherwise. The goal is to weave an ever-tighter web of specialized competencies so that any conceivable contingency can be handled, as long as one is able to pay the admission fee that allows a person to enter the web to begin with.

Returning now to the basic question of the possible discrepancy that exists between the goals of an individual school and those of the system as a whole, we can begin to see that under the goal of maximizing the growth of technological knowledge, what may be perceived as a problem on one level may not be accepted on the higher level as a problem at all. If a particular school fails to train a large number of youngsters into the intellectual disciplines, or neglects to develop their ethical and aesthetic sensibilities, or refuses to recognize them as rational individuals, if the routine of the school is nothing other than rigid, mechanical, and boring, this does not mean that the school system as a whole is failing to provide the conditions needed for maximizing the growth of technological knowledge. Whether this is occurring depends on another set of factors. These factors include such things as the number of people who do not have sufficient skills to enter the labor force at any level. Such skills include certain behavioral patterns as well as minimal reading skills. Yet even these are perceived as problems only when the economy is unable to absorb such people, or when the undesirable spinoffs such as crime and welfare go beyond the level that is accepted as tolerable. Another index of the success or failure of the system as a whole is its ability to produce sufficient high-level manpower when the material base is able to absorb it. As far as other matters are concerned, such as developing students with intellectual curiosity or youngsters who are able to solve problems and think abstractly in many different areas, the school system can often tolerate a good many failures without significant concern.

Given this analysis, we can now return to look at the implications of some of the seemingly competing views on the limits of educational reform. In light of the previous analysis, we should be able to see how many of the empirical disputes about the limits of educational reform simply evaporate because the general goal of the project remains unquestioned. As we have already seen, since the goal of maximizing the growth of technological knowledge requires that an ever-larger number of people be able to work in bureaucratic settings directing their energies to accomplishing stipulated goals, and since members of some groups adapt to such behavior more readily than others, it does not especially matter whether an IQ examination measures innate intelligence or whether it is culturally biased against some groups. If such examinations are to be functionally adequate, they will do two things. First they will select out those individuals whose cultural development renders them dysfunctional for work in bureaucratic structures. Whether the dysfunctionality results because of low intelligence or from cultural styles that would be in conflict with those of the present members of the organization is somewhat irrelevant when functional matters alone are to be considered. After weeding out individuals whose cultural development renders then antagonistic to bureaucratic structures, the second function of IQ examinations is to rank those remaining according to their fit with the knowledge-generating structure. Incidentally, both of these functions help to explain the presence of peculiarly normative items in IQ exams such as the ones that ask why we need policeman and why it is better to pay one's bills with checks rather than cash.[12] If one believes that IQ scores are environmentally rather than genetically determined, there will be more enrichment programs proposed for the early years, but it should not be surprising if some of the gains made here are lost later in school. Of course, one may explain the drop as the result of genetically determined factors, but these factors might easily be looked upon as no more than indices of human tendencies. What might be much more revealing is the way these tendencies are treated, and here the increasing pressure for early selection and the resulting differential programs as the child moves through the elementary grades to high school are much more revealing factors than the hypothesized quality of a genetic pool.

With the above comments in mind, it should be easy to see the essential similarity between the theories put forward by scholars like Jensen on the one hand and Banfield on the other. Thus even though each locates the limits of educational reform in a different place, Jensen in the intelligence of the child and Banfield in the culture of the parents, their proposals for change are governed by essentially the same considerations. Banfield's solution to the problems of schooling is to have the slower youngsters leave school earlier and enter the work force at low-level jobs, for he believes that once the schools have trained these youngsters into the routine of the workforce, there is little else that can be done. As with Jensen, and granting a few exceptions, the more interesting aspects of schooling are to be reserved largely for youngsters from the middle class and above.

Banfield's analysis has conceptual problems equally as difficult as those we saw earlier with Jensen. We can treat them here only briefly. Banfield believes that the most powerful limitation on reform is a person's class membership, and he defines class in terms of certain psychological traits, such as a person's orientation toward the future. His analysis is interesting, not only because of his somewhat unique definition of class but because in his *use* of the concept, as distinguished from his definition of it, his indices are fairly conventional ones, such as income and status. The overall impression is one that strongly suggests that people have low incomes and status largely because of their own psychological makeup and that this makeup is simply transmitted from generation to generation through such things as child-rearing practices, which schools cannot affect. Again there is a certain ring of truth to some of this, but the interesting thing is the way in which Banfield's analysis isolates family practices from all other aspects of a person's social situation and general life chances. One would suspect, for example, that an extended future orientation would be dysfunctional for a large number of roles in this society, but this is not looked at. In any event, by failing to analyze the general work roles and structure of the society, Banfield's proposals for schools could, as with Jensen, do little more than intensify the division between classes, and has the effect of simply servicing the existing direction of that division. When trying to decide between the relative merits of Banfield and Jensen, it would be well to guide the deliberation by the pragmatic dictum: If there is no difference in practice, there is no difference at all. It should not be thought, however, that liberal educational reforms are in any way exempt from the pressures issuing from the division of labor, although advocates of these reforms are generally less comfortable guiding their educational policies by these pressures. Nevertheless, one need only examine the different ways in which progressive educational reform was translated into practice for children of different classes to understand how forceful these pressures are. For example, the difference between the middle-class progressive schools of the 1930s and the working-class, life adjustment ones of the 1940s was significant in terms of both subject matter, method, and purpose.[13]

Given the failure to address the relationship between education and the division of labor, it is questionable how much improvement we can expect in education through empirical research and the reform guided by it. Certainly if there were to be a large expansion of challenging and interesting jobs, we might expect at some point to see similar changes in the schools, but this kind of expansion has not yet become the goal of consciously directed policy, and some research suggests the direction of work to be otherwise.[14] Without these changes, then, even if empirical educational researchers help us to devise better and more effective ways to improve teaching and to help children learn, it is likely that the improvements will be delivered in such a way as to help most middle-class children to improve their conceptual skills and most lower-class children to improve their ability to learn by rote – and this is so whether or not we accept Jensen's view about Level I and Level II learners. Certain programs and styles of teaching, such as that developed by Bereiter and Engelmann, will be labeled "lower-class" and kept far away from white, middle-class schools, and other programs, such as the "new math," will be labeled as middle-class and kept away from the lower-class schools. For some who go along with Jensen and Banfield this is likely the best of all possible worlds. But to use a more rustic classification scheme, one that runs implicitly through their writings, to accept a scheme where the dull get duller and the bright get brighter is surely questionable, even if it does serve to maximize the growth of technological knowledge.

Conclusion

One of the difficulties with contemporary empirical research discussed in this and previous chapters arises largely because the goals of the educational system are taken for granted by the researcher and there is thus a failure to critically penetrate the framework in which the research program is carried out. In Chapter 7, we will see that some of these very same problems arise (and for the same reason), among more radical critics of schools. In this case, however, a different set of sensibilities is at work, but its impact is blunted precisely because it shares with traditioned scholars the inability to develop a framework in which the goals of schooling provide a central focus for analysis. The focus instead is on the presumed intention of the school reformer. Now, however, we need to turn away from the empirical tradition and examine the inability of recent educational philosophy to critically grasp the implications of empirical research.

6 The philosophical tradition and its limits for educational understanding

Because the empirical tradition takes its central values from the school and borrows its major methods and concepts from the parent disciplines, it has failed to develop an independent analysis of education. Moreover, its claim to value neutrality simply neglects to consider the network of institutional meanings and values that are taken for granted in formulating research problems and in deciding which aspects of the total educational situation are to be taken as candidates for choice. In this neglect it has a strong tendency to reinforce the dominant values of the society by removing them from the realm of rational deliberation.

One of the major supplements to the empirical tradition has been the work of philosophers of education in England and the United States known as analytic philosophy of education[1] and sometimes referred to as ordinary-language philosophy, linguistic analysis, or conceptual analysis. This work attempts to clarify concepts that appear to be centrally related to the idea of education itself. It differs from the empirical tradition in the sense that it is not concerned with questions of fact, but with those of meaning and usage. As with the empirical tradition, this one too maintains a claim to value neutrality – but in a different way. Many of the concepts that are treated by this tradition have clear and recognizable value implications, and part of the work of these philosophers has been to spell out just what these implications are. In this respect, conceptual analysis has been concerned, among other things, with clarifying concepts, such as "motivation," "punishment," "reinforcement," and others, that guide empirical research. It has also been concerned with understanding and clarifying some of the unique characteristics that concepts take on when developed in the context of specifically educational discourse. In this latter concern, the line between the neutral analysis of values and implicit advocacy often becomes blurred. There is also, as we will see, a difference between analyzing a concept that is thought of as specifically educational in some way and identifying a domain for understanding education.

The philosopher's concern with clarifying concepts, including those that are

96

clearly related to human values, would lead one to expect a penetrating analysis of the value implications of empirical research. For the most part, however, a critical analysis of the evaluative framework of empirical scholarship has been absent from the philosophical debates, and this absence requires an explanation. Moreover, in many instances conceptual analysis has, like empirical research, operated within a framework that tends to assume and reinforce certain deeply held values. The purpose of this chapter is to highlight that framework, and to suggest some of the reasons why the analytic tradition has been unable to reflect upon its own implications. In the course of this analysis, I will also begin to suggest why, without a more adequate notion of the domain of educational studies, conceptual analysis must be limited in this respect.

Educational philosophy, as conceptual analysis, actually has its roots in a number of different, but closely related traditions that are grounded in British philosophy. Rather than examine each of these traditions separately, we can look at a few of the kinds of concerns that occupy the attention of educational philosophers.

The general concern of conceptual analysis is to achieve clarity in the use of concepts. This concern often involves distinguishing the different ways in which a particular concept can be used. For example, a good deal of early work in this area was concerned with distinguishing the difference between "knowing that" and "knowing how." More recent work has been concerned with notions of authority and the distinction between being *in* authority and being *an* authority. Although many of these analyses can become quite complex, it is not difficult to perceive the usefulness that such distinctions can have in clarifying disagreements that arise from conceptual confusions of the sort mentioned above. It is the concern to clarify these confusions that explains the seemingly labored attempts to correctly identify the nature of the concept that is being examined and hence to avoid inappropriate comparisons or analogies. This explains, for example, the large literature dealing with the issue of whether "education" is a task or an achievement concept.[2]

The role of analytic philosophy of education is not limited to distinguishing the various meanings of concepts. Borrowing from speech act theory, some philosophers of education are concerned with what a particular utterance does. Thus, following J. L. Austin, utterances like "I thee wed," said under the proper circumstances, are important because of what they do – in this case complete a marriage ceremony.[3] Although these latter concerns are more closely associated with philosophy of language than with linguistic or conceptual analysis,[4] many of the insights developed in this area have been incorporated into the work of educational philosophers as part of the tools of conceptual analysis.[5]

Analytic philosophers of education view their concern with values as but an incidental aspect of their concern with concepts. Thus, as Richard Peters writes,

" 'education' is different from ordinary cases of tasks and achievements" in that "it is inseparable from judgments of value."[6] And then clarifying the point, he elaborates:

"Education" is like "reform"; for it would be as much of a contradiction to say "My son has been educated but has learnt nothing of value" as it would be to say "my son has been reformed but has changed in no way for the better." This, by the way, is a purely conceptual point. The connection between "education" and what is valuable can be made explicit without commitment to content.[7]

Thus as Peters sees it, the role of analytic philosophy is not to serve as an advocate of a set of values, but rather to show just how concepts like "education" entail judgments of value.

There are, however, two features in the actual practice of educational philosophy that complicate the relationship between values and the analysis of concepts. First, the strictly formal treatment of concepts such as "education" has been very difficult to maintain, and educational philosophers have often gone beyond the limits that one might expect would be imposed by the simple task of analyzing concepts. Second, the treatment that is offered of "education" is almost always framed in terms that limit the analysis to single individuals or to an intended transmission between individuals. Thus, it provides few, if any, guidelines for understanding the relationship between education and other social institutions. It often appears as if the function and practice of education, as analysts define it, is simply a matter of good judgment and conceptual clarity.

As understood by its practitioners in education, analytic philosophy does not stand as an alternative to the empirical tradition, but as a complement to it and as a way to avoid confusing many of the noneducative functions of the school with education itself. Moreover, although the analytic philosophers proclaim a neutrality with regard to human values similar to that of the empirical researcher, their work attempts to aid our understanding of such values. These philosophers believe that although their enterprise does not and should not dictate which values people ought to choose, it can clarify what values are entailed in using certain concepts. Thus, whereas the empirical tradition attempts to avoid dealing with questions concerning human values entirely, the ordinary-language tradition is quite willing to address such issues, but it strives to do so in a neutral way. The following passage by Richard Peters illustrates the concerns and methods of this approach:

Much of the confusion about "aims of education" comes about through extracting the normative feature built into the concept of "education" as an extrinsic end. Given that "education" suggests the intentional bringing about of a desirable state of mind in a morally unobjectional manner, it is only too easy to conceive of education as a neutral process that is instrumental to something that is worthwhile which is extrinsic to it. Just as gardens may be cultivated in order to aid the economy of the household, so children must be educated in order to provide them with jobs and to increase the productivity of the community as a whole.

But there would be something inappropriate about this way of speaking: for we would normally use the word "train" when we had such a specifiable extrinsic object in mind. If, however, we do specify an appropriate "aim" such as the development of individual intellect and character, then the aim would be intrinsic to what we consider education to be.[8]

The tradition that Peters represents begins with the idea that there are certain standards entailed by the concept of education itself that must be met if an activity is to be thought of as educative, and that at least in a formal sense these standards are to be derived independently from the perceived requirements of particular institutions. For example, whether schools are adequately meeting certain perceived "manpower" needs or whether they are providing for adequate mobility for talented members from all social classes is not to be confused with the question of whether they are fulfilling their educative function. Analysis is perceived to be value-neutral because it does not address the question of whether schools, or any other institution, should have an educative function. Rather, it provides a set of guidelines for determining what schools, or any other institutions, would be doing if they were educating.

In contrast to the empirical work that characterizes the earlier models, the work of this tradition is intended to operate on a conceptual level and to rely upon our informed intuitions about the use of the English language. For Peters, the first task is to analyze the kind of concept that "education" is and to then distinguish it from concepts of a different kind. He notes that the concept of education, unlike some other concepts, such as gardening, does not pick out or refer to any *specific* activity. People can educate themselves, they can be educated by tutors or by attending large lectures. In this sense he notes "education" is more like "reform" in that "it picks out no particular activity or process. Rather it lays down criteria to which particular activities or processes must conform."[9]

The approach is designed not so much to add to our knowledge but to remind us of and to underscore that which we already know implicitly. Thus, whereas most of the conclusions of this tradition are not startling, they are intended to highlight activities that can often go unattended in the daily pressures of school life. Peters, for example, reminds us of the need for the educated person to understand not just an array of facts, but also the principles behind such facts, and he distinguishes the merely knowledgeable person from the educated one by the degree to which knowledge is used to inform everyday life. Thus, the works and much of the virtue in this tradition can be seen as providing a basis for discussing the values that the empirical traditions had taken as unproblematic.

One of the problems with conceptual analysis as used in education is that even as it attempts to isolate values and concepts that are to be thought of as belonging specifically to education, it has not provided any explicit articulation of a domain that could properly be thought of as an object for educational understandings. Indeed, a major difficulty that conceptual analysis has is to explain why some concepts are selected for analysis and others not. However, the mystery is dissolved when we remember that conceptual analysis is understood by its practioners as a supplement to empirically oriented research. This has meant in practice that analysis will be exercised on either those concepts that are presently being employed on some (undefined) domain of education by practitioners of empirical research, or else it will be employed on commonsense ideas that are used in informal discussions about education. It is therefore not surprising to find, for example, educational philosophers treating psychological concepts in the first instance, such as "motivation" and "conditioning," or commonsense notions such as "play" and "work" or "freedom" and "indoctrination" in the second. Yet it is not at all clear whether these concepts are selected because they are somehow tied in an essential way to the domain of education or because they happen to dominate educational talk at the moment. For the most part, however, philosophical analysis in education follows school talk.

The fact that conceptual analysis begins by isolating its concepts from any specific institutional practice means that a certain critical potential is retained. Unlike empirical research, the ordinary-language tradition does not mistakenly assume that the domain of educational understanding is to be limited to a single institution such as the school, and it does not take uncritically every school-defined aim or problem to be an educational one. Education may occur in schools but then again it may not, and if it does not occur in schools, then it may occur elsewhere.

Yet this points out the weaknesses as well as the strengths of the tradition. Empirical research is treated as problematic only if its basic concepts are unclear, confused, or contradictory. There is, however, little impulse to move beyond these kinds of problems and to try to understand just why certain kinds of problems occur in certain research programs and what the connections may be between these contradictions and deeply held social values. The IQ debate treated in Chapter 2 is a case in point. There is no reason why conceptual analysis would not be able to point to the ambiguous use of the concept of "intelligence." Indeed, a few analysts have done so. Yet there would also be little reason for the analyst to probe that ambiguity in order to try to critically understand the values that render it inconsequential for contemporary society. Thus, although such philosophy has a critical force, it is a limited one.

Although ordinary-language philosophy serves as a supplement to empirical research, its analysis of education is limited by its own approach to issues. That the concepts that are inspected by language analysis initiate from commonsense talk and from the work of other disciplines in education means that it is going to be tied in both its insights and its oversights very closely to those understandings and to the values that they rest on. In this sense it, like the empirical sciences, has difficulty in maintaining its claim to value neutrality. More important, it too has difficulty in understanding this shortcoming. Yet the shortcoming is extremely important in attempting to understand the way in which a methodology unconnected to a theoretical domain and applied on an ad hoc basis serves to circumscribe the way in which education is understood. By looking at an example of the way in which analysis circumscribes the educational relationship, we will be able to see how its own relationship to the disciplines arbitrarily and perhaps unwittingly places certain issues beyond the boundaries of educational research. Later as we begin to mark out an area for educational research we will look at some attempts to correct this oversight. As an example of this problem we begin with the treatments of "indoctrination" offered by two ordinary-language philosophers, John Wilson and Richard Hare.

Conceptual analysis and the indoctrination debate

The debate over the question of indoctrination is one of those instances in which language analysis exercises its method over a commonly understood (rather than a discipline-generated) concept. The question of indoctrination and how it is to be understood has been raised by ordinary-language philosophers because of the central place it is thought to have in understanding "education." The assumption is that "indoctrination" is a concept that marks off an area that is beyond the boundary of "education" and that if we were able to understand the concept of indoctrination, then we would better understand the concept of education.

This debate has a history that dates back at least to the 1930s when it was centered around some major political and educational problems. More recently conceptual analysts have tamed that discussion by removing the issue of indoctrination from any concrete political context and have elevated "indoctrination" to the level of a concept pure and simple. Yet by taming the discussion in this way, recent philosophy has been unable to reconstruct the connection that is necessary in order to bring the issue back to the world of political life where it had its beginning. It has ironically circumscribed the debate in such a way that political and social relationships have been relegated to background considerations that enter only through the rear door. Yet such background considerations are especially important in illustrating the way in which ordinary language philosophy implicitly has limited educational studies to a certain form of transaction. They are also important in assessing the philosopher's claim to be treating values in a neutral way. In order to see these issues it is important here to reflect not only the formal arguments that are to be found in this debate, but on the tone of the debate as well. The tone rides free along with the labors of the formal argument, but in riding free it also provides the cues that direct how the formal argument should read.

We can see these points by examining the formal and informal arguments of two representative essays, the first by John Wilson entitled "Education and Indoctrination" and the second by Richard Hare, "Adolescents into Adults." Wilson initiates the debate by announcing that his concern is to map out a logical geography for the term "education" by contrasting it to similar terms with different meanings. "Indoctrination" is such a term because it depicts a set of activities that may, under some circumstances, be mistaken for education but that Wilson thinks are clearly distinguishable when presented in a paradigmatic form. The paradigms that Wilson offers are such acts as brainwashing people to believe in communism, teaching Christianity by the threat of torture or damnation, and forcing people by early training to accept social roles, as in Huxley's *Brave New World*.[10] The problem is to find out what it is that marks off certain activities as indoctrination, and thus by contrast to learn something important about the meaning of "education."

Wilson considers two candidates for indoctrination. The first has to do with the use of methods that somehow go beyond rational appeal whereas the second has to do with the nature of the content that is taught. Wilson rejects the first candidate, arguing that there is a difference, for example, in hypnotizing someone to believe in the doctrines in communism and hypnotizing him to do A-level physics. The first is obviously an example of indoctrination, but the second is not. Yet because the methods are the same, he concludes that the problem must reside in something about the content that is taught. The problem of indoctrination arises, Wilson argues, when we teach, as certain, beliefs for which there is no publicaly accepted evidence, "evidence" that, he says, "any rational person would regard as sufficient."[11]

Wilson is not arguing that rational people do not hold beliefs that if taught as certain would be considered indoctrination. He emphasizes that "there are rational people who believe in Communism, Roman Catholicism, and free love, as well as rational people who believe in liberal democracy . . . and the sexual conventions of the western world."[12] However, these beliefs he notes are such that neither are they certain nor do we know what would count as evidence for or against them. Thus, we need to distinguish beliefs about such things as the existence of God or the morality of homosexuality from beliefs about life on other planets or black holes in the universe. His argument is that whereas the second set of beliefs can be taught in terms of probability regarding the first, even the category of probability is not applicable, and surely to teach such beliefs as if they were certain knowledge is indoctrination.

In favor of his conception of indoctrination, Wilson argues that it avoids some of the problems that are likely to be raised when the context of the situation shifts from teaching youngsters who have already reached an age of reason to that of teaching prerational children. This speaks in favor of his method because in the latter case, nonrational methods are sometimes unavoidable, and if our criteria of indoctrination were to be decided primarily on the basis of the *methods* used in teaching, we would have to label all such teaching indoctrination. Wilson believes that this approach clearly will not do.

In what follows, however, Wilson's argument begins to falter, for inadvertantly he has made his criterion of what is to count as indoctrination so inclusive as to rule out the possibility of raising young children without indoctrinating them, a view that he is attempting to avoid. As he puts it: "This principle consists in only educating children to adopt behavior patterns and to have feelings which are seen by every sane and sensible person to be agreeable and necessary."[13] He proposes that when such behavior derives from factors inherent in reality itself rather than as a projection of adult fears and distortions, then it is not to be judged as indoctrination. And then stating the criterion again, he writes, with a slight shift in emphasis:

Indoctrination begins when the behavior we teach children is behavior demanded by ourselves and not by reality at all: when we force on the child a particular interpretation of reality which we may think good but which an ancient Greek or medieval Chinaman or a modern Red Indian would think wicked, absurd or unnecessary.[14]

Yet clearly this injuction, when applied to behavior patterns, is much too strong if one wishes, as Wilson does, to avoid the idea that indoctrination is inevitable. This is because it would make any decisions regarding such things as toilet-training, weaning, and dietary habits virtually impossible to make since some group is bound to see a particular practice as either wicked, absurd, or unnecessary. Indeed it is extremely difficult to think of any behavior that is demanded by reality alone unless one includes social as well as natural reality. However, if this inclusion is made, then the distinction between demands made by reality and demands made by ourselves collapses, as does the distinction between indoctrination and nonindoctrination. Wilson does not wish to take us in this direction, and although he seems to sense this difficulty, he does not articulate it. Indeed, the above-mentioned shift in emphasis is the prelude for a larger shift from "behavior patterns" to "interpretations of reality" to "the kinds of reasons" that should be given in getting a youngster to behave in a particular way. Regarding this latter point, Wilson suggests that we should avoid giving reasons that appeal to irrational fear or guilt. The problem, however, is that as the principle for identifying indoctrination shifts, so too does the context in which the principle is to be applied. When one is speaking strictly of behavior patterns, then one is clearly including in that context prerational and also prelinguistic youngsters. However, when one is referring to the kinds of reasons that should or should not be given, then the context includes only those youngsters who have at least reached a stage where they can understand reasons, even if they cannot yet evaluate them. This subtle shift in context is important. Either Wilson has made the criterion of nonindoctrination so narrow as to include as indoctrination almost all child-rearing practices, as is the case when he insists that the behavior patterns to be taught be agreeable to every sane and sensible person, or else his discussion is not really about prerational children at all. If the latter is the case, then his claim for the superiority of his principle does not really apply to the situation that he intends. For part of its value rests upon his belief that the principle does not exclude, as indoctrination, nonrational practices essential for the rearing of pre-rational children. This shift is important for another reason as well. It indicates his assumption that a distinct separation between what is indoctrination and what is education is possible and it overlooks that necessary function of education that is social reproduction.

Hare's treatment of indoctrination begins with his attempt to correct some of the problems that he observes in Wilson's presentation. His objection is that by focusing so narrowly upon the rationality of the content, Wilson unwittingly allows methods that are intended to produce the strictest possible conformity to pass as education. Hare notes with Wilson that there are times when the methods of the educator and the indoctrinator may be the very same, but he is not willing to grant that the distinction therefore lies in the content of instruction. The content may be rational and the activity may still be seen as indoctrination. Rather, Hare proclaims, indoctrination depends upon the aim of the instructor. As he puts it:

Indoctrination only begins when we are trying to stop the growth in our children of the capacity to think for themselves about moral questions. If all the time we are influencing them, we are saying to ourselves, ''Perhaps in the end they will decide that the best way to live is quite different from what I'm teaching them; and they will have a perfect right to decide that; then we are not to be accused of indoctrination.''[15]

It could be objected that by emphasizing the aim of the teacher, Hare's criteri-on of indoctrination leaves open the possibility that given two teachers using essentially the same methods, teaching the same content, and achieving essen-tially the same results, one could rightly be accused of indoctrination and the other not, depending only upon their aims.[16] If the response to this is that the aim must eventually make a difference with regard to the methods, content, and results, then not only might we ask for a clearer statement regarding the nature of this difference, but we might also ask why ''indoctrination'' could not be charac-terized in terms of these manifest differences alone rather than in terms of the aim of the teacher. This could, of course, lead us into accepting some form of behavioral objectives. Although Hare properly does not propose this, the im-plications of his argument lead in this direction.

If the meaning of the concept of indoctrination comprises the major theme of these essays, then the question of what identifiable practice is to be taken as the most serious form of indoctrination is the major subtheme of this debate. Yet taken together these two themes ring an uneasy chord because in the essays by

Wilson and Hare the two themes appear totally disengaged from one another. In other words, it would be quite easy to conceive of someone holding Wilson's view on the meaning of indoctrination and Hare's views on the most serious source of indoctrination, or vice versa. If we pursue this gap, we will be able to see some of the major problems that the use of this approach entails for the understanding of education.

Wilson begins this debate on a promising note. He places education in the context of modern society. Although his analysis of this context has little to do with his analysis of the *meaning* of indoctrination, it does provide Hare with another point of contention. Wilson writes:

We live in a society whose chief aim is to preserve and if possible expand a technological culture, whose end product is the private possession of consumer goods. Nearly all questions of government home policy are concerned with this, and nearly all citizens acquiesce in it and indeed insist upon it. The significant alternatives are not choices between communism and western democracy, socialism or conservatism, public service or private profit: they are between a technological and acquisitive culture, as we find in all industrialized countries, together with all the moral and political values of such a culture, and whatever other kind of culture we have the imagination to think of and the guts to achieve.[17]

Hare, in defending modern culture, chooses to focus on advertising. He writes:

Take advertising for example. If all the advertisements were advertising the same brand of soap, as might be the case in a communist country, then it would be time to get worried though even in that case good would come of encouraging people to wash. But since they are all advertising different brands, the consumer very soon realizes that there is not much difference between the brands, and, though of course he will probably go on buying *some* heavily advertised brand, he will not care very much which. The same applies to more important things than soap. Advertisements keep branded goods before our attention; and if this is not done, we shall probably stop buying them and buy some other brand. But in choosing between the brands which are competing in this way, does not the multiplicity of the advertisements make us stop caring which we buy, unless indeed, we think there is a real difference between the brands. If we do, and we think it is important to have the best one, do we not make some effort to find out which the best one is? This at any rate is what the schools ought to be teaching their pupils to do; and I do not think it is so difficult. Listen to any two young men discussing the merits of two kinds of motor-cars. Which influences them the most – the blurbs in the advertisements or the reports of performance in the technical press?[18]

What Hare overlooked is not difficult to see, given recent events such as the oil crisis and the continuing inflation. With our hindsight knowledge of these events, his remarks not only fail to refute Wilson's position, by implication they support it. If the advertisements for different kinds of soap provide us with an opportunity to choose between Palmolive, English Leather, and Camay, they make it that much more difficult to resist the myriad of products that are competing to clean our hair, shine our teeth, deodorize our armpits, and powder our toes. Certainly it is not out of line to ask philosophers to look at the moral issues involved in diverting resources to these products when the majority of the world's people often live on the border of starvation and where the prospects for the future do not look promising. Hare may be right when he remarks that very few young men would go out and buy a Ford or a Plymouth or a Morris just because they saw an advertisement for one. But take all the advertisements for Fords and Plymouths and Morrises and one might wonder about the chances for cheap, energy-efficient public transportation. Hare's and Wilson's use of ordinary-language philosophy, however, proves an awkward vehicle to address these issues because it confines rational argument to an overly narrow sphere.

If we put aside the specific issues that are in question in the debate between Wilson and Hare, we can begin to see the way in which the formal treatment of the issue of indoctrination has implicitly limited the domain of educational understanding to the transaction between a person taking on the role of a teacher (including a parent) and a child. Moreover, we can also begin to understand just how this implied domain molds our thoughts about what is to be taken as educational.

By focusing upon the transaction between a teacher and a child both Hare and Wilson have mistaken what must best be taken as the moment of education or indoctrination for the activity itself. We can see this best by remaining within the same implicitly normative framework in which the debate has been conducted and by noticing an area that neither Wilson's or Hare's treatment of indoctrination is able to address. Each has focused only upon the manner in which beliefs are issued to the child by the teacher. In doing so they have completely neglected the problem of those questionable beliefs that a child may continue to hold, not because such beliefs have been issued by an intending and conscious agent, but because they represent the child's understanding of an institutional and social arrangement that has never been challenged for her and that has thereby come to be taken for granted. As an example, we may think of the beliefs about the quality of different races of people that a child might be expected to hold by virture of living in a society where the members of one race are restricted to holding the most menial kinds of jobs. More to the point of the debate, we may conceive the development of materialistic values in our own culture in many ways, some of which need not be taught in a manner that, under Wilson's or Hare's conception, could be thought of as indoctrination but that we nonetheless might consider to be indoctrination after all. Although Wilson's own example raises this issue, his conception of "indoctrination" does not in fact cover it.

The problem with the formal analysis of the concept of indoctrination is that the narrative has framed the factors of significance only in terms of the transaction between a teacher and a student. Here, ordinary-language analysis is concerned with what the teacher does, or aims to do, to the student. The student, however, is treated as an empty category whose function in the analysis is only to receive what the teacher has to offer. And if what the teacher offers is not false, irrational, doctrinaire, designed to elicit dependency, or presented as certain knowledge when it is not, then indoctrination is not thought to be taking place, and, presumably, if the student is learning true, rational, nondoctrinaire beliefs, then the teacher is meeting her responsibility. The difficulty with this formulation is simply that when it is placed in the context of existing practices and policy, it allows the teacher to escape responsibility in those areas where a student could be expected to hold false beliefs or to maintain irrational values, but where the beliefs and values are not the direct result of the classroom interaction. It is as if we held doctors responsible only for insuring that patients not contract a disease while they were inside their office, but did not hold them responsible for treating the diseases that were developed on the outside. Indeed, this view of teaching has much in common with the way in which we absolve physicians from the responsibility of addressing environmental factors that are likely to produce disease.

Conceptual analysis and its limitations

What is important to notice about the indoctrination example is the way in which the analysis proceeds by separating out concepts that in actual practice are bound together. Yet once having separated them, this tradition can provide little understanding of why they are bound together in the first place. Hence, if the philosopher wants to understand the concept of education, he begins by distinguishing it from concepts that he believes are often mistaken for "education." "Indoctrination" is one of these; "training" is another. Yet this approach can tell us nothing about why such "mistakes" are so frequently made and what it is about educational practice that brings these concepts into such close association with each other to begin with.

Even though conceptual analysis begins by recognizing the need to clarify concepts that it sees as specifically educational, it has not been used in explicitly identifying a coherent domain for the study of education and may not be the best way of doing so. The very way in which many ordinary-language philosophers approach their own concern provides an inadequate understanding of what is to count as educational, and thereby imposes a very specific normative ideal onto "education." Yet because this ideal remains hidden by the analysis itself, it is difficult to challenge it on normative grounds. This can be seen by turning to the other side of the indoctrination question – the problem of the justification of liberal education, and to the treatment of this issue that is provided by the British philosopher Paul Hirst.

To put the matter briefly, liberal arts education (for Hirst) is to be understood as the other side of indoctrination. Whereas the latter is conceived of as false education, the former is presented as real education, and Hirst's problem is to find a justification for it. Yet as we will see, his analysis presupposes a certain normative view of the nature of liberal education, a view that is not well supported by argument and that excludes a good deal that is important. The point of the following critique, however, is not only to reveal this inadequacy but also to highlight the way in which, in the absence of a coherent domain, important normative issues can remain concealed.

Hirst's concern is to provide a justification for liberal education that will both serve to mark it off from other kinds of study and will provide a guide for deciding which courses of study are to be included as liberal ones. In contrast to other modes of instruction, perhaps best thought of as training, and primarily designed to serve some external function, Hirst proposes that liberal education is the label for that form of education that is based on the nature of knowledge itself.[19]

Hirst begins his analysis by rejecting a number of the arguments that have been traditionally provided for liberal education, including those that have been based on a certain view of reality, or metaphysics. He proposes instead that the justification must rest upon an understanding of knowledge in its various forms. The forms of knowledge are most easily thought of as embracing the traditional disciplines, and Hirst distinguishes them from one another by the claim that to each belongs a unique set of concepts, logic, and method. The forms of knowledge represent for Hirst the way in which a mind would organize its experience if it were to be truly rational. Thus for Hirst the very request for "the justification of any form of activity is significant only if one is in fact committed to seeking rational knowledge."[20] This, argues Hirst, is precisely the commitment of the liberal arts.

His argument is stated inadequately, since one may seek justification for many reasons (to find out whether an act will increase one's pleasure, for example), and the knowledge that one receives may in some cases be thought of as simply a by-product that is obtained in seeking some other goal. Hirst is thinking that what is needed is an intrinsic justification for liberal education. However, by requiring such a justification Hirst's argument arbitrarily limits what is to count as educational and implicitly limits the domain of educational studies. We can begin to illustrate this point by looking at Hirst's remarks on the nature of mind as these are used to justify his views about liberal education.

Hirst begins the discussion of mind and knowledge with the observation that "the phrase to have 'a rational mind' . . . implies experience structured under some form of conceptual scheme."[21] This means that if we are to understand experience, we must understand it in some particular way, and that this way of understanding is provided by our various conceptual schemes. Although a conceptual scheme is among the first conditions of knowledge, it is not, for Hirst, its defining characteristic. If a conceptual scheme is to take on the characteristics of knowledge, it must first be embodied in some publicly acknowledged symbol system – a language of some kind that then enables people "to come to understand both the external world and their own private states of mind in common ways, sharing the same conceptual scheme by learning to use symbols in the same manner."[22] The ability to share experience through a public symbol system is what we commonly call understanding, and is what makes knowledge possible. Knowledge itself arises because such conceptual schemes also have made possible certain public criteria that can be assessed against experience itself, and "it is by the use of such tests that we have come to the whole domain of knowledge."[23] Thus, the forms of knowledge upon which Hirst bases his notion of a liberal education are said to be "the basic articulations whereby the whole of experience has become intelligible to man." He also says that "they are the fundamental achievement in mind."[24] He further believes that there are a limited number of such forms, each of which is identifiable by such things as a unique set of concepts, logic, and methodology.

Obviously there are problems that can be raised about Hirst's formulation. For example, it is not clear whether the experience against which knowledge claims are tested is the same experience that is unintelligible except insofar as it is organized by conceptual frames. If it is somehow a different experience, then Hirst seems obliged to tell us how it is that experience is suddenly able to appear sufficiently intelligible to provide a check against knowledge claims that the conceptual frames generate. If, however, it is experience as organized by conceptual frames that he is referring to, then he would seem obliged to tell us how such experience could ever provide an external check upon itself. Just how serious these difficulties are is an open question, and others have suggested procedures for assessing knowledge claims without totally moving outside our established conceptual frameworks.[25] (It should be noted here also, as Dennis Phillips has pointed out, that Hirst has never really successfully elaborated the "unique" logic, method or set of concepts that is supposed to belong to individual forms of knowledge.[26])

The difficulty that Hirst has in dealing with the structure of experience brings us to the central problem in his view of education. He writes: "To acquire knowledge is to become aware of experience as structured, organized and made meaningful in some quite specific way, and the variety of human knowledge constitutes the highly developed forms in which man has found this possible."[27] Clearly what Hirst presents us with here is a static, textbook view of knowledge. Even though he initiated his discussion earlier by noting that the forms of knowledge are the way in which human beings have come to organize their world, knowledge is presented here as a world already organized into neat and tidy compartments. It is the world as organized, not the world being organized, that Hirst emphasizes. As Phillips points out, Hirst has been unable to specify the key elements that mark off the various forms of knowledge. This is but one indication of the problem of seeing knowledge as fixed in the way that Hirst does. Indeed, recent work in the philosophy of science has quite convincingly shown that even those forms of knowledge that we take to be relatively fixed, such as physics and mathematics, often are the result of struggles in which the political dimensions are as prominent as the conceptual ones and where the two are separated only by hindsight.[28] Nevertheless, to return to our original concern, the implications of Hirst's treatment of the forms of knowledge is that the domain of educational studies is to be found in the settled concepts and theories of established disciplines.

Hirst's mistake results from a confusion between techniques that may be useful for introducing a youngster into the accepted forms of knowledge on the one hand with questions concerning the nature of knowledge on the other. It is precisely the same mistake that leads to the problems in the analytic treatment of indoctrination. Both arise from making a radical separation between things that are in fact not radically separate: Between liberal and specialized education on the one hand and between education and indoctrination on the other.

To see this point in a different way we must return to Hirst's notion of the discrete forms of knowledge, which seem to include among other things mathematics, the physical sciences, the human sciences, history, literature, and philosophy. Hirst says there are seven or eight such forms.[29] Although Hirst admits to some interrelations between these areas, he generally treats them as equal and discrete disciplines. The liberally educated person has sampled them all. Although Hirst recognizes some interrelations among these forms, he does not seem to recognize the possibility of conflict that can exist between them. Nor does he recognize the territorial battles that may take place at the margins.

The absence of conflict in Hirst's treatment of the forms of knowledge is puzzling given his earlier, although too brief, recognition that these represent the ways in which people have come to structure their experience. For surely the process of structuring experience is rarely conflict-free, and the power to define reality is a prize that many see as worthy of the fight. Yet none of this appears in Hirst's serene treatment of the liberal arts. Indeed, although he denies that any particular case can be made for the curriculum on the basis of metaphysics, his oversight could be justified only if reality were such as to be neatly sorted into the forms that he articulates, that is, by a certain kind of metaphysical commitment. It is as if the world were created in such a way as different parts of it would be amenable to different forms of knowledge, and no form would ever have to trespass on the territory of another. Such a view of the nature of the world and of knowledge would seem to have implications that are a long way off from the value neutrality claimed by language analysis. Hirst's confusion between knowledge as a world of experience already organized and knowledge as a process of organizing experience is indicative of oversights that are found in the entire debate over indoctrination.

Once knowledge is identified only with a set of well-established categories and methods through which experience has been ordered, at least by some, then there is little reason to probe the process that individuals actually do use as they are engaged in ordering experience as it confronts them. In other words, whereas Hirst's formulation would enable people to be initiated into the forms of academic knowledge, it would provide little room for them to reflect upon the category and methods of thought that they already use to organize their everyday experience. Yet a statement about what is to count as education that leaves out such reflection is surely deficient.

It is the large separation between knowledge and education on the one hand and indoctrination and training on the other, and the failure to understand on what level of analysis the distinction is appropriate, that accounts for the problem that ordinary-language philosophers have in developing a reasonable analysis of these concepts. Yet this difficulty itself reflects some popular thinking that life is one thing and education another (even though Hirst might disagree with this formulation), and the method of analysis, wedded as it is to current language use, could not be expected to go beyond such thinking. Thus, whatever the merits of this approach may be, and clearly there is a need to distinguish the concepts at some level, it is almost guaranteed to overlook any important relationships that may exist between these concepts. Yet once the normative implications underlying these debates are brought to the surface, we can begin to see that the relationship is more problematic than is usually granted.

Most of the analytic literature on the question of indoctrination begins with the unstated normative assumption that under most circumstances it is possible and also desirable to avoid indoctrination and therefore it is also possible to distinguish the concepts of "education" and "indoctrination" from one another. Thus, the only problem is to clearly distinguish between these two. However, the conceptions of indoctrination offered are unable to handle many activities that must occur in any society in the interaction between older and newer generations and yet are more or less consistent with the characterization given to indoctrination by the ordinary-language philosopher. This is clearly the case with Wilson (although he fails to acknowledge it) when he proposes that indoctrination begins when "we force upon the child a particular interpretation of reality" that would not be universally agreed upon. While few if any practices will be universally agreed upon, people must function within a society under some generally shared interpretation of reality. Even very simple acts such as gesturing must be interpretable in a common way (as, say, a greeting or a threat) if communication is to be possible. Yet in providing such interpretations for children, we are not providing one that is likely to be universally accepted as good or necessary,[30] which is the criterion that Wilson uses for nonindoctrination at this level.

Hare's analysis is grounded in a similar oversight. When he writes that "indoctrination only begins when we are trying to stop the growth in our children of the capacity to think for themselves about moral questions,'' he is beginning at the point at which a certain practice has become a moment of conscious choice. Yet clearly many of the most important social practices, whether we call them ''indoctrination'' or by some other name, are learned through less than consciously designed procedures or institutions, such as the way in which children are expected to behave at a dinner table or the different games that boys and girls are expected to play. These practices do in fact limit the way in which children are likely to think about moral questions, such as rights and entitlements. Such activities do not fall neatly under the category of indoctrination (as described by Hare) because they do not occupy the focus of conscious decisions, and this is an indication of the very restricted range of events upon which the analytic philosophers' attention has been focused.

Behind the concept of indoctrination, as it is treated by Wilson and Hare, is a view about the nature of knowledge that, at least in broad outline, is similar to that put forward by Hirst. Wilson's view that there is a firm distinction between knowledge, which entails publicly accepted evidence, ''evidence which any rational person would regard as sufficient,''[31] and indoctrination, which means taking as certain that for which there can be no publicly verified evidence, is parallel to Hirst's view that true knowledge entails certain public criteria that can be tested against experience itself. This view is not challenged by the other treatments of indoctrination. Yet the nature of this experience remains problematic even as it is used to decide whether one person is indoctrinating another.

There is, however, a different way to look at the issue of indoctrination, a way that will enable us to view the question of the nature of education in a different light. Suppose that we begin with a rather broad categorization of indoctrination as involving the uncritical acceptance of a set of standards and norms that guide the judgments of everyday life, an acceptance that may or may not involve the presence of an indoctrinator.[32] Let us suppose too that in the very process of becoming a functioning and productive member of a society, some form of ''indoctrinatory'' development is inescapable as a result of the very fact that people must learn to communicate in certain ways, rather than others, to hold certain beliefs without full, rational justification, and so on. Such beliefs would include ideas about what constitutes the rules of ownership, the nature of personhood, and so forth. The prerequisites of becoming a functional member of society would also involve coming to hold a shared set of rules about the form that elementary manners must take in order to enable communication to proceed or continue. Such prerequisites would include, as well, a set of interpretive devices to determine when an individual might be exhibiting these manners and when she might be mocking them at the same time as she is exhibiting them. Functional social membership requires as well a set of judgmental categories to determine whether the manners are appropriate to mock or not. It also involves the fundamental standards that come to comprise an individual's conception of honesty and rationality, along with a set of beliefs, often unarticulated, about when such standards are appropriate to apply and to what degree. For example, when trust has broken down between two individuals or between two groups of individuals the normally accepted standards of honesty and even of rationality will undergo certain shifts and changes, and certain rules will be viewed by each party as nonapplicable in this situation. Or again, some groups may believe that the right of privacy enables them to legitimately conceal certain feelings whereas others may believe that to hide such feelings violates fundamental standards of openness and honesty.

It is useful to note that most of these instances can easily be fit into Wilson's and Hare's schemes of indoctrination because few rules will be viewed as universally rational, and many of these rules will usually be taught without conscious deliberation about whether a youngster might, will, or should think otherwise when he grows up. Yet from a different point of view, they can also be viewed as the knowledge that is necessary in order to function socially. To look at the issues in this way is to allow a wider conception of knowledge than that which the ordinary-language philosopher, in his understandable concern to escape relativism, has stressed. On the one hand, it allows the everyday rules that people must learn in order to function socially, and that are verified by their functioning successfully, to count as knowledge. The network of such rules (along with guidelines for their application, the rituals that reflect them, etc.) may be thought of as a tradition. On the other hand, it suggests the possibility that at some point education may include reflection back upon the categories of thought and system of rules that have been presented as fundamental for everyday social life.

Part of the shortcoming of the analytic school's proponents arises because they have not provided an acceptable treatment of the relationship between the activity of education in their sense and the fact that the activity in the usual sense is always embedded in an ongoing society. We are thus presented with an image of the educated person as one who is broadly trained, flexible, aware of the larger principles that govern fleeting events, and whose activity is informed by the concept of logic that is to be found in the major "forms of knowledge." Contrasted with the educated person is the narrow, the doctrinaire, and the merely trained one. Just how the former traits are derived from the concept of "education" itself is a mystery until we realize that it is the concept as *used* by twentieth-century Western academics that is being discussed. Yet this tradition in education provides us with little if any insight into the role that such traits play in contemporary society or the reason and extent to which a society would support their development. Nor does it allow us to understand the extent to which the development of different traits may be rooted in aspects other than the educational system of a society, aspects that may have as much to do with the nature of work and one's place in the work force as with school and curriculum.

Even though analytic philosophy has served to capture the meaning and use of concepts, it has failed to capture the significance of those concepts in a total system of practice. (Conceptual analysis is limited because it can capture meaning and use but not significance. That is, it has not explained the role that a particular concept plays in practice and why some concepts take on importance at certain times and not others. For example, when open education was fashionable, it became popular to analyze the concept of play, and as it retreated from fashion, so too did the analysis of the concepts connected to it.

The question needs to be raised whether these limits are a function of conceptual analysis and its methods, or whether they arise simply because of the way in which analysis has been used. The problem is not just that analytic philosophers have tended to be insensitive to their own political and social commitments and thus have exercised their technical skills within certain unreflectively held ideological boundaries. It is also that analysis itself rests upon a sharp separation between conceptual adequacy and empirical truth, and thus, except where conceptual issues are obvious, has not found the levers to address the normative implications of empirical research. Similarly, because conceptual analysis begins by examining concepts that have become crystallized in the speech patterns of certain groups, it is unable to capture the extent to which concepts change over time in response to concrete social and political practice. Finally, because it deals with crystallized concepts, it directs attention away from the struggles over meaning that occur prior to crystallization. In the next chapter, one that examines a much more critical movement in education, we begin to examine some of the factor that are involved in the struggle over meaning and the attempt to cement or to challenge a given interpretation.

7 History and the interpretive understanding of education

The ideal of value-free educational research reflected in the empirical tradition has been implicitly challenged by some historical scholars. These individuals recognize that the interpretive framework and the values of the researcher form the pattern out of which the historical narrative is woven. History, Clarence Karier writes,

is an imaginative art in which pictures of the past are painted in the contemporary world by the historian out of the artifacts of the past. Much of what the historian creates, including chronology itself, is a consciously developed illusion. The historian writes his story of the past as if he lived in the past as an observer and recorder of events. He then moves the reader along from past to present creating the illusion that he and the reader have been there. . . . The verbal reconstruction of the past thus involves an imaginative, creative act. History, however, is more than pure fiction and illusion. A picture of the past leaves the world of fictional writers when the historian insists on documentary evidence to establish the validity of his story.[1]

Karier then goes on to discuss some of the present concerns that inform his treatment of history. Karier's remarks do not, as may appear, necessarily represent a major break with the empirical tradition. Empiricism even in its most positivistic form is also able to allow imagination and values to guide the researcher's quest, to determine the problems that are selected for investigation, and to move from the bare facts to the first approximation of an explanation. As with Karier, evidence for the empiricist largely enters the picture when one seeks to ground a validity claim. And, with Karier, many empiricists could agree that neither the test of social usefulness nor empirical creditability "leads to certitude with respect to historical judgment." There may be some parting of the ways when Karier writes: "There are . . . many pictures of the past that are judged more or less true and more or less useful by the living present."[2] However, since it is not clear whether it is the values and opinions found in the present or the

Sections of this chapter appeared in an earlier version in *Teachers College Record,* Vol. 78 (3), February 1977.

115

standards of empirical exactitude upon which this judgment is to rest, the remark provides insufficient reason for agreement or refutation.

Whether or not Karier's remarks are to be thought of as a major departure from traditional empirical research, they do provide an emphasis on the significance of interpretation that is not usually found in empirical research. Thus the remarks are important not because of the issues that they settle, but because of the questions that they bring to the surface for discussion.

Other historians have also stressed the importance of interpretation. "All any of us can do," writes Arthur Schlesinger, Jr., is "descry a figure in the carpet – realizing as we do that contemporary preoccupations define our own definitions."[3] Schlesinger's metaphor is apt for capturing the way in which many historians understand the role of interpretation in historical scholarship. The configurations present in the carpet can yield many different figures (although perhaps not an infinite number), and those that it does yield will be determined by the contemporary preoccupations of the historian. In other words, the real carpet provides the check against which we can determine whether or not a particular figure is represented in the configuration, but it cannot help us to decide which of the many possible figures is the most accurate one. It is the preoccupation of the historian that determines which figure will be selected as appropriate. Thus, interpretation has an initial role in the historical enterprise of selecting evidence and putting it together to form a coherent story. The carpet or the artifacts from the past serve as an external check on whether the story is grounded in fact.

Schlesinger's view of interpretation is reasonable as far as it goes, and is incidently consistent with Karier's view on this matter. This fact alone is interesting given many of the conflicts in their presentation of the past. However, neither Karier nor Schlesinger provides an avenue for reconciling their own differences – assuming, of course, that the figures drawn do represent some feature of the configuration found in the rug.

Both Schlesinger and Karier, speaking in their role as historians, represent reasonably well the historical enterprise as understood by many of its practitioners. Yet to say "all any of us can do" when speaking to historians should not be taken to imply that other things cannot be done. Interpretation does indeed enter the historical enterprise at the level at which data are selected. However, more stress needs to be put on the fact that the interpretive framework of the historian is also woven into the story that is told and that this story punctuates the evidence and tells us how the description is to be taken. Whether we accept a historical presentation cannot depend alone on whether it conforms to the evidence available, since many competing explanations can conform equally well. Nor should it depend strictly on whether it is in agreement with our own values. This is because our acceptance of it as history is in terms of its accuracy, not in terms of its conformity. Indeed, good history often has the effect of changing values, rather than simply reinforcing them. What the historian's self-under-standing leaves out of consideration is the way in which the narrative punctuates the evidence and hence tells us how it is to be read.

The following sections in this chapter are intended to explore some of the ways in which historical scholars shape the evidence in order to tell a particular kind of story. The point is not to deflate the story of education that is told because it is in many ways both powerful and correct. It is rather to show the limitations that occur in interpretive research when the domain of education remains unspecified and assumed. In this instance we are looking at aspects of consciousness within which competing interpretations attempt to ground themselves. This issue will be examined directly at the conclusion of the chapter. The earlier sections will examine the historical studies of American schools that have been developed by two scholars who have been labeled as revisionist and will show some of the ways in which their evidence is punctuated by their narrative and thereby directs our reading.

The nature of revisionist scholarship

For a brief time during the 1960s and 1970s, educational scholarship turned in a different direction and began to mold a new understanding of the role of the school in American society. The new direction was not initially forged by tradi-tional empirical disciplines or by philosophical analysis. Rather, it had its begin-ning in the more interpretive study of history and especially in Michael Katz's first book, *The Irony of Early School Reform.* Subsequent to Katz's work a number of other studies appeared that were implicitly critical of the past and present character of the American school, challenging its persistent class charac-teristics and its insensitivity to the integrity of minority cultures and groups. At the center of this challenge was a rejection of the widely shared belief that universal schooling has been an obvious benefit to all members of this society, rich and poor, black and white. Because of this challenge a different light has been cast on both the role of the American school and the activity of its leadership.

Much of the newer, "revisionist" history has focused its attention on the relationship between the public school and various depressed groups in American society, such as the working class, the immigrant, and the black, and within this focus there have been two major lines of attack. The first has examined the class interest of the early leadership of public education in this country, along with the opposition that the formation of public schools generated. The second has looked at the consequences of schooling as they have a bearing upon the status and well-being of particular groups in the society. The general view tying together both of these perspectives is that the schools did not, nor were they designed to, serve the needs of the poorer groups in American society. Rather, they were established and maintained to further the development of corporate capitalism by establishing in the young the attitudes and values needed to work in an industrial setting. In addition, the point has been made that at least during the earlier years of public education the poor themselves resisted the expansion of public education and did not, as suggested by many traditional historians, welcome it as an unmitigated blessing. The revisionist points out that in a number of instances expansion was resisted and the resistance was overcome only by outmaneuvering the poor in the political arena and by softening the rhetoric to make the inroads for school reform easier.

Those who have been called "revisionist" disagree among themselves about many aspects of school reform. Some argue, for example, that the rhetoric was a mask to hide the deeper and more questionable reality that underwrote American education, while others believe that the rhetoric itself is a key to understanding the development of public education. Nevertheless, whatever the differences may be among the revisionists themselves, they have been muted by the criticism from outside. A major concern of the revisionist's critic has been that the new history has erred by examining the past from the standpoint of the present and that the new historians' interpretation of the past has been governed by their views about many of the problems of the present. The thrust of this criticism is that by shifting the context of the examination of school reform from the past to the present, the revisionist has clouded the fact that school reform was a response to certain problems and pressures that do not have a direct analog in the problems of today. The upshot of this criticism is that the significance of these earlier problems and pressures is lost when reform is looked at only from the point of view of issues that are uppermost in our minds today. Although such criticism fails to take seriously Karier's and Schlesinger's earlier-mentioned point, it does suggest some larger issues.

On the surface, the debate appears to be about the nature of the past happenings of American education and therefore is presented as concerned largely with matters of fact. However, the debate is about more than simply questions of fact. It also involves questions of interpretation and questions about the appropriate perspective through which the past is to be viewed and the proper set of values by which it should be judged. Yet the perspective and the values constitute the unspoken context of the debate, often allowing the argument to be carried forward as if only matters of fact were at stake.

The strength of the revisionist treatment is to be found in the extent to which it is able to penetrate the perspective and values of the traditional historian. This advantage, however, is weakened by the very way in which revisionists misunderstand the nature of their own enterprise and are thereby unable to consciously address the very *perspectives* from which different factual accounts are generated. Thus while revisionists provide new insight, they provide no new theory in which such insights can be grounded and therefore have been vulnerable to superficial but sometimes persuasive criticisms from traditional sources.[4] Whatever their scholarly merit, the persuasiveness of these criticisms can be understood partly in terms of a shared perspective between critic and audience and partly in terms of the failure of revisionist writers to confront that perspective directly. Debates about the past are carried on as if they were debates about the facts and nothing but the facts.

Yet the work of revisionist historians has penetrated the established view in productive ways. However, because they have misunderstood the relationship between history as a descriptive enterprise and history as an interpretive enterprise, the penetrations have been seriously limited. The fact that this misunderstanding is shared with more traditional historians requires that we look at it more closely, and here some extrapolation is necessary. For revisionist and most other historians the goal of the historical enterprise is thought to be accurate description of events past. Interpretation has a place in the historical enterprise because the past leaves us only with fragments and these fragments need to be pieced together in order to tell a story, one that will be as accurate with regard to the facts as possible. Values enter the picture by way of determining which fragments are most important, but unless they dictate that certain facts remain systematically unaccounted for, they are themselves not subject to serious challenge. Hence a wall is built around the historians' values and the facts that they illuminate. Interpretation is analogous to putting together the pieces of a puzzle, and could the puzzle be fully pieced together, presumably we would have the historical ideal – full and accurate description.

The problem with this view is found in the idea that interpretation is simply a puzzle-solving activity in which pieces are tied together into some preexisting whole and where the whole remains only to be discovered and described. Rather, the act of putting the pieces together as well as deciding just which pieces are significant issues from a perspective that is itself part of the interpretive process. Moreover, the story is not complete until that perspective has itself been raised to the level of a problem that requires discussion, analysis, and criticism. There is little doubt, for example, that a Marxist will describe certain features of Reconstruction differently than a traditional liberal. However, the difference will not lie in the facts alone, but in the way that they are tied together by a given perspective into a narrative. To place this perspective beyond the realm of discussion is to give the appearance that historical disputes have only to do with the facts of the matter and to reinforce the positivists' perspective, which many historians ritualistically reject.

The historian's understanding of education has been limited by the fact that the point of view out of which the story of the past has been told has itself been bracketed and placed beyond the realm of discourse and analysis. Thus differences among historians appear to be differences of fact only, and questions of value and perspective serve only to license the description that is issued. When the object in question is the role of schooling in American society, the perspective will include some general ideas about what educational institutions can and ought to do. This perspective will guide the way in which historians tell us what they have, in fact, done. Thus interpretation is not just a matter of piecing parts of a puzzle together. It involves as well a judgment about just how the final fit measures up to some implicit idea of how the pieces ought to look when they are functioning properly. In other words, interpretation in education is carried on against the background idea of what schools would be doing if they were carrying out their appropriate function, however that function may be conceived. When such appraisal remains implicit, it forms the unstated context in which interpretation takes place. Only when it becomes explicit can it become the object of a public discourse. The examination of the writings of Katz and Greer that follows will allow us to see how shifts in contextual considerations (from revisionist to traditional) can yield different interpretations of the essentially same "facts." This examination is intended to show the need to go beyond the historical "description" and to examine the contextual backdrop from which judgments are generated.

A summary of the historical critiques of Michael Katz and Colin Greer

The intent of both Katz's and Greer's revisionist history is to explode some of the myths that they believe surround the history of schooling in American society. Katz's earlier work, *The Irony of Early School Reform,* is concerned with showing that in the formative period of American education, public schools did not have the wide degree of support that is commonly assumed, and that the establishment of free, public education was often opposed by poor and working-class parents who viewed it as an imposition fostered by the upper classes. In a later work, *Class, Bureaucracy, and Schools,* he extends these insights to some of the specific problems of the late 1960s and shows how the battle between the black community and the professional educators in New York City can be seen as a continuation of some of the earlier struggles. Greer, in *The Great School Legend,* attempts to refute the widely held belief that schools have served as a vehicle of upward mobility and equality of opportunity for the immigrant and the poor. Like Katz, Greer also extends his analysis to some of the problems of contemporary times as he attempts to show that the large number of school failures is not unique to blacks in the latter half of the twentieth century. Thus the analyses of Greer and Katz, while different in many respects, complement each other in at least the following way. Whereas Katz is concerned with showing that the schools did not meet with the universal approval of their clients, Greer's analysis suggests that given historical hindsight, we can now see that there were very good reasons for various groups to withhold their approval.

In addition to offering complementary analyses, both Katz and Greer believe that it is important to correct the impression and the methodology of older, more traditional historical treatments. Katz illustrates the tone of this earlier historiography by a quotation from Alice Felt Tyler's *Freedom's Ferment:* ''It was not until the common man became conscious of the privileges of which he had been deprived and used the suffrage he had acquired to demand education for his children that the state turned to a consideration of the common school. This movement was in accord with the humanitarianism of the time, and the reformer joined the workingman in seeking remedies for the defects in the educational system.''[5] Greer initiates his critique by focusing upon a similar work, a report sponsored by the National Education Association that he tells us was largely written by the educational historian Lawrence Cremin. Greer quotes as follows: ''A source of profound strength lies in the American educational heritage, . . . designed especially for their task, public schools have stood – and now stand – as great wellsprings of freedom, equality, and self-government.''[6]

Katz of course challenges the view that the common man supported the establishment of public schooling with such zeal, and Greer argues that schools were not the wellsprings of freedom and equality that they are reported to be. Both historians also challenge the historical methodology supporting these quotations by arguing that these traditional historians have taken the rhetoric of the school reformer too seriously and have failed to analyze the empirical information that could serve to support or refute the reformer's claims. Thus, both of these revisionist scholars believe that by focusing upon different sources of data, we will arrive at a new, more adequate and critical interpretation of school reform. Part of the analysis of revisionist scholarship offered here is designed to show that the data, while not at all insignificant, are not sufficient to arrive at the interpretations suggested. Thus we begin by looking at some of the empirical corrections that have been offered to counter the traditional interpretations of education history.

A sketch of the evidence used in support of revisionist critiques

In contrast to Tyler, Katz argues that the common school was not seen as a universal blessing by the poorer groups of society, and that more often than not these groups were opposed to the expansion of public schooling. He supports his view by examining the political activity related to a vote taken in Beverly, Massachusetts in 1853 to abolish the high school, and then by looking at similar issues as they unfolded in other towns at approximately the same time. Katz found that in Beverly the vote to abolish the high school divided clearly along lines of wealth and occupation, with the wealthier, more prestigious citizens supporting the school and the poorer ones opposing it. On the basis of this analysis, Katz concluded, ''Educational reform and innovation represented the imposition by social leaders of schooling upon a reluctant, uncomprehending, skeptical, and sometimes . . . hostile citizenry.''[7]

Katz's analysis of the vote in Beverly and his description of events in other towns, such as Groton and Lawrence, are intended to show that by focusing only upon the rhetoric of the reformers, the historians have been misled into believing that the working classes rose up in support of the expansion of public schooling. Instead Katz argues that the reformers were motivated by a quest for power and that the rhetoric that later historians took to be so important was simply a mask to hide this quest. In other words, Katz argues that the real function of schools in their formative stage was to consolidate the power of the middle and upper middle classes over the poor. In Beverly as elsewhere, the poor perceived the high school as a luxury that would be unavailable to those families that needed the income of an adolescent to make ends meet, and thus the arguments of the reformers, based as they were upon economic well-being and upward mobility, could not easily take root. The question of whether or not the schools actually did serve to further upward mobility is left somewhat open by Katz, but there seems to be little question that he does not side with the traditional historian on this issue.

The evidence that Greer uses is intended to show that in fact the reformers were wrong and that the schools did not serve to further upward mobility for the poorer groups in American society. He proposes that had the schools actually served the goals of upward mobility and equality of opportunity for the urban poor of an earlier era, then "poverty, under-employment, large-scale and long-term immobility for lower class groups would be primarily – almost exclusively – black," and that even "Puerto Ricans and blacks, the new urban immigrants, should by now be moving wholesale across the cities they live in and out into the suburbs."[8] Although some of the evidence cited by Greer in support of his contention that this movement has not generally occurred is to be questioned, the thrust of this examination will be that even if his evidence is correct, it need not be taken as support for his interpretation.[9]

Greer's argument that the schools have not served as significant vehicles of mobility is supported by his claim that a significant number of groups, such as the Irish and the Italians, have not left their urban enclaves in large numbers and moved into the outlying suburbs to join the middle class. He later links this observation to the performance of immigrant children in school. He examines performance of these children in school around and after the turn of the century when, as he writes, "immigrant children were entering the schools in increasing numbers."[10] Here he finds that more children failed in school than succeeded and that a majority of the children were classified as either below average or retarded.[11] Greer does admit that a few groups such as the Jews and the Greeks and selected individuals from the less advantged sectors were able to escape into the middle class, but he attributes their success to factors independent of schooling. The Jews and Greeks were successful because their skills and values were generally consistent with those demanded by American life. However, he observes that these attributes were largely developed in the old country, and were not learned in the schools of America. As for those successful *individuals* who came from other groups, from Italian, Irish, or Polish stock, Greer believes that their success can be attributed to institutions other than schools, institutions such as business or labor, or perhaps even crime. The general point that he is making in this discussion is that there has been less success among immigrants than has often been supposed and that the success that there has been cannot be attributed to schools. Rather, as Greer summarizes his point, ''things seem to have worked in quite the reverse order, with cultural background and economic status being reflected and reinforced in the school, not caused by it.''[12]

While the brevity of the above sketch cannot do justice to all aspects of the argument and evidence, it does outline some of the major points to be found in Katz and Greer, and I will return to these points shortly. However, before doing so, it is necessary to establish a perspective for the remarks that are to follow.

Some remarks on the problem of historical judgment

The point has been made a number of times that the revisionist can be faulted for writing of the past from the point of view of the concerns and pressures of the present. This criticism is meant to point out the moralistic tone of the recent history and to account for it in terms of a distortion of significant aspects of the past. The general idea is that by placing events of the past in the context of the concerns of the present the newer history highlights considerations that were not in the minds of the historical agents and suppresses others that were. The unstated principle that seems to govern this criticism is one that claims that people must have adequate knowledge before they can be held responsible for their acts, and since much of the knowledge and experience available to the newer historian was not available to the educational reformer, it is unfair to judge their activities in light of contemporary considerations. Whatever one may decide about these questions, the considerations are important for assessing the impact and for judging the merits of revisionist history.

The issue is not, however, a completely arbitrary one. In the first place, people can and do make judgments about historical action, and although some of these judgments are not moral ones, many others are and should be. Thus, the major question is not whether judgments should be made, but rather on what basis they should be made. Here it is important to remember that one of the most powerful, although often implicit, charges of the revisionist against the traditional historians is that they have *failed* to make judgments where in fact judgments needed to be made. This is partly the impact of the criticism that sees the traditional historian accepting the rhetoric of the school reformer at face value. However, even here it is not quite accurate to say that no judgment has been made. Rather it is more correct to say that because of an initial methodological decision to "enter the skin" of the historical agent, and to view the world entirely from that point of view, pragmatic and prudential considerations replace moral ones. And in this instance, the historian encounters the danger of coming to think that *because* a certain agent *thought* his acts were morally commendable, in fact they were. This traditional stance can go a long way in explaining how it is that some traditional historians have often overlooked the racism and class bias in early school reform.

At least in principle, the question of historical judgment can be resolved, and when the principles are looked at the revisionist comes off no worse for adopting the view of the present than the traditional historian does for "entering the skin" of the historical agent. To a large extent judgments about historical acts are made on the same basis as judgments about any other kinds of acts. In the first place, we decide whether the act calls for any judgment at all by noting whether it seems to violate some generally acknowledged human norm or principle and by then deciding whether the agent had any realistic choice in the matter, such as whether there was a course of action that was available that would not have violated an equally important norm. At times our initial judgments need to be qualified because we find that more than one principle was at stake, and because we find that in the instance under examination, action for one principle had to mean action against another. At other times we need to judge the merits of two competing principles considering such factors as consistency with other acts of the agent, the comprehensiveness of the different principles, and so forth. Obviously, judgments like these are always open to some challenge. However, the fact that historical ambiguity cannot always be removed in the making judgments about the past does not mean that it can never be removed. Historical agents can, for example, *believe* that they are serving some higher principle, and yet the evidence will suggest that they were deluding themselves while serving their own self-interest or the interest of a narrow group. At other times the agents' activity might be antagonistic to a principle that, although recognized in our own time, was not generally recognized in theirs. Because the agents acted without knowledge or insight into this principle and because there would be little reason to expect them to have such insight, moral judgment is properly deferred, but we may use the agents' activity as an example of the stage of consciousness and intellectual development of their own time. We do not, for example, fault educators of the Middle Ages for failing to act in accord with principles of equality of opportunity. Rather we show how their activity was consistent with principles held at that time. If we do find some people who wanted to further this ideal, we praise them for being ahead of their times, but we do not as a rule scold their contemporaries for being behind *our* times. Nevertheless, once a norm is acknowledged, a historical *act* can be judged, as with any other, in terms of whether or not it violated the norm. And if the act violated the norm, the *agent* is judged in terms of a number of considerations. He or she can be judged in terms of his or her intentions, which themselves are measured partly by the alternative courses of action that were dismissed and by the pattern established through a series of acts. Some agents are self-serving, calculating, and hypocritical, and others are not. The difficulty in judging the intentions of historical figures is sometimes complicated by the unavailability of some evidence, but not always. In some cases it is easier to judge the intent of a historical agent than it is to judge that of contemporary figures simply because of the availability of evidence such as diaries. The fact that it may be difficult to evaluate intentions does not mean that they cannot be evaluated at all. And it needs to be recognized that traditional historians are no less prone to making judgments of this kind than their revisionist counterparts. When Cremin writes of progressive education that it began as "a many sided effort to use the schools to improve the lives of individuals,"[13] he is making no less a claim about intentions than when a revisionist claims that the schools were established for purposes of manipulation and social control. Even with the question of intentions aside, acts of historical agents can be judged in terms of the knowledge available to the person, as when they say that a person made a mistake or a miscalculation; they can be judged in terms of the knowledge that should have been available but that the person did not comprehend, as when we judge someone to be incompetent; or they can be judged in terms of knowledge that was readily available to the agent but that he chose not to seek out for personal reasons, as when we judge a person to be irresponsible.

The point of the above discussion is simply to illustrate that there is nothing wrong per se in writing history from the standpoint of the present. And if judgments are initiated by determining whether certain norms have been violated, then, even if one recognizes that such norms were not available to the historical agent and uses the initial judgment simply to illustrate the intellectual climate of the times, we are still beginning from our own present standpoint. Indeed, if one were to take Dewey seriously on this point, the present is the only standpoint from which history could be written.[14] Where many revisionists and traditional historians may be faulted is in their failure to spell out clearly the factors that have entered into their judgments, and this is the matter of context that we will return to shortly. In any event, a thorough analysis of revisionist writings on these points would likely show that their judgments are in need of some refinement, but this is true of traditional historians as well who are often too willing to enter uncritically into the skin of the historical agent.

Historical evidence viewed in the light of shifting context

The purpose of the above remarks is to caution that the examination of Katz and Greer that follows is not intended to support the charges levied against revisionists by traditional historians. Rather, what I want to show is the way in which different contextual considerations involving issues of perspective and values, that is, issues of consciousness, have helped to generate different judgments of similar movements and to then follow this up by addressing some of those contextual considerations as guides for educational understanding. In order to understand the role that contextual factors do play in historical judgments we turn to the writing of Katz and Greer to show how, given a different set of considerations and different modes of punctuating the narrative, their evidence could be used to generate somewhat different evaluations.

Consider first Katz's two books on school reform. In both he makes the major point that the expansion of public education did not have the wide degree of popular support commonly assumed. Moreover, in both books he suggests that this lack of support was the case not only at the beginning of the public school movement, but is still so today. However, despite these similarities, there is a decidedly different tone to the two books even though they were published only three years apart. The second book appears to be more sensitive to the ambiguities involved in school reform and is not nearly as critical of the educational reformer as is the first. Yet this shift in tone could have been anticipated by a conceptual ambiguity that runs through Katz's first book but that is never explicitly identified in either one. The confusion involves the question of imposition, what it means, and how its occurrence is to be identified.

Katz begins the conclusion of the first book by noting the similarities between the concerns of the early school reformer Horace Mann and those of the more contemporary educator James B. Conant. Both reformers, he tells us, "were stirred to action by the 'social dynamite' they saw in the slums,"[15] and both were concerned to use the schools as instruments for social control. He then laments that given the impulse to use the school in this way, "We have still to see a movement driven by a desire to bring joy and delight to the life of the individual, to enrich experience solely for the purpose of making life more full and lovely."[16] He then continues in the same paragraph to talk about the similarities between the earlier and later reforms. "The goals of both movements have been extrinsic; they have stressed the needs of society and the economy. They have also been utilitarian, stressing the concrete cash value of schooling to the individual. In both movements goals have been formulated with scant regard to the indigenous culture, even the aspirations of the working class groups to be reformed. Very largely both movements of urban reform have been impositions."[17] What is important to observe in this passage (and I have divided it in order to highlight this point) is that there are two things that Katz counts here as "imposition," and that these may not always go together. In the first place there is the imposition that is set upon the child when, according to Katz, his education is designed for external, societal ends rather than for the goal of "making life more full and lovely." In the second place there is the imposition set upon the parents when their culture and aspirations are overlooked. One form of imposition has to do with a certain kind of education, whereas the other has to do with the aspirations of a certain group of people.

Given these two different treatments of imposition, some distinctions need to be made. The first is that the two need not go together conceptually. A parent's aspirations may, for example, dictate that he or she wants an education for the child that is guided by the demands of the society, as determined by what the society is willing to reward. Secondly, although it is possible for these two conceptually different modes of imposition to coincide historically such that at any given time a parent may want the child's education to be designed "solely for the purpose of making life more full and lovely," Katz has not shown this to be the case with any of the historical periods that he deals with.

Whereas Katz's first book glosses over the tension between these two kinds of impositions, his second book dramatically recognizes it. Here Katz recounts an incident where members of a poor community decided to select one of their members to run for the school committee, and he tells us that this initiative was supported by a group of radical students "who saw in the mothers an indigenous community movement representing educational radicalism and participatory democracy."[18] Yet when pressed to come up with a platform, Katz reports that the candidate "advocated the reintroduction of report cards and corporal punishment; she opposed sex education."[19] Here Katz is unhappily forced to concede that "educational radicalism is itself a species of class activity. It reflects an attempt at cultural imposition fully as much as the traditional educational emphasis on competition, restraint, and orderliness, whose bourgeois bias radicals are quick to excoriate."[20] Yet given his implicit definition of "imposition" Katz may be understating the case. For if competition (in the form of reports cards), restraint, and orderliness composed the platform of his local candidate, then in this instance it is not very clear how he can call *these* "bourgeois values" imposition – unless, of course, he is willing to overlook one of his implicit definitions. What is important to notice here is that Katz's conceptual scheme, grounded as it is in the values of the minority group, has no way to explain or resolve this issue. This is because his framework allows little room for judgments of false consciousness to be made by the historian, and thus his own mode of punctuating the narrative unwittingly denies the use of an important critical tool.

Katz's problem, and his eventual retreat, result partly from a faulty understanding of the concept of "imposition." There is more to the concept than simply doing something against the will of another person, a definition Katz simply imposes on his data. Perhaps equally important in determining cases of imposition is a normative decision about the nature of the rights that each party has over the object being acted upon. When it comes to questions concerning young children, we do give prima facie consideration to the parent's desires, and for many good reasons. However, this does not mean that the parent *owns* the child, and in certain situations, such as child abuse, to interfere with an act of the parent is not generally looked upon as an imposition at all. It is simply protecting the rights of the child. Indeed, the assumption here is that the parent has gone beyond the scope of his or her own rights and that interference is justified. Thus, whether Katz has correctly labeled these situations when he cites them as instances of "imposition" is an open question, but for now it is sufficient to point out that his data do not compel one to adopt his interpretation of it, and that his own conceptual scheme blunts the possibility for a more probing, critical analysis.

A different kind of tension exists in Greer's work, but it points to the same kind of interpretive ambiguity. After arguing passionately that the schools have not served to provide upward mobility for poor people in American society, be they immigrant or black, he then turns around and writes that "schools could be an agent for major change in this society. Basic as they are to maintenance of both the humane and democratic rhetoric of society, and of wide-scale socioeconomic inequalities, the public schools could be a vehicle for some of us to push the contradictions inherent in the severe disjunction between school rhetoric and school reality to the point of absurdity."[21] The remark is jarring precisely because it comes as the summation of an argument designed to show that the schools have initiated little if any fundamental change in American society. Thus we are left to ponder the question of what it is about the future that might make the role of the school so different than it has been in the past.

The remark is jarring for another reason as well. Whatever else may be the shortcomings of the traditional historians, they began with the belief that the major advances made by American society, including its educational system, were to be found in the fact that the ideal of equal opportunity *could* be used as a critical lever here in a way that it could not be used elsewhere. To these historians Greer's proposal is nothing new. It is precisely what the schools and other institutions have been doing all along, and will probably continue to do. Unlike Greer, these historians do not have the problem of suggesting in what way the future will be different than the past. From their point of view, what Greer suggests should be the case has, in fact, been the case. Obviously, there is more than an empirical difference here. Nevertheless, there are empirical questions involved in this dispute.

The traditional historian believes that there was a basic commitment to equality of opportunity in the formative years of American society, a commitment that was not present in other, more established nations. According to this view, this commitment, which may have begun as a vague feeling that the oppressed of other nations could be judged here on their merits, later became translated into the social, legal, and educational institutions of the country. And when it was, the traditional historian argues, it was used precisely as Greer suggests it should be, as a critical lever to highlight and address distinctions that were made on grounds other than talent and achievement. I use the word "distinction" rather than "discrimination" here because what underlies the positive treatment of American society by the traditional historian is the belief that the major ethical contribution of American society was that it turned judgments that elsewhere would have been looked upon as acceptable distinctions into unacceptable acts of discrimination.

Whether the more established interpretation of America's past is an accurate one is surely open to some question. Yet given the size of the immigration into this country, and given too the belief on the part of many immigrants that opportunity was more plentiful here than elsewhere, it would be unlikely to find that the belief in equal opportunity did not become a critical ideal by which to judge the progress of American society.

It is probably important to point out that the ideal itself may have been much less unique to American society than it was to a certain historical level of capital development and potential and to the manpower needs that this generated. To say this, however, is to grant what Greer implicitly denies, that the ideal came to be seen as a way to judge whether or not existing society was measuring up to its social and economic potential.

To a certain extent the difference between Greer and the more traditional historical account of American society can be found in the differential emphasis placed on the role of schooling as the vehicle for economic and social mobility. Although Greer is correct in pointing to the important role that educational historians believed the school played in developing equal opportunity, schooling has not generally been thought to be the most significant vehicle for the realization of the ideal. American history has always reserved a special place for the singular hero whose success was achieved in spite of deficient schooling – the Edisons and Fords, to cite but two examples. The more usual interpretation of equality of opportunity in American society was expressed by the simple belief that given sufficient energy and talent, a person could overcome much of his ethnic and social class background. The particular institution that was to serve as a vehicle for such mobility was of secondary importance. It might be the school, but then again, it might be labor unions, business enterprises, or government. The dream of many first- and second-generation Americans was neither a college nor a high school education for their children, but rather a small business where they could be independent and could use their talents to their own advantage. For others the ideal was a union card and the security that they hoped it would bring. These were the dreams of many who believed in the ideals of American society, and until only relatively recently, schooling was not thought to be a major factor in their realization. Generally the traditional historian has not needed to invoke the specter of schooling in order to picture what the ideal meant for some of the newer Americans. Oscar Handlin captures more accurately than Greer the spirit and beliefs of some of the newer immigrants by quoting from the diary of Samuel Gompers, who left England as an immigrant to later become head of the American Federation of Labor.

It was typical of the feeling among English wage earners of my boyhood days that the two most popular songs were "The Slave Ship" and "To the West." I learned both and sang them with a fervor in which all my feeling quivered and throbbed. I could throw back my head and sing:

> To the west, to the west, to the land of the free
> Where mighty Missouri rolls down to the sea;
> Where a man is a man if he's willing to toil,
> And the humblest may gather the fruits of the soil.
> Where children are blessings and he who hath most
> Has aid for his fortune and riches to boast.
> Where the young may exult and the aged may rest,
> Away, far away, to the land of the west.

The song expressed my feeling of America and my desire to go there rose with the ringing chorus:

> Away! Far away, let us hope for the best
> And build up a home in the land of the west.

Years afterward Andrew Carnegie told me this song had inspired his father to come to America.[22]

The fact that this song inspired both Gompers, the labor leader, and the father of Andrew Carnegie, the industrialist, indicates how different were the groups that shared this belief, and the fact that both of these people were "self-made men" indicates just how incidental schooling was to the initial expression of this idea. These rather commonplace observations should not be taken here as an endorsement of the ideal itself. They are mentioned only to place "the great school legend" in the wider perspective in which it belongs. Once this perspective is established then it can be argued that much of the evidence Greer offers, such as the percentage of children who had failed in urban school or who had fallen behind during the early years of immigration, is simply beside the point. Once the legend is revised in this manner, we can begin to see how it is that the traditional and the revisionist historians can often speak past one another by punctuating their narratives in different ways, and we can also begin to see the role that context plays in historical judgments.

By this time it must be clear that the traditional and the revisionist historians do not really share a common basis for comparison. For the traditional scholar the appropriate basis for judging life in America was the differences between the opportunities that were available here for the immigrant and those available in Europe. For revisionists like Greer, as we shall see, the proper point of comparison is to be located elsewhere.

We need only to glance back at the Gompers quotation cited by Handlin to understand the importance of the European experience for the traditional interpretation of America's past. Yet when we look at the way in which Greer treats similar material from traditional sources, we can begin to understand how insignificant the European experience has become from the revisionist perspective. Greer, for example, begins his first chapter with a quotation from Henry Parkinson that essentially *compares* the extent to which Americans and Europeans came to rely upon schools during the days of the early republic. However instead of addressing this comparison, he chooses to link it to a National Education Association report that argues that schools have been essential for American democracy and prosperity. It is this latter quotation comprising, as he sees it, the major part of the "great school legend," that Greer chooses to concentrate on.[23] The contrast becomes even more obvious when Greer examines specific information that could in fact lend some support to the claim of the traditionalist that there was a significant difference between the American and the European experience. The following quotation, where Greer is attempting to explain the success of the Jews in American society, is but one example. Here he alludes to an important traditionalist's point but does so only in passing, and thus fails to acknowledge its significance. Greer writes:

In the period between 1870 and 1914, approximately two-million Jews – or one-third of the whole Jewish population of Eastern Europe – emigrated, almost all of them to the United States and a very high percentage to New York City. Moses Rischin suggests convincingly that many Jewish men and women had experienced the life of the sweatshop well before they emigrated. When poverty intensified – in the 1800s, 6,000 Jews reputedly starved to death annually in Galicia – and after forerunners had reported from the United States that life was possible there along lines not altogether dissimilar from those known in Europe, but with no starvation, massive emigration began. Over 66 percent of those gainfully employed in America at the turn of the century had had "industrial" experience in Europe; no other immigration approached such a percentage.[24]

For Greer, the important item in this passage is the fact that most Jews who came to this country from Eastern Europe had some kind of industrial experience. It is this experience, and not public schooling, that he believes explains their reputedly disproportionate success in American life. However, what would likely be more important for the traditional historian in this passage would be the reported fact that six thousand Jews a year were starving in Galicia, and that once they found enough money to buy passage to the United States they could not only find food for all, but eventual success for a goodly number of them.

For Greer, however, the significant point of comparison is not the different opportunities between the earlier European and the American experience, but the relative positions of different groups in American society. On the one hand, this point of view has the major advantage of giving recognition to the fact that not all groups in the United States originated in Europe – a point traditional historians all too often ignore. On the other hand, when used as a way to measure the upward mobility and the opportunities of groups that did immigrate from Europe, the use of this comparison has been somewhat misleading. For example, Greer claims that if the immigrants really were given equal opportunity, then we could expect that the long-established urban groups would by now be moving into the suburbs. He claims, although on the basis of some questionable evidence, that this is not the case, and therefore concludes that equal opportunity has been but a legendary aspect of American life. The corollary of this conclusion is, of course, that schools have not fulfilled their obligation to equal opportunity. Yet Greer's argument simply rests on a different platform than that of the traditionalist, and even if his evidence is found to be correct, it would not establish his case against them. We can see this point rather quickly by looking at some of the arguments that Greer uses in attempting both to support his case and to counter some of the stronger evidence for the traditional point of view.

We have already seen that Greer attempts to explain those instances that appear as exceptions to his argument on the grounds that mobility here derives from factors other than school. For groups such as Jews and Greeks, who he admits have experienced a fair degree of mobility, he suggests that their success can be explained in terms of an initial congruence between their values and those of industrial American society. The success of individuals from other groups that as a whole have experienced little mobility is explained in terms of institutions other than schools. Yet it is fairly easy to see how these very same observations can be used equally well to support more traditional interpretations of mobility in American society.

In the first place, the traditional historian will generally see school as only one possible vehicle for the achievement of mobility, and in the second place, equal opportunity is not measured by the relative positions of different groups, but by the chances that "talented" and "energetic" people have to rise out of their initial situations. Certainly these are somewhat loose measures, but once they are acknowledged, it is easy to see how Greer's observations can be used to support traditional perceptions. If we are not concerned about the relative positions of groups as a whole, then the fact that some individuals have been able to move from positions of relatively low status and income to much higher positions can be easily used to support the claim that there is reasonable equality of opportunity in the United States. That such achievement may have been the result of institutions other than schools does not affect this claim as long as one remembers that schools have been thought to be only one of the institutions through which mobility could be obtained. Moreover, once the traditional measure is accepted, the recognition of the fact that the success of some groups can be accounted for in terms of a congruence between the values of the group and those of industrial society does little to counter the traditionalist's claim. What is important here is that mobility *did* take place, not *how* it is to be explained. That schools advanced those who were able to conform more readily to the values of the larger society should be surprising to no one. Nor should anyone be surprised that those who were able to advance through the schools were also those who had an initial headstart at home. What is disturbing from the traditional point of view is to find talented individuals who, despite their conformity to the dominant values, were discriminated against because of their origins in a particular subculture. That such discrimination has occurred is undeniable, but it is questionable whether this kind of discrimination was practiced less frequently against Jews and Greeks than against Irish or Polish-Americans. Greer's observation that the members of some groups were able to overcome this discrimination more readily than members of other groups could easily be cited as evidence that the ideal of equality of opportunity was indeed useful as a critical lever that aided the mobility of those who measured up to some widely accepted standards of performance.

What is therefore important to the more traditional interpreter of the American experience is not that some groups were left behind, but that others, starting from the same social level, were able to move ahead and, for whatever reasons, overcome the barriers that were initially placed in their way. This, however, is not what is significant for Greer. Indeed, the difference between his own analysis and the traditional one is so large that even when he uses more traditional sources, he fails to acknowledge the conflicting interpretation. For example, in discussing the mobility pattern of Irish Americans, Greer has occasion to quote, as support for his views, the following passage from the sociologist Kane: "There may be some kind of lower middle or lower class orientation among them to education and occupation which tends to anchor Catholics in the lower socioeconomic groups which appear to offer more security, albeit less prestige and income."[25] The quotation is interesting in its own right because it seems to explain the reputedly low positions of certain groups in terms of factors within their own culture, a perspective that is in fact quite conservative. However, Greer's use of this quotation is also interesting because it points out much of the conflicting interpretive base of the traditional and revisionist historians. We can see this in the brief comments that follow the quotation. He begins by offering census data to support Kane's observation to the effect that "ethnic differences still predominate, leaving Irishmen and Italians considerably less advanced than Russian Jews."[26] Yet after offering this rather neutral information, Greer then, without acknowledging the difference between his own interpretation and Kane's, shifts the locus of explanation from the subculture to the society at large. He writes: "Census data in 1920 and in succeeding decades up to and including 1960 make it clear that even when immigrants became Americans, neither school nor society offered quite the mobility imagined."[27] Granting that this last passage is slightly ambiguous – its meaning depending upon how much mobility was imagined – nevertheless in the context of the rest of Greer's work, it suggests quite a different interpretation of the data than Kane's original quotation suggests. The quotation seems to locate the source of immobility in certain characteristics of the particular culture rather than in terms of what the school and the society had to offer. Greer really misses the very essential difference between his own view and the view that seems to be indicated by his citation of Kane. What Kane seems to suggest here is that what characterizes American society in general is opportunities for mobility, and what therefore needs to be explained as somewhat surprising is the relative immobility of certain groups. Greer, however, is claiming exactly the opposite. His claim is that what characterizes American society in general is immobility and what needs to be explained as surprising is the mobility of a few exceptional groups such as the Greeks and the Jews. In reality, however, all that we know is that some groups have advanced at a quicker pace than others. The explanation for this difference cannot become a settled question until more attention has been given to the problem of context and especially to the points of comparison that are being used.

The failure to address these fundamental issues unwittingly renders much of Greer's intended revisionist critique compatible with generally conservative treatments of educational reform. In order to illustrate this point, we need only take what for Greer stands as an implicit standard of analysis – the relative positions of different groups in American society – and alter its function from that of the basis of comparison to simply a descriptive observation about the distribution of success and failure among different groups in the population. Since Greer never explicitly argues for his standard, the move is fairly easy to make. However, once it is made, then the question of whether the variations in the distributions of success and failure indicates a lack of opportunity depends upon some empirical assumptions about the distribution of talent and the relative compatibility of different cultures to conditions of modernity. In addition, once the move has been made, then the debate has been cast in a framework that likely gives advocates of IQ examinations an influential voice. Certainly Greer himself would quickly see that there is too much at stake here to allow the influence of the psychometricians to decide the case, but there is little in his analysis that would guard against precisely that influence.

Of course, it is possible, as we have seen, to argue against the merits of IQ tests on their own grounds, and there are many good reasons for rejecting the claim that IQ tests measure some genetically based intellectual capacity. Yet granting these arguments, Greer's quotation from Kane, cited earlier, suggests where this compatibility would be located. The quotation from Kane seems to anchor his explanation not in anything that would characterize the general social order, but rather in the qualities of particular subcultures, and this point does not seem very far from other, more conservative positions expressed by people like Moynihan and Banfield. Here the argument is that the disproportionate number of blacks found in the lower classes is explained not in terms of racism, but rather by certain psychological and cultural characteristics that mark off lower-class culture from the middle and upper classes and that are transmitted from generation to generation. Now Banfield and Moynihan have both been criticized for developing positions that by implication, simply blame blacks and other lower-class groups for their own condition, and this is surely not a position that Greer would be comfortable with. However, the point is that his own analysis does little to offset this interpretation, and the evidence he uses to support his own point of view could be used equally well to support the other side. As we have seen, all that is needed to make the shift is to take Greer's standard for evaluation and turn it into a simple descriptive account of the relative positions of different cultural groups imposing thereon a different standard of comparison. That is, all that is needed is to punctuate the ''evidence'' differently.

Although Katz's analysis of school reform avoids some of the methodological problems of Greer's work and is more sophisticated in reporting the results of empirical research, it shares with Greer some of the same problems of interpretation. Katz begins *The Irony of Early School Reform* by highlighting a fact that he believes has been generally overlooked by school historians. Thus he shows by his analysis of the Beverly vote and other sources that school reform, at least on the secondary level, had much less support among the lower classes than has normally been believed. Yet even this simple fact opens up some unaddressed questions. A number of historians of more traditional persuasions have reported on conflicts between the leaders of public education and such groups as the Irish Catholics, conflicts that in the 1800s led to the establishment of parochial schools. That such dissident groups contained a large number of working- and lower-class members is an important consideration for determining the uniqueness of Katz's analysis, for this analysis focuses almost entirely on class and occupational factors and does not examine religious considerations. Yet it is possible that many of these class conflicts were treated by the traditional historians under a different set of categories. That is, it is possible that they saw them as religious rather than as class conflicts. To a certain extent this is an empirical issue, and it may turn out that the opposition in Beverly was essentially of the same faith as the school leaders and that in fact the conflict could be explained only by class factors. It is also possible that even if religious differences are found, a reasonable argument could be given that the conflict surrounding the school was primarily a result of class differences and that religion played very little part. Yet no matter how the empirical side of this question is worked out, the fact that traditional historians have observed conflicts between differently advantaged groups and yet have chosen not to describe those conflicts in terms of one group imposing its will upon the other suggests that between Katz and the traditional historian there is an unshared interpretative element.[28] We can begin to understand what this element is by returning to examine Katz's analysis of the vote in Beverly, Massachusetts together with his subsequent supporting description of events as they unfolded around the same time in Groton and Lawrence.

The analysis of the vote in Beverly, together with the description of other similar struggles in Groton and Lawrence, is designed to show, among other things, that traditional historians were misled by the rhetoric of the reformers and that the working class did not rise up in unanimous support of public schooling. Yet if it is true that the traditional historian accepted the rhetoric of the reformer at face value and too quickly, it can also be said that Katz's analysis suffers because he dismisses this rhetoric too soon. Katz's analysis is designed not only to show something about the limited support for public education, but also something about the motivation of the reformers, and here he is on somewhat shakier ground. His suggestion is that the reformers were motivated by a drive for power and that talk about the public school as the mainspring of democracy was just so much rhetoric designed to conceal the quest.

Even though Katz's analysis of ideology is one of the weaker aspects of his book and does not measure up to his treatment of other issues, it is also one of the most revealing. It is through this issue that we can begin to understand some of the different interpretive factors at work in traditional and revisionist histories and also the way in which the contextual limits of revisionist history could be broadened.

While Katz is not as clear as some might like about what is to count as ideological, it would be quite reasonable to say that generally he uses the term to indicate the use of democratically oriented rhetoric to cover up an educational innovation that is being imposed upon a group of people. In Groton, for example, the school committee argued for the establishment of the high school on the grounds of its democratizing influence. However, Katz contends that this was really an ideological cloak used by the school committee to conceal its real motives, which were to control and centralize the school system while destroying the veto power of the smaller districts. Yet his analysis is problematic at this point. Before it can be decided whether the rhetoric was in fact ideological or whether the establishment of the high school was an imposition in any strong sense of that term, we need to know the answers to some other kinds of questions. As we have seen earlier, one of these questions concerns the criteria that should be employed in identifying acts of imposition. It will be useful to briefly return to this point.

When we are trying to judge whether or not something is an imposition in the strong sense of the term, we generally make a distinction between a clash of wills in which one party simply prevails through reasonable but not necessarily ideal means and a clash of wills in which there is some kind of objectionable means. The paradigm case here is perhaps illegal force, but there are others as well. We may use the term "imposition" in both cases if we wish, but a generally neutral observer who is trying to judge whether or not some kind of blame is warranted will reserve his use of the term for the second kind of case. When the term is in fact used to describe the first kind of case it is usually because it brings with it the powerful connotations of the second and is useful in generating negative judgments. The interesting aspect of Katz's analysis is that he uses the term without addressing the question of means, and here he uses it only selectively. He does not use the term, for example, in those situations where the antischool forces won out (e.g., in Beverly, at least for a while). There is a danger in pushing this linguistic analysis too far and thereby obscuring a very important point which Katz suggests. Yet it is necessary to make the linguistic point because Katz's use of the term "imposition" serves to cut off the analysis at precisely the place where it should be extended.

We can begin to see part of the problem with Katz's use of the term "imposition" by *imagining* a situation somewhat similar to Groton but where in fact the rule of decentralization holds, where one district can have veto power over all and where wealth is very unevenly distributed among the districts. Thus any district can retard the development of programs that are desired by each of the remaining districts, but which need the cooperation of resources between districts. Here the casting of a negative vote might be perfectly in accord with established means, but whether one wishes to use the term "imposition" in order to generate a negative judgment might depend largely upon how one felt about the program that was being proposed. What this suggests is that the term "imposition," although often used to mold a judgment, also points to the need to evaluate the goal of an activity. Before examining this point, however, it will be useful to return to the question of historical context. By so doing we will be able to see more clearly the way in which different sides of the historical debate bypass each other, and to also understand some of the important issues that are obscured by the shifting focus. In order to see this point we need to look again at Katz's treatment of the issues on Groton and Lawrence.

When Katz looks at the school committee member's statements in Groton he classifies them as ideological, as "a kind of cloak with which they [the Groton school committee] could cover their less idealistic motives. Ideology became the rationalization of interest; and it served well, for the committee won."[29] Suppose, for the moment, as the traditional historian would likely do, that we emphasize the point somewhat differently and assume that the members of the school committee really believed their own rhetoric about social harmony and that they also felt that the only means to insure such harmony was to bring scholars from different districts together. Now their belief might have been wrong and the goal of social harmony may be questioned in terms of class interests, but in this kind of situation and given Katz's implicit suggestion of conscious concealment as an element of ideology, it is questionable whether we could, under Katz's terms, call their rhetoric ideological. We can see the problem in a different way by turning to Katz's treatment of the strike in Lynn. Katz tells us that one writer proclaimed to the mechanics of Lynn that "those occupying a position in society different from yours have wantonly and ill-advisedly insulted all that is manly in your breasts." Katz's only comment here is that "in a very real sense the strike was about manliness, about the preservation of honor."[30] Thus, unlike his treatment of the Beverly "reformers" where Katz saw behind every utterance a self-interested motive, here behind every act he sees a lofty ideal. It does need to be said that in spite of his position of advocacy, Katz is making an important point, but his differential treatment of the school board members and the strikers obscures the implications of that point.

The point is that for many working-class children, attending the high school was not a real possibility since their parents needed the income that their work brought in. Nevertheless, without further empirical analysis the significance of this point is difficult to judge since the reformer could easily claim that although not everyone could *yet* be accommodated by the high school, nevertheless it would allow many parents who could not affort the tuition of a private school to send their youngsters to the public one. And then, hopefully and in time, all parents would be able to free their children from work to enjoy the benefits of public education. Whether these ideas were actually in the minds of the reformers is of course pure speculation, but the speculation highlights one of the more significant omissions in Katz's analysis. His analysis at least suggests that the dispute was not over *what* the high school had to offer children; it was over who would in fact *receive* the offerings. To understand the reasons for this, perhaps we need only return to Oscar Handlin's quotation from Samuel Gompers and to remember that what inspired Gompers also inspired Andrew Carnegie's father. What Katz overlooks is that workers and owners sometimes shared a large part of the ideological superstructure of American society. The political platform of the local school board candidate that Katz tells us about in his *Class, Bureaucracy, and Schools* is but a recent manifestation of this shared ideology. Katz's failure to recognize this fact can go a long way in explaining the retreat that one finds in this second book.

To a large extent the power of *The Irony of Early School Reform* is the result of Katz' unwillingness to meet the traditional historians on their own ground and his tendency to look at schooling more from the point of view of the client than of the agent of reform. Yet in much the same fashion as Greer, Katz's unwillingness to meet on the ground of the traditional historian also limits his analysis, and eventually the complexities of the issue force a retreat. For when the ideas of the reformer become also the ideas of the client, then the categories of "imposition" and "ideology" lose their critical force, and Katz's analysis can go no further. Only by returning to the standpoint of the traditional historian should we be able to continue the analysis.

In some brief remarks intended to convey the commitment of the school reformer to industrial development, Katz provided a reasonably impartial statement of the goal that guided the early reformers' efforts. He writes:

The ideal school system was graded, promotions were equally open to all solely on the basis of merit, teachers were hired for their professional qualifications; this ideal school system reflected a belief that status based on achievement should pervade society. . . . To cope adequately with its business an industrial, urban society must award relative priority to achieved rather than ascribed qualities.[31]

Katz offers this comment as background for his more major point that school reform was designed to *impose* the values of industrial society onto the young- sters of the poor and that the rhetoric of the reformers was designed simply to make this imposition more palatable.[32] Yet in making this point Katz bypasses the basic rationale of the reformer – to develop a society that rewarded "achieved rather than ascribed qualities," and in so doing we are left in uncer- tainty as to how this rationale should be considered. To dismiss it as simply an ideological cloak that is designed only to conceal self-interest is to fail to recog- nize that within broad limits industrial society does strive to reward achieved qualities.[33] Yet to accept that this was the true reason for the reformer's activities and to say nothing more about it is implicitly to grant the view presented by the traditional historian of the reformer as visionary. Moreover, given this traditional view, the fact that the reformer went against the winds of public opinion would enhance, not detract from, his visionary status. Either one of these positions would be difficult to accept, and if no more could be said about this ideal, then Katz's dilemma would be unresolvable, and we would be forced to accept the traditional interpretation of educational reform. Fortunately, however, more can be said, but to see how this dilemma is to be worked out we need to return again to the question of historical judgment.

To a certain extent revisionist history is, as the traditionalists claim, moralis- tic. To agree to this label, however, is not to deny its insights, nor is it intended to support the widely prevailing view that there is something wrong in principle with moralistic history, It is simply to say that both explicitly and implicitly through the use of categories such as "imposition" and "ideological," moral judgments are being made. However, while there is nothing wrong in principle with moral history, there is ground for debate about whether the revisionist's judgments about particular agents are reasonably accurate. Regarding this issue we need to know more than we do about both the knowledge that was available to the historical agent and the methods used to effect the reformer's will. Yet even if all of these factors worked out to the revisionist's advantage, there remain other considerations. We also need to know what principles did govern the reformer's activities and the extent to which these principles are compatible with other, generally acknowledged ones. For example, Katz uses the category of imposition as a critical lever by which to judge the work of the reformers, hence granting implicit recognition to the principle of participation, whereas Greer grants similar recognition to the principle of equality of opportunity. However, in making judgments about the past, it is important to recognize that there are conceivable situations, and early school reform may be one of them, where the two principles of participation and equal opportunity may not be compatible. In quoting Kane about the possible roadblocks to mobility that exist within a culture, Greer implicitly grants this point even though he does not explicitly acknowledge it. If Kane is correct that factors within the subculture itself inhibit achievement, and yet if equal opportunity is accepted as the goal, then the implication would seem to be that something must be done to counter the influence of the subculture, and this of course does not speak well for the goal of participation. Of course, Kane may be wrong, and if so, then the dilemma may not be a real one for the instance that he describes, but then there are many other possible instances that could arise where the dilemma fits. When it does fit, then the task would seem to be to go beyond the evaluation of the historical agent and to analyze the ways in which equality of opportunity may be disfunctional for certain subcultures, and here is where we need to move beyond revisionist critiques.

Toward a new focus for educational critiques

In order to move beyond these critiques we need to recognize that there is a difference between judging the works of the educational reformer and judging the structures, possibilities, and understandings that guided those works. This latter issue will be examined in the next chapters and is one of the reasons for articulating a domain for educational studies. In the former case we need to establish just what knowledge was available at the time and to make some reasonable guess about the reformer's intentions. While this is not an impossible task, it requires more analysis than has yet been done by either of the historians disucssed here, and it remains still a matter of debate whether our present knowledge about the consequences of school reform is reasonable to attribute to the schoolmen of the past. In the latter case, however, the knowledge that we possess, although not absolutely sufficient for an evaluation of the principle, is nevertheless an essential starting point. For we know, as well as it can be known, something that the reformers of the past could only guess at. We know how these possibilities worked out in practice, and it would be foolish not to use such knowledge in reflecting on the reforms themselves. The remainder of this chapter is primarily concerned with considering some of the present factors that would be involved in an evaluation of past reforms.

When we look at reforms, such as those described by Katz, from the vantage point of the last quarter of the twentieth century, it is not difficult to see them as the initial sequences in a series of change that together served to maximize technological development as was mentioned earlier. The schools came to serve this function in two different ways: First, as Katz suggests, by reducing the resistance to urban and industrial development; and second, by providing a structure that would eventually come to maximize the growth of the knowledge needed to maintain and expand technological development. This structure of course includes not only the primary and secondary schools, but now the colleges and universities as well.

Although the idea of maximizing the growth of technological development by maximizing the growth of technological knowledge was clearly not the focused goal of each and every reformer, it was the goal of many of them, and forms a consistent thread throughout the history of contemporary school reform. William Torrey Harris warned in 1885, "Either educate your people in the common school or your labour will not compete with other nations whose people are educated up to the capacity of inventing and directing machinery."[34] And his warning was echoed by many other critics throughout the next decades. Arthur Bestor, for example, repeated the message in the early 1950s when he wrote: "It is a curiously ostrich-like way of meeting life needs to de-emphasize mathematics at precisely the time when the nation's security has come to depend on Einstein's equation $E = mc^2$."[35] Later in the same decade Conant repeated the theme in his recommendations for the children of America, those 15 percent whom he identified as academically talented and the 85 percent whom he did not.

Before returning to the critiques of Katz and Greer, one additonal point needs to be emphasized again. To say that the direction of educational reform over the years has been toward maximizing technological development is not to say that this was the conscious intent of each and every reformer. Surely many recent reformers have spent their energies trying to open up opportunities for poor youngsters from minority groups just as many earlier reformers were working to help the immigrant children mature in an age when urbanization was bringing about far-reaching and not always healthy changes in urban life. Even though these are of course general statements, they are important to make if we are to remain conscious of the many sides of school reform. To recognize this complexity is not, however, to deny the dominant and encompassing direction of school reform. Even though the above mentioned reforms were directed toward making happier the lives of individuals, they were also serving, intentionally or not, to further technological growth in certain directions, and under certain forms of control. Whatever their personal concerns may have been, reformers were serving this goal. The opportunities that they attempted to open up were, after other roadblocks were hopefully removed, determined largely by the ability of the youngster to demonstrate his integration into the web of corporately directed technological development. The important point to keep in mind is that in order to identify and analyze the outstanding direction of school reform, we need not assume that every reformer directly intended to further this direction. What would be more significant would be to show how most major reforms, regardless of intent, were colored or limited by this mode of development.

While Katz and Greer's analyses reveal a number of interesting and important aspects of school reform, their failure to meet the traditional historians on their own ground also obscures something important. What they fail to see is that the equality of opportunity, which Katz dismisses as a rhetorical weapon and which Greer claims was a goal that the schools never did accomplish, is in fact the individual side of the schools systems' social function of maximizing technological development. In short, the most efficient way to maximize technological development is to hold up opportunities to those who, for reasons of cultural development, intellectual ability, or just simple compatibility with bureaucratic structures, are able to demonstrate congruence with the technological thrust of the larger society. If people are denied advancement, either in education or employment, it may be because of intellectual or cultural factors, but it may just be for other reasons as well – "the staff would rebel if a woman or a black were put in charge."

This last point helps us to understand why some of the critiques by revisionist scholars are dismissed as insignificant by people who are committed to instruments such as IQ examinations. Given the goal of maximizing technological development, it matters little whether a test expects a youngster to reject black features and to accept Anglo ones as the standard of beauty as one IQ test did.[36] I have already noted that if such tests are doing what they are supposed to do, then they first will identify and exclude people whose cultural norms would create friction on certain levels of the bureaucracy, and second they will rank people according to their ability to absorb technological knowledge as defined by those structures. Although it is true that members of older, more established cultures initially maintain control over these selection instruments, the existence of the instrument and the seemingly objective criterion they embody can serve as a two edged sword. They control access to the higher levels, but they also provide an avenue for members of newer groups to enter those levels. As some members of the newer groups "choose" to gauge their own performance on the basis of such instruments, they not only begin to demonstrate greater congruence with the general values of the society, but they also come to use such instruments to maintain their own positions against advances from below.

Once we begin to understand the limitations of revisionist critiques and the fact that they have failed to highlight the overall goal of the school systems, then we can also understand some of the paradoxes that arise within the histories of revisionist scholars. The ghetto parent who found no reason to build a political platform on the basis of joy and delight in the classroom, but who chose instead to campaign for order, discipline, and control, was simply recognizing, in a way that Katz did not, the impact of modern society on the aspirations and life chances of ghetto children. If some of these children are to have a reasonably secure, even though uninteresting, job, if they are to escape the squalor of the ghetto and not be victimized by the crime that is found there, if they are to be able to afford tolerably healthy surroundings and decent, perhaps even humane medical care, then they will have to enter the workforce at the level at which the society will likely allow. Thus the campaign for "basic" skills is perhaps carried on not because these skills are seen to have any epistemological priority, but more likely because they reflect the priorities needed to work at a certain level in industrial capitalist society. What these parents may quite instinctively see, and what the "radicals" that Katz describes did not, is that the ability to follow orders unquestioningly, to accept routine, and to work hard at boring, meaningless tasks are at least as basic as the ability to read and to write, which are skills that can be taught in a variety of ways, using a variety of techniques. If these parents reject an education that teaches their children how to "feel" and "to be," perhaps it is not because they believe feeling and being are incompatible with reading and writing, but rather because they implicitly know these are incompatible with the level of work and routine that will likely be required of their children later in life. Implicit in the parent's desire for an education in the "basics" may very well be an important understanding of one of the implications of technological growth, and that is that a commitment to maximize the growth of technological knowledge does not entail a commitment to improve everyone's life situation. For many people in a capitalist society the condition for a tolerable life requires that one possess the skills, attitudes, and frame of mind needed to compete for routine positions toward the bottom of the industrial hierarchy.

Greer's analysis also suffers from his failure to see that the rhetoric of the school, and one might here add of the society as well, is simply the other side of the drive for technological efficiency. Thus to highlight the rhetoric would be an unlikely way to change the reality because there is in fact little contradiction between the two. Equality of opportunity as it is commonly understood is, within certain limits, a reasonably efficient way to maximize technological development.[37] Thus, if the rhetoric is simply highlighted without analyzing its implications for different strata of the society, it is in fact likely to remain a powerful force maintaining those aspects of education that Greer finds so objectionable.

The conflicting viewpoints of revisionist history

In order to summarize the implications of this analysis for educational reform and revisionist history we need to return to a point made earlier. To a large extent the force of revisionist history revolves around two independently critical pivots. There is first a commitment to upward mobility and equality of opportunity for all members of the society and second a commitment to local authority and community participation in the affairs of education. Sometimes a heavier emphasis is placed on one of these sets and sometimes on the other, yet in the works under study here both are present.[38] For a historical study, this dual emphasis may be perfectly appropriate, because it is quite possible that both of these values have been denied at any given point in history. Although it is possible for both of these values to be denied, much remains to be said about the conditions under which they both can be affirmed.

As long as a society chooses to arrange its institutions so as to maximize technological development, and as long as there are some cultures that place greater stress on other values, then equality of opportunity and local control will remain incompatible. Equality of opportunity as it is presently defined is a goal that is intended to open up opportunities for individuals. It is not designed to advance directly the well-being of local communities or cultures. (In this respect, there is little difference between the concept of equality of opportunity and the concept of equality of results.) When the norms and authority of the local community conflict with the norms and authority of the larger society, the person for whom opportunities are made available is precisely the person who moves beyond the structure and values of the local community and marches to the tune of the dominant groups. How this conflict is to be evaluated depends to a large extent upon the characteristics of the local community and the characteristics of the world outside it. However, as long as the overarching goal of schools remains that of serving to maximize technological growth, these two goals will be incompatible, and any critique of American education based upon both of them will remain unstable and likely inconsistent.

Conclusion: The implicit domain of the traditional and revisionist historian

Revisionist scholars like Katz and Greer are limited by their failure to develop the implications of their own critical point of view. The force of their criticism depends upon and is grounded in the effects of schooling on individuals and in the reaction of individuals to the workings of the school system. Equal opportunity and mobility, for example, are functions that relate to the access and advancement of individuals. Acts of imposition are ultimately judged by the extent to which the establishment of an institution is congruent with the desires and inclinations of a client group. Yet there is little room in the explicit analysis for the historian to exercise a critical judgment when, for example, the access of individuals may have been reasonably well served (as in the case of Jews and Greeks, according to Greer) or when the client generally agreed with goals that from the outside may appear to be more repressive than necessary. Of course such judgments are made by these historians, but they are not an explicit part of the analysis. Instead these judgments depend upon such things as playing upon the ambiguity of terms like ''imposition,'' as in the case of Katz, or shifting the reference of ''equality of opportunity'' from individuals to groups, as in the case of Greer.

The interpretive ambiguity serves a purpose, of course. In the absence of an explicit framework that can allow the researcher to make judgments of mistaken interest or false consciousness where it exists on the part of the client, some way is needed to punctuate description with a critical force. Yet it is precisely because people can be mistaken about their own interests and because their expressed desires can be molded inappropriately from the outside that a full understanding of education needs to be able to maintain its critical force without just appealing to what people want or desire. In some cases we need to understand why people want or desire in the particular way that they do. This requires, as we will see, that much more attention be given to deliberations about the domain of educational understanding than the revisionist critics have done.

We have seen that although the ideal of mobility and equal opportunity refers to individuals, it also has another side. It relates to the structure of jobs that are available to individuals outside the school system. Unfortunately, few revisionist scholars have examined the implications of this connection for educational research, and where they have been examined by traditional scholars they are often treated in a way that would, by implication, blunt the force of the revisionist critique.

Cremin, for example, is one of the few scholars who explicitly attempts to extend the focus of historical research in education beyond the schools. For him the domain of educational scholarship would include any institution in which there is a deliberate attempt to transmit knowledge, skills, and values. Churches, families, businesses, and other institutions become appropriate materials for educational studies, and thus, in Cremin's view, the polarity between school and society that he sees as implicit in progressive education is overcome. Schools are not the only institutions that educate, and they are not the only focus for educational research.

One might think, given Cremin's attempt to broaden the scope of educational research and to loosen the distinction between school and society, that we have the conceptual basis for the revisionist impulse mentioned earlier. Indeed, in his treatment of the multiplicity of educative institutions Cremin notes that we must think relationally and view each institution in terms of its mediation with the others. Thus the messages provided by the school are mediated by family, church, industry, community, and so forth. Now this is a conceptually productive move as far as it goes, because it does connect the school to other influential institutions. Yet there is an element of this mediation that needs to be examined more closely. Cremin's discussion focuses upon mediation only in terms of the transmission function of an institution as it stands in relation to individual learners who are the focal point of messages sent from that and other institutions. Yet there are other ways in which mediation occurs.

Institutions exist in structural relation to each other, and the influence of some of these institutions on the educative process extends quite beyond any direct role that they may have in the transmission process. Moreover, institutions that have the most prominent and visible role in direct transmission, such as schools, may have a much less significant role than other institutions in influencing the range of acceptable alternatives that are appropriately included in the transmission process. The first case constitutes the visible educative function of institutions; the second is often much less visible and much more difficult to reveal. Yet Cremin's emphasis is on the visible aspect of education. As he puts it:

Every church and synagogue has a curriculum which it teaches deliberately and systematically over time. . . . And every employer has a curriculum, which he teaches deliberately and systematically over time, and the curriculum includes not only the technical skills of typing or welding or reaping or teaching but also the social skills of carrying out these activities in concert with others on given time schedules and according to established expectations and routine.[39]

Clearly Cremin is correct as far as he goes, but the emphasis directs us to the visible aspect of the transmission process. The influence that different institutions have on the mode, content, and purpose of transmission as it occurs outside their own immediate pedagogical functions is underemphasized, as are the power relations that exist between institutions in specific societies. Indeed the emphasis on the transmission process as the focal point of educational history again presupposes that the primary relationship for educational understanding is to be found in the individualized transaction between a student and a teacher (or surrogate). What recedes into the background are the larger economic, intellectual, and social purposes toward which the transaction is aimed. Receding also are the struggles between different groups in directing the reproductive process in such a way that these purposes continue to be served or are superceded by others.

Yet it is precisely the examination of this influence and the purposes that it serves that should constitute the strength of the revisionist insights. What such scholarship implicitly calls for is the need to attend to the structural place of schooling in contemporary society and the role of the school in the larger issue of intergenerational continuity and change. The concern over the judgments and intentions of individuals, as important as those are, is not a substitute for a conceptual scheme that highlights the structural relations within which individual choice is circumscribed. However, the adequacy of such a scheme will depend in part on its ability to account for the perspectives of different individuals and groups. In the next chapter such a scheme is suggested and some of its features developed.

Part II

Education as social reproduction

8   The domain of educational understanding: Education as social reproduction

Both the empirical tradition and the work of analytic philosophy overlook the need to identify the domain of educational studies and to situate the domain in a social and political context. The empirical tradition commits this oversight by accepting, as unproblematic, societal and school-defined goals as its own. The analytic tradition commits the same oversight by radically distinguishing what it takes to be essential features of "education" from other aspects of social life such as training and the development of common understandings. The effect has been to view the problems of schools in isolation from the larger political, social, and economic context in which they occur. The traditional empirical researcher has tended to accept these latter factors as fixed constraints that limit the range of acceptable explanations to educational problems. The political and economic context in which schooling occurs is thereby *treated* as a quasi-natural feature of education, one that is subject to little alteration, and because of this it is treated only as a background factor in deliberation about schooling. The tradition of analytic philosophy reinforces this perspective. By insisting that philosophy restrict itself to analyzing educationally related concepts, many of which are generated by empirical research, the philosopher has in practice implicitly disavowed the need to question the relationships between educational and other institutions that are taken for granted by traditional empirical research.

In other words, whereas empirical research has developed under an implicit notion of the factors that are appropriate to emphasize in the analysis of educational problems, recent philosophical scholarship has failed to develop an independent theory that is able to capture, explain, and criticize this implicit notion. The latter discipline, in restricting itself to the analysis of concepts, has been unable to develop adequate ways in which to understand the relationship between concepts and the reasons why certain modes of empirical understanding take on the significance that they do in given historical moments. This failure is consistent with the self-understanding of analytic philosophy – an understanding that insists upon a radical division of labor between the analysis of concepts and the development of empirical generalizations. This radical division of labor, however, is unable to capture the deeper concerns even of many of the practioners of analytic philosophy. Rather, such concerns must occupy the subterranean, unofficial features of the analysis, as was shown in Chapter 6.

In contrast to the other modes of research, the revisionist historian has developed an interpretation that has enabled us to highlight as significant some of the factors that traditionally have been underemphasized by educational research. It has done this by stressing, as a counterpoint, factors that have largely been taken for granted. However, the framework through which this interpretation has been developed functions only as a tool and has not been elevated into an object of analysis. This failure has reduced the force of the revisionists' interpretations by rendering them unable to analyze alternative, more traditional interpretations when these are able to account equally well for the "facts." This difficulty becomes especially problematic when those alternative interpretations are held by groups whom the revisionists identify as the victims of schooling and whose viewpoint they are attempting to articulate. The problem is that while the revisionists have developed a critical viewpoint that is useful in countering the interpretations of dominant traditions, they have not developed an apparatus for critiquing false consciousness that may sometimes constitute the particular judgments of oppressed groups.

Recent changes in educational scholarship

Recently a movement within education studies has arisen that has addressed some of these issues in a fruitful way. This movement has links to the empirical tradition. However, it does not begin by taking the school as an isolated unit, but rather attempts to highlight the relationship between the school and outside institutions and to address those structural features that both define and constrain the educational process in contemporary society. This movement spans a number of discreet disciplines. Out of it has come studies of both classroom activities and of the relationship between schools and other social, economic, and political institutions.

The starting point for many of these studies has been the problem of inequality in Western society. Those who look at the relationship between schools and other institutions have tried to explain the constraints that inhibit schools from significantly furthering employment mobility and economic equality. Others have looked to the classroom in order to understand how the educational institutions of contemporary society lead people to accept both a democratic ideology and the facts of political, social, and economic inequality.[1]

These studies differ from traditional empirical research in a number of ways. First, they do not accept the practical framework of the school as the source of their research program; second, they do not treat schooling or traditional educational research as a value-neutral activity, and third, the problems that they address arise from a theoretical perspective that insists on viewing schooling as internally related to other institutions. This research is concerned with understanding the institutional and structural limits to educational change, and one important such limit that is sometimes mentioned is the very research model used by traditional scholars. Thus these newer scholars insist on situating education within a complex of other institutions and attempt thereby to understand the relationships between schooling and these other institutions. For example, rather than viewing the projected manpower "needs" of a society as a target for educational institutions to reach as some traditional empirical research does, this research might insist upon viewing such targets as an important part of the contemporary educational process itself, one that both influences and limits what it is that schools can do. Thus Bowles and Gintis in their study, *Schooling in Capitalist America*,[2] argue that one of the major limitations on educational reform is the role that the schools are expected to serve in reproducing the relationships of production that are essential to a capitalist society. Such things as the hierarchical characteristics of schools, the different personality traits of various classes of students, and the relative immobility of certain groups in the society are explained in terms of the functions that these serve for maintaining the capitalist relations of production. Their study has had a strong critical impact as they have shown that the way in which production is structured in advanced capitalist society limits the extent to which liberal educational goals such as personal growth and equality of opportunity can be achieved. Hence, rather than providing a wedge for changing the social order by reducing inequalities, this research strongly suggests that schools serve to reproduce and legitimize the social order, and that given the present economic system, they can realistically be expected to do little else.

The importance of Bowles and Gintis's work in the context of contemporary debates about education is in terms of the challenge that it raises for those who believe that ability and schooling are significant factors in the social and economic mobility of individuals. Instead, their analysis suggests that the most important determinant of placement is not native ability, but rather social class origins, and that schooling but serves to reinforce the benefits and liabilities that arise from being a person from one kind of background rather than another. Moreover, they argue that this is explainable in terms of the role that schools play in a capitalist society – especially that of reproducing the personality traits that are required for work at different levels of the corporate enterprise.

Whereas Bowles and Gintis's work offers a significant challenge to contemporary beliefs about schooling, it also can bring us significantly closer to identifying a more inclusive object of educational studies. What is needed, however, is a refinement of the reproduction thesis, and this can be accomplished by looking at two different kinds of challenges that have been offered to the Bowles and Gintis thesis. The first of these involves questions raised by some traditional scholars about their use of evidence. The second, raised by other reproduction theorists, concerns their belief that the fact of differential schooling can be *explained* by the needs of the enterprise in a capitalistic system.

Although little significant criticism has been directed against the overall message of *Schooling in Capitalist America,* that schools tend to reproduce the social order, there have been some technical criticisms raised about whether schools tend to do so precisely along the lines suggested by the authors. This is not surprising given the fact that most research has found social class variables to be less significant than the weight that Bowles and Gintis's analysis discovered, and no doubt the question of statistical technique will continue to be debated. It is important to notice that this dispute takes on its significance only in the context of certain ideas about what schools should be doing, ideas that at another level Bowles and Gintis wish to address but that here provide the shared ground for the argument. To put the issue in another way, the critics of Bowles and Gintis are not arguing that the schools do not reproduce the social and economic order; they are only taking issue with claims about the factors that are most significant in that reproduction. In other words, the debate here is about which individuals are likely to wind up in a given social and economic slot and how they happened to get there (by virtue of level of intelligence and education, or by virtue of social class background). Yet, to return to the issue raised in Chapter 1, it is because Bowles and Gintis are able to rub their analysis of evidence against the liberal intuition about what should count in favor of advancing a person that their analysis takes on the critical form that it does. It is this moral intuition that allows their argument to take on a critical tone rather than simply to be considered as a neutral description (whether accurate or not) of schooling in American society. Take away this intuition, as for example in societies that believe that people *properly* achieve their social status from the status of their parents, and the critical force of the argument recedes and is replaced by a description with positive overtones.

This is not the only set of intuitions that Bowles and Gintis rub against in order to carry the critical component of their argument forward. In one respect, but in one respect only, the analysis provided by Bowles and Gintis about what the American educational system does is remarkably similar to what a number of researchers have claimed that the system ought to do. That is, it prepares people to work at the different levels of the industrial enterprise. Indeed, for the political scientist and the economist working under a manpower model of education, one of the cardinal sins of schools is to prepare people with the knowledge and personality traits required for higher levels of work when the economy cannot absorb people at those levels. The result of such "overeducation," it is claimed, is underemployment and political unrest. Yet when Bowles and Gintis observe that schools prepare working-class children for passive roles in the industrial enterprise by encouraging conformity and submissiveness to rules, the critical force of this observation requires an acceptance on the part of the reader of the liberating *obligation* of educational institutions.

Thus what generates the critical features of Bowles and Gintis's analysis is their reliance upon certain key judgments and critical intuitions that constitute part of the liberal frame of mind in contemporary society. Yet these may be as much a product of the process of contemporary schooling or education as is the inequality that the authors observe, and these too need to be included within the domain of educational studies.

Bowles and Gintis's analysis of schooling in capitalist America is a powerful, albeit still controversial, critique of the American educational system, and it also comes closer than any of the other works we have looked at to identifying an appropriate domain for educational research – that of social reproduction. Since this was not their primary purpose in addressing the problem of educational inequality, there are obviously some adjustments that need to be made before this domain can be brought clearly into focus. In order to do this, we will need to look more closely at the role that economic and social reproduction plays in their system.

Bowles and Gintis's argument that schools reproduce the functions required by the economic system is presented as a way to explain the fact that educational outcomes remain unequal and highly related to social class background. Whereas most of the statistical debates have centered on the question of just how much individual inequality is really explained by social class,[3] the most important, although less surprising, aspect of their work has gone largely unaddressed by their statistical critics. The idea that schools do reproduce the traits required by the economic system has rarely been raised to the level of controversy. Yet clearly even if the question of the influence of social class were resolved to the advantage of the critics, Bowles and Gintis would still find the level of social inequality to be a serious problem with American schooling. Indeed, this would likely be the case even if inequality were randomly distributed across generations. What the author's work quite appropriately points to is the systemic limits to the possibility of providing what many take to be a decent education for all children. Yet here the question that needs to be addressed is the extent to which the idea of reproduction can properly be said to *explain* such inequality and the extent to which it may also serve to suggest a different focus for the study of education in the wider sense in which I propose to conceive it.

What we need to see first is that the idea of reproduction serves as an *explanation* of inequality only within the rather narrow context of traditional liberal views of education. These views propose that inequality is explainable by a variety of isolated factors such as inadequate funding, inappropriate teaching methods, variations in intelligence, and so forth. It is in relation to these other individual variables that Bowles and Gintis's findings regarding the strength of social class factors take on their significance. Against the liberal view that ability and achievement should count more than parental background in determining social position and reward, the finding that social class background continues to have a strong consistent weight *demands* an explanation in a way that other findings would not. Once the weight of social class is accepted, then it becomes quite reasonable to count as an explanation of that fact the view that schools are required in some sense to reproduce the skills and personality traits demanded by the economic system.

What Bowles and Gintis call the correspondence principle therefore may be taken as a reasonable explanation of the persistence of social class factors. However, it is important to see just *what kind* of explanation it is. The correspondence between the social relations of the school and the social relations of the workplace tells us the function that such inequality serves, and, of course, when rubbed against the meritocratic concerns of the liberal establishment, it also unfolds as a powerful critique of American education.

Yet one of the things that their analysis does not explain, as Michael Apple has pointed out, is just how such inequality is created and how it is that many youngsters come, through schooling and other socialization experiences, to accept their place in this unequal scheme of things. Nor, incidentally, does it explain how it is that some youngsters do not come to accept their place in this scheme of things. In other words, it does not explain what happens within ''education'' to produce this correspondence. Nor does it explain itself. That is, it does not explain how that which could be taken as a neutral description of the relationship between school and society – that schools tend to reproduce the social order – can also be issued as a critique of both schools and society. It is the fact that description can be turned into critique (in this case) that would allow for the possibility that reproduction could be developed along different lines.

It is precisely through exploring this oversight that Bowles and Gintis's analysis can be helpful in bringing into focus the appropriate domain of educational understanding. What they have captured, first on the level of description and second on the level of critique, are the two essential moments of education – the reproduction of the skills and habits needed for an economic system to function and the reproduction of the ideological apparatus that is required to harmonize the different perspectives that economic reproduction leads to. Their own analysis functions as a critique precisely because they are able to point out a large area in which the norms prescribed by the latter are not able to adequately capture the reality produced by the former. This observation leads to the heart of the matter. Reproduction is more than just an explanation of inequality, although in some cases it may well be that. It is the focal point of educational understanding. It is, in other words, the domain of educational understanding as conducted within a theoretical framework. Yet in contrast to the largely economic critique of Bowles and Gintis, educational research does not begin by singling out one line of identity (in this case the economic one), but by examining the lines of social continuity and discontinuity wherever they might occur. In order to see this we have to expand the idea of social reproduction beyond its use by Bowles and Gintis.

Education as social reproduction

To speak of education as social reproduction in the larger sense is to recognize its primary role in maintaining intergenerational continuity and in maintaining the identity of a society across generations even in the context of many significant changes. To highlight this essential institutional function of education is not to deny its possibility as a vehicle for developing transcendent forms of human enlightenment such as critical reflection. It is only to situate that reflection within the context of an ongoing society and to recognize that reflection, among other things, is the process that helps explain just how a society can maintain its identity without maintaining each and every pattern of activity in precisely the same way from one generation to the next. In other words, reflection is a process that may serve to mediate the existing with the emerging patterns of thought and behavior.

The study of education as social reproduction is the study of the patterns and processes through which social identity is maintained and within which social change is defined. Education in this sense has two functions. First there is the reproduction of skills that meet socially defined needs. These skills include not only those related to specific economic functions, but also those habits and behavior patterns that maintain social interaction in a certain structured way. Here we include the "appropriate" patterns of interaction in everyday life, such as turn taking, greeting, physically distancing, and so on. However, they also include the patterns of behavioral relationships that occur among people with different skills, such as interactions between owner and worker, doctor and nurse, and so on. Second there is the reproduction of consciousness or of the shared understanding (whether formally articulated or not) that provides the basis for social life. These two moments are to be found in any society and, along with some degree of shared historical understanding, account for the maintenance of social identity across generations. Whereas schools are an important means of reproduction for contemporary society, they but represent the formalization of the moments of reproduction into a structured curriculum, with a stipulated method of instruction.

At the most basic level, the study of education involves an analysis of the processes whereby a society reproduced itself over time such that it can be said of one generation that it belongs to the same society as did generations long past and generations not yet born. Whether such a process is incorporated into specialized institutions called schools or is carried on elsewhere and in less formal settings, the task of unraveling the patterns and mechanisms of intergenerational continuity is the first function of educational research.

When, for purposes of analysis, the process of reproduction is broken down, it can be viewed from two different perspectives, an objective and a subjective one. From the objective side, social reproduction entails the process whereby individuals learn to *behave* in ways that are compatible with the continued functioning of those institutions that carry on and coordinate the productive activities of the adult members of society. It is through the educational process that children learn to take on various adult roles in the society, such as parent, worker, consumer, and so on. From the subjective perspective, or more accurately the intersubjective perspective, education entails the process whereby individuals are initiated into a common *consciousness,* a shared set of *meanings,* and a *sense* of what constitutes significance. This process enables everyday interactions to proceed and provides a context in which routine conflicts can be contained and resolved. This process is commonly but imprecisely called cultural transmission or socialization. Before looking more closely at the study of education as social reproduction, it will be useful to distinguish this as the object of educational research from these two closely related concepts, "socialization" and "cultural transmission."

In a social context, the shorthand distinction between socialization and reproduction can be stated simply. Individuals are socialized, but a society is reproduced. "Socialization," in Dollard's terms, attempts to account for "how a new person is added to the group and becomes an adult capable of meeting the traditional expectations of his society."[4] Sometimes, as Sills reports, the concept of socialization is used synonymously with the concept of cultural transmission, but at other times socialization is restricted in application to the learning of social roles whereas the concept of cultural transmission has been used to include the learning of beliefs and values as well.[5]

Whichever of the two concepts is used, however, the emphasis in traditional socialization theory (including cultural transmission) has been on the development of habits, behavior patterns, and/or the beliefs of individuals. The study of socialization seeks to explain how an individual comes to accept and to adequately perform a given role such as that of father, mother, or worker. Or it may seek to describe how individuals within a given society come to reach an acceptable level of social behavior, such as the focus on weaning methods or toilet-training. This focus accounts for the influence of both behavioral and psychoanalytic theory in studies of socialization, since each is concerned with the development of patterns of behavior and responses in individuals.

The established concepts of socialization and cultural transmission are usually either treated as synonyms or else entail but a shift in concern from the learning of role behavior to the learning of cultural beliefs and attitudes. However, there is a deeper distinction that can be made, and to follow this distinction through will enable us to see that there is a level of analysis that is not covered by either the concept of socialization or cultural transmission. This, of course, is the level of social reproduction.

If socialization is understood in the narrow sense of the learning of a given role or set of roles along with learning the behavior that is appropriate to that set, then cultural transmission (or better, inculturation) involves learning how one's own role functions in relationship to other roles and learning that in any specific situation appropriate role behavior is defined relationally. This means that one of the key factors entailed in learning the set of behaviors that define a given role is learning when it is appropriate to exhibit a specific subset of that behavior.[6] However, what this suggests is that when socialization occurs what is learned is not just a set of behaviors, but a set of categories and definitions that are understood relationally to one another.

Through an expanded concept of cultural transmission it would be possible to understand the way in which individuals learn these relational categories and definitions. What still remain to be understood, however, are the patterns of relationships and understandings themselves. It is these very patterns that implicitly guide the researcher's understanding of what constitutes a society and that are presupposed in any application of the concepts of socialization or transmission. Yet the structure or pattern of these relationships is not itself usually the object of study in either socialization or transmission studies. However, it is these very patterns of relationships that the activity of socialization strives to reproduce. Unfortunately, the concept of socialization does not equip us to understand them.

Traditional socialization research begins by accepting the structure of social relations as fixed and unproblematic. The focus of understanding is directed at the individual and seeks to explain just how that individual takes on the roles that society defines as appropriate. The taking on of a role is understood largely in terms of developing the habits and dispositions that are appropriate to a defined social function. Thus, whereas the society is accepted as fixed and unchangeable, the individual is treated as adaptable to any structure that has developed (or can develop) a sufficient socializing apparatus.

What is missing from this account is the fact that society itself is continually re-created (but not exactly or always in the same way) through a shared understanding in which all of its members, to one degree or another and within different frameworks, participate. The cohesion of a society will depend upon such things as the compatibility of the different frameworks and on the way in which members participate in the shared understanding. The production of the society, however, is a function of the development of the shared understandings, and this development is the primary function of education, first as a process and later as a specific social institution.

By losing sight of the element of common understanding, traditional socialization theory overemphasizes the role of habits and behavior as a factor in the social process. Even the expanded concept of transmission overemphasizes the individual transmission of beliefs. In order to see this, return to the point made earlier, that the same role will generate different behaviors in different relationships. The problem with most treatments of socialization that emphasize behavioral and habit patterns is that they cannot explain why this happens. That is, they cannot explain how, given the fact that a new relationship always requires new behavior that constantly requires the modification of established habits, a society is able to generally avoid chaos and maintain itself. Yet the usual day-to-day circumstance is one in which chaos is avoided even though this fact cannot be explained by an appeal to habits, or behavior patterns, or even previously inculcated beliefs. Of course, what happens in a new relationship, as the symbolic interactionists have suggested, is that a set of responses is negotiated, and not, incidentally, without an eye toward the power components that the factors of the relationship suggest (a point the symbolic interactionists generally overlook).

Yet to say that new relationships are negotiated is too general a description, for the metaphor of "negotiation" suggests an essentially public activity in which each side lays its demands on the table. A part of the process that we are talking about here, however, is private, although the features of the process are shared by (but not with) the parties involved. The process itself involves attempting to fit this new and problematic situation into the general pattern of social relationships that is commonly understood and in this context to assess the legitimacy of the demands that are being made. In this sense successful socialization implies a cognitive process in which shared social norms are understood and accepted and where actions can be appraised in terms of whether or not they are instances or violations of those norms.

The difficulty that traditional socialization theory has in acknowledging the cognitive and normative elements involved in the understanding of new social relationships points out the shortcomings of the concept as a basis for understanding education. Social life is not to be understood as a string of behaviors circumscribed by roles. There is no *social* behavior that is not first understood in a certain way. It is the understanding that makes the behavior social.[7] What we understand when we understand such behavior is the way that it fits or is supposed to fit a set of role relationships. We see someone raise a hand and we count it as a vote rather than counter it as a threat because we perceive that person as acting within the role of citizen. We consent to accepting a moderate dose of poison, to having our abdomen slashed open and some vital organs inspected and perhaps discarded, because we perceive that the person doing these things is acting in the role of a physician rather than in the role of a criminal.[8] Yet it is not only our individual understanding that makes the behavior what it is, but our socially shared understanding, an understanding embodied in institutions. Physicians are physicians because of medical schools, hospitals, and other institutions where roles related to health care are defined and worked out. This understanding includes presumptions about the ultimate purpose of an activity and about the right of those who exhibit it to do so. The first task of education as a social activity is to develop these forms of understanding, and the first task of educational scholarship is to understand the nature of these forms and the process of their development.

The task of educational scholarship, however, is not simply to reflect such forms or to understand them in precisely the same way as they are understood by those who participate in them fully. In contrast to the unreflective and naturalistic understanding of the participant, the function of educational scholarship is to reflectively understand these relationships as social constructions with historical antecedents and thereby to initiate an awareness that these patterns are objects of choice and possible candidates for change. Thus educational scholarship adds a consciously critical dimension to the social activity of education. It is incidentally the *consciously* critical element that is left out of any account that conceals its own interpretive framework.

When conceived of in this way, educational scholarship contains a number of distinctive moments. First there is a descriptive moment whereby the scholar tries to capture as accurately as possible the participant's framework of understanding. Second, and inevitably woven into this descriptive moment, is an interpretive one whereby the scholar sets the mood in which we are to take the participant's form of understanding. Finally, there is a critical moment in which the participant's framework is raised to the level of an object to be examined. The critical phase also can provide the researcher with the opportunity to engage his own framework of understanding, allowing part of it to become an object for critical examination.

As an example, take the historical event of Woodrow Wilson premiering *Birth of a Nation* in the White House. Insofar as this event reflects a form of consciousness, it comprises a proper object for educational analysis. For Wilson the film was likely shown because of the technological breakthrough in cinema it represented, and to capture this understanding would be to engage in the descriptive moment. Yet the film was also a glorification of the Ku Klux Klan, and it is this glorification that provides its significance for our own times. Given these clashing perspectives, it would be difficult to describe the event today without implicitly or explicitly commenting on it – without also providing an interpretation as to what should be taken as significant. Even the scholar who fails to mention the Klan and simply concentrates on the film as an instance of new technology is telling the reader what to take as important. If, on the other hand, a scholar decides to stress the racism of the film, another mode of interpretation is being provided, one that highlights a significance of a different kind. In this case, however, the interpretation is woven into a critical framework where we are told that what is most important about the event is that Wilson was not even capable of recognizing the film as racist. The point here is that Wilson's framework did not enable him to see the glorification of the Klan as significant and, further, that it is this failure that should be taken as significant by us. This last stage also opens up the possibility for bringing into focus our own framework of understanding while trying to see some of the tensions and contradictions that it might entail. We might, for example, look at the values that Wilson associated with modern technology and the way in which many of these have become taken-for-granted elements in our own mode of understanding.

Education as reproduction: The research program

The study of education is to be understood as the study of the aims and processes of social reproduction as reflected in the practices of institutions and indivduals. Insofar as education is concerned with developing the skills for operating upon and making sense of the world, that is, insofar as it is concerned with work, social interaction, and consciousness, it is concerned with knowledge. Insofar as different forms of work, different roles, require different skills and influence the development of different modes of consciousness, the study of education is concerned with the distribution of knowledge.

Thus, for the purposes of understanding education, knowledge and the question of its distribution are to be understood in relation to institutions. It is important not to confuse this, as the focus of education understanding, with other issues such as the criteria for distinguishing knowledge from belief or false knowledge claims from true ones.[9]

For the purpose of understanding education, knowledge is to be thought of as any representation of the world (including the methods prescribed in order to obtain a representation), that is maintained by an institutional network that serves (1) to provide procedures for informally verifying the representation in everyday life and (2) to facilitate the naïve member into the representation and thus into the structure of work and consciousness of the society.

The above conception of knowledge provides us with a way in which to focus upon the processes and aims of education, and is not intended to respond to issues about the nature of true knowledge, or to assess formal criteria of verification. Rather, it begins by assuming the point of view of the social participant in order later to arrive at the point of view of the reflective social analyst and critic. Thus it begins by establishing a thin criterion of verification whereby a representation counts as knowledge if it enables individuals to function in and to make sense of their social world. More formal and elaborate criteria of evaluation, with their concern to weigh competing explanations by controlled observation and so on, are not in competition with this scheme, although they would play an important role in evaluating the researcher's analysis of education in any given society. However, it must not be thought that more formal procedures operate independently of the institutional concerns that are the subject of this inquiry.[10] The idea here is to begin by putting aside the question of real or true knowledge and to examine what is *taken* as real knowledge and the routes by which it is obtained. This focus thereby provides a framework for understanding, among other things, the institutional factors that are involved in the distribution of knowledge.

The study of the distribution of knowledge is not therefore an assessment of individual achievement. Rather it is an analysis of what is taken to count as achievement in any given society. It involves an analysis, not of what people actually know, but of what they are presumed to know as a result of their relation with the educational process. It is, in other words, an analysis of what the social "consensus" gives people a license *as knowing,* of the way in which knowledge is divided into different spheres and of the significance that is given to certain kinds of knowledge.

A comprehensive analysis of education and of the distribution of knowledge in any given society would include an examination of the structure of knowledge to which individuals are initiated as participants, as well as the process that enables them to participate in that structure at different levels. Such an examination would include a detailed investigation of the scope of different knowledge functions or the range of activities and ideas over which various individuals are presumed to be aware. It would also include an analysis of the level of awareness that an individual is presumed to possess over a given range of activities as a result of his or her participation in some part of the educational structure.

The idea of level may be understood in terms of a continuum that on one end is represented by a presumption of a passive awareness. Here a person simply knows that such and such is the case, but such knowledge is presumed to be accompanied by a framework in which the individual case is thought to be the result of an unchangeable function, such as the will of God or the laws of nature. Here there is perceived to be a one-to-one relation between that unchangeable factor and its manifestation. On the other end of the continuum the presumption is made that an individual is able to perceive and evaluate a given case in light of a series of alternatives, and is able to understand the case in terms of the principles that generate it and the procedures for changing it. Whether individuals actually conform to a given point on this continuum is always an empirical question, as is the more interesting question of the spread that is assumed to exist between individuals in any given society. However, the knowledge system of a given society can be *understood* in terms of the factors of scope and level, and the educational process, whether formal or not, will reflect this system and define the knowledge of individuals according to it. For example, in contemporary society the presumed knowledge of both physicians and nurses would share the same scope, but the presumed knowledge of the disease process and its treatment would differ in terms of level, and this difference is reflected in the formal education of each group.

Given the general concepts of scope and level we can begin to understand the basic function of the educational system in terms of the reproduction of skills and the reproduction of consciousness. Moreover, an analysis along these lines can serve to correct some of the imprecisions of functionalist explanations that attempt to understand differential roles and the education required to pursue them only in terms of the basic activities and skills required to maintain any form of human and social life. Such functional explanations are unable to capture the different ways in which a society distributes such skills and can describe their function in only very general terms such as healing, food gathering, and so forth.

In contrast to the functionalist approach, the present analysis begins by looking at a social role in terms of the clustering and exclusion of certain skills and in terms of certain corresponding ideas about the rightful ownership and exercise of such skills. For example, it is possible to think of the healing skills as related in a number of possible ways,[11] some of which are entailed by our contemporary ideas about the role of a doctor, others of which are not, even though some of the skills that we exclude have been included by other societies. The range of a physician's activity may be distinguished along different lines. It may be distinguished in terms of the activities performed such as cutting, bandaging, sewing, prescribing drugs, and so on. It can be distinguished in terms of the object on which the skill is exercised (i.e., people), and it can be distinguished in terms of the ideal or distinctive goal of the activity (i.e., healing). It is the intersection of these different areas in a certain way and not in another way that characterizes the healing profession in contemporary society. Thus the activity of cutting flesh is not clustered, as it once was, with the activity of cutting hair, and the aim of the physician's healing is directed at people and excludes horses.

Whereas scope factors describe the nature of a field in a given society, level factors differentiate the roles within that field and provide an understanding of the variations in status that attach themselves to different roles. Hence, for example, while one of the physician's major functions is to prescribe medicine, he or she is not usually prohibited from dispensing it (at least in small doses), and the institutional assumption is that the knowledge involved in dispensing is available to the physician if he or she chooses to make use of it. The role of the pharmacist, however, is restricted to dispensing on order from the physician and the *institutional* assumption is that the activity of prescribing is beyond his or her trained capacity. One can often understand the conflicts between established and aspiring professions as involving an attempt to alter these institutional definitions and thereby to gain a tighter control of a market.[12] The situation is similar in terms of the doctor–nurse relationship whereby the physician is presumed to possess an understanding of the principles underlying different diseases and by virtue of this understanding is thought to be able to respond to unexpected and complex contingencies. The nurse is presumed to have a practical understanding and to be able to follow the directives of the physician. The *institutional* assumption is that the knowledge that the physician has is essential in order for nurses to carry out their responsibilities, whereas the knowledge that the nurse has would be quite accessible to physicians, but would, if acted upon, largely interfere with their more important activities.

The educational system (formal or informal) functions to reproduce and to distribute such skill clusters and thereby to maintain the work relations in society. However, included with the reproduction of skills are the reproduction of ideas about the ownership of knowledge and the reproduction of ideas about the rights and responsibilities of those who possess certain forms of institutionally granted knowledge. The reproduction of skills together with the reproduction of consciousness are the major components in maintaining the range of possible relations describable in terms of roles (social classes can be understood at least partly in terms of the relationship that different roles have to each other, to the socially distributed knowledge, material conditions, and rewards of a given society).

The reproduction of consciousness is the other side of the reproduction of skills. It is the factor that enables the clustering of skills into specific roles and the clustering of roles into specific classes to persist relatively unchallenged in a stable society. It is also the factor that must change if any significant alteration of the skill cluster is to be accomplished. The reproduction of consciousness serves to maintain a given distribution of skills in a number of ways: First, by developing an intuitive understanding and acceptance of the principle of social order by which a given distribution of skills is established; second, by providing acceptance of the institutional routes by which the present cluster of skills are developed and legitimized or licensed; third, by providing institutional protection for, and ideological justifications of, the rewards that are attached to the exercise of a particular skill cluster; fourth, by providing an acceptance of and sentiment for the symbols that maintain appropriate responses to a given cluster such as the ''costumes'' of the witch doctor, the wig of the barrister, or the blood-stained robe of the surgeon; and fifth, by providing a sense that the selection of individuals for a given role is both just and fair in the larger scheme of things.

Whereas the exercises of different skill clusters will often be accompanied by perceptions and norms that are specific to that role, reproduction of the general social consciousness will entail a more or less stable consensus about the level of knowledge that is appropriate to each role and also to a general category of roles, such as manual laborer, professional, and so on. Moreover, it will entail beliefs about the consequences of a group having access to knowledge that is thought to be inappropriate for it. As one Englishman wrote, arguing against the development of charity schools in the eighteenth century: ''If a horse knew as much as a man, I should not like to be his rider.''[13] Such beliefs are reflected of course in policies that are designed to provide groups with only enough knowledge to manage and function in their given station, and are illustrated by laws prohibiting slaves to learn to read as well as by proposals to use IQ examinations to group children according to their performance, and thereby to teach them in different ways and for different goals.

In any society in which there is a hierarchy of roles, the institutional reproduction of consciousness will strive to develop in each individual an acceptance of his or her own position. It will also strive to develop an understanding and acceptance of how this position relates to those above and below it. This is a major condition for stability, and it generally holds whether a society approaches a situation of zero mobility or a situation of total mobility in which there is a completely random distribution of positions across generational lines.

The institutional interest of stability requires not only that individuals in one social position know how they are related to those who occupy positions above and below their own, but also that they accept the general principles governing these relations. Without such an acceptance, each perceived violation of the relationship would be an occasion for challenging the distribution of skills and the privileges and responsibilities accompanying it. Thus, along with an understanding of the activities appropriate to a given role, institutional means are developed to provide a generalized awareness of the reasons for encouraging intellectual efforts in one direction rather than another and for distributing knowledge in a given way. Societies can be related to and distinguished from one another in terms of the patterns of intellectual development and usually in terms of the reasons that are provided for the established pattern. Moreover, the identity of a single society over time can be traced in terms of the conflicts that arise within an established knowledge code and the changes that take place in the pattern of development and distribution.

The role of formal educational institutions in the distribution of knowledge

Formal education can be understood as a consciously designed and institutionalized system of instruction that functions to maintain a given knowledge code and to further the pattern of intellectual development that is associated with it. The concept of a knowledge *code* is intended here only to suggest the fact that education involves not just learning certain skills, but also involves learning other factors that are associated with possessing such skills. We learn, for example, what is high- and low-status knowledge and we also learn how to identify, either through manner, modes of expression, dress, or physical environment, the dfferent values that are to be placed on those persons with different modes of knowledge. We learn the range of activity over which a person with a certain level of knowledge is to be granted authority. Thus a knowledge code binds together the reproduction of skills and the reproduction of consciousness. The knowledge code itself is to be understood as an interrelated body of arguments and beliefs about the importance of a certain set of information and skills that are ideally coherent and serve to propel intellectual energies in one direction rather than another, and that are woven into and supported by the dominant social institutions. To say that a knowledge code is ideally coherent is not to say that it is devoid of internal inconsistencies or that it provides the most adequate explanation for all experience. It is simply to say that the inconsistencies will be taken as signs of the limitations of present understanding rather than as signs of the inadequacy of the body of arguments and beliefs. An obvious example of such a code is a systematic body of religious beliefs that have implications for the conduct of everyday life and the governance of society.

Because different groups and individuals, depending upon their particular developed skills, stand in different relations to a knowledge code and view it through different frames, a knowledge code has built into it a potential instability. (A *frame* here is to be understood as the perception of the code from a point of view associated with a given skill cluster.) Most segments of society will be expected to take on faith the fact that the definition and distribution of high-status knowledge is justified, but with the exception of the initiated, most will only be able to view such knowledge from the outside. As long as there is a general acceptance that the clustering of skills and the definition and distribution of high-status knowledge comprise a natural process or are of functional benefit to all, stability will likely remain. This stability is an indication of a tight bond between a code and its relevant frames. Stability can also be maintained even if certain groups accept a different hierarchy of knowledge, if they do so only within the isolated realm of their own culture.[14] Here a code is maintained through the indifference of potentially relevant frames.

Yet because a frame provides a perspective for viewing a knowledge code, it is always possible that the dominant code or some aspect of it (such as the way in which high-status knowledge is distributed) will be denaturalized and looked at as *just* another framework, one that belongs to and rationalizes the position of the dominant social group. In such instances the potential instability of a knowledge code threatens to erupt because it has become decoupled from its relevant frames. For example, the soldier who simply *fears* reprisal for deserting his post is in a more unstable relation to the dominant code of the military than the one who, having deserted, feels *guilty* about his act. Yet instability is not simply a function of the way in which a code is perceived through its relevant frames; it is also a function of the extent to which those who perceive in this way are able to communicate their individual framework to one another. Such communication is often the major weapon of informal cultural groups. Thus, for example, the efficiency engineer can describe in detail the formal, task-directed behaviors of the workers on the shop floor. However, as Willis suggests, what is much more difficult for him to understand are the swaggers and the posturing with which his very presence is greeted. It is this posturing, however, that serves as the gestures through which individuals communicate to one another their shared framework of antagonism.

Formal educational systems offer protection for knowledge codes that are threatened by a number of different situations and where a tighter bonding between a code and its relevant frame seems to be desired. Among these are situations in which the conditions of work and family life are no longer thought able to accommodate the instruction of children toward an acceptable level of consciousness. Examples of this would include the shift from small farming to large industries and the reaction against immigration that occured in the Ur˙ ed States.

Yet these are not the only situations in which formal education serves to protect a favored code. Weber cites the use of formal education to protect the favored status of the knowledge of the Chinese literati when under challenge by the well-developed *code* of the military, another highly organized body.[15] Moreover, threats can arise from within the code itself as, for example, when the items within the code become too diverse, unwieldy, and inconsistent, thereby threatening to destroy the coherence of the code and thus the authority of those who possess it. This kind of threat often accounts for the movement of professional areas away from apprenticeship forms of training and toward training within a formal university structure where knowledge is no longer carried in the somewhat random activities of the practitioner, but rather in the systematic form of a textbook. An example would be the shift from the law as carried on in the accumulated decisions of individual judges to the codified law as presented in textbooks, journals, and similar materials.

In addition to protecting an established code, formal institutions serve other functions as well. They are used, for example, to signal the end of a dispute between experts about a given issue within an accepted code and to communicate an image of smooth and unbroken progress within the code. Science textbooks, as Thomas Kuhn points out, typically neglect the weight of the counterarguments that were proposed prior to a theory's general acceptance and underemphasize the strong features of countertheories. Formal institutions are also used to crystallize the development of new codes as, for example, when one country colonizes another or when there is a shift in the mode of leadership, power, and rules within a country, say in a major revolution. Formal systems of education are used to insure that the skills that are perceived to be effective in meeting defined social needs are preserved from generation to generation. Preservation is accomplished by providing a setting for the transmission of skills that are defined as especially important and that are thought to take a considerable amount of time to learn or that for some other reason are thought to be fragile. In addition to providing a setting for their transmissions, protection for such skills is accomplished by teaching the general population to recognize them *as* important, to consent to the provision of special incentives for their continuation and development, and to believe that their development requires rare and specialized abilities.

We can see the relationship between a knowledge code and a formal system of education more concretely by returning to and recasting Max Weber's treatment of the education of the Chinese literati who, he reports, occupied the ruling stratum of Chinese society for more than two thousand years and constituted the major force for a unified Chinese culture.[16] Weber's description of the power and influence of the literati focus heavily on the educational system which produced and maintained this class.

The education of the literati consisted of a recognized core of knowledge, a core which was organized around the ritualistic features of Chinese culture. For example, Weber notes:

> For two years before he was introduced to their meaning, the pupil learned merely to paint about 2,000 characters. Furthermore, the examiners focused attention upon style, the art of verification, a firm grounding in the classics, and finally, upon the expressed mentality of the candidate.[17]

Weber reports that calculation and any hint of technical skills was lacking from the curriculum,[18] and that "the schools were concerned with neither mathematics nor natural science, with neither geography nor grammar."[19] Training in the classics, as far removed as it seemed from the tasks of administration, provided the literati with the credentials to administer large territories and to serve as central advisors to the rulers. "The Chinese prebendary official proved his status . . . through the canonical correctness of his literary forms. Therefore considerable weight was placed on these forms in official communication. . . . The actual administrative 'work' could rest on the shoulders of others."[20]

The education of the literari in the forms of the classics illustrates the capacity of a well-developed and exclusive knowledge code to protect itself from external challenges. Weber tells us that during the period of the literati a number of challenges arose to their administrative rights, but that except for short spans of time, such challenges were always defeated. Natural and political disasters were successfully blamed on the break with tradition. Hence the burden of proof was always placed on those who challenged the bearers of that tradition.

The education of the literati was based upon a written script that was largely unconnected to the oral vernacular, and entrance into the educational system was governed by rigid examinations that in theory were open to those from any class, but that in fact required much leisure time to prepare for. These factors, together with rigid institutional control over the employment prospects of the literati, meant that the knowledge code maintained an exclusive character that was closed to knowledgeable challenges from the outside. The relative openness of the examination system provided the selection process with an atmosphere of fairness, while the difficulty of the examination provided "proof" that entrance into the ranks of the literati required rare and specialized abilities. Weber also reports that by virtue of being largely pictorial and descriptive in its media, by relying heavily on concrete memory, the education of the literati tended to discourage the development of other knowledge systems, such as abstract science, which requires more speculative thinking.

Accompanying these factors was a network of visible, institutional support that mutually functioned to enhance the authority of the dominant knowledge code. Thus, as Weber reports, "A province considered it an honor and an advantage to have one of its own sons selected by the emperor as the best graduate of the highest degree and . . . all guilds and other clubs of any significance had to have a literary man as a secretary, and these and similar positions were open to graduates for whom office prebends were not available."[21] It is not difficult to see how a mutual network of support was thus established whereby the guild gained material benefit from its added stature, and the attractiveness of a literati education was enhanced by this added prospect of support.

Because of the neglect of innovation and practical technique, the education of the literati may appear to us to be disconnected from the functions of administrators, but in fact the skills that were developed in school were very closely associated with the performance by which administrators were judged. Hence, the skill cluster that defined the administrator's function placed a heavy emphasis on the form and correctness of the written language while discouraging advocacy procedures and oral pleading. The latter skills were largely excluded from the requirements of the administrator's job and hence were not reproduced through the training of the literati class. Since the preferred standards were generally consented to and shared by each and every administrative district, they provided powerful "proof" of the importance of the education of the literati. It is likely that a deeper explanation of the training of the literati would point to the need to develop a common dispassionate framework of interpretation for a dense population with scarce resources. Whether it also served to retard the further development of those resources is a crucial but open question.

What Weber's treatment of the literati signifies is the very close relationship between the reproduction of skills and the reproduction of consciousness that exists in a given society. The fact that a particular cluster achieves dominance means that it has gained the capacity to materially demonstrate its efficacy, to successfully ward off challenges and thereby to imbed its "rightfulness" in the everyday consciousness of a sizable segment of the population. To understand education as social reproduction, however, we must understand the way in which these moments of skills and consciousness are held together and to be able to evaluate them in light of other possibilities.

Reproduction in contemporary society

The treatment of the Chinese literati as offered by Weber likely runs the danger of neglecting the force of some of the challenges that were directed at the education and the influence of the literati. Yet it illustrates the way in which the reproduction of skills and the reproduction of consciousness are interwoven and serve to mutually support one another, and it demonstrates how the status of a knowledge code is thereby maintained. These features are easier to see in terms of the code of the literati than is the case with education in contemporary society because we are able to view the code of the literati with the intellectual distance that such a remote position allows. They are perhaps also easier to see because the content of the curriculum of the literati was relatively fixed over long periods of time, and the skills reproduced are apparent and visible. With the more frequent changes in the content of contemporary education, it is necessary to move beyond the content and seek the principles that may help to understand the changes and to highlight the constancies alongside the changes.

Nevertheless, once the domain of educational studies is recognized as social reproduction, it becomes possible to shift the concern of educational scholarship without erasing its interdisciplinary character. The study of education as reproduction shifts the basis of unity of these disciplines from a strictly pragmatic one that is designed to repair dysfunctions in the present systems to an organic one in which each discipline focuses upon a different moment in the reproductive process. Hence, for example, educational economics would no longer be concerned only with projecting future manpower requirements onto the school, but would be concerned with understanding the relationship between the material forces of a society and the process of cultural reproduction. It would also be concerned with seeing the way in which material conditions are understood and with analyzing how this understanding may constrain the process of reproduction.[22] Educational psychology, to take another example, would involve the study of social reproduction as reflected in the framework through which individuals interpret their world, and educational sociology would examine the way in which the frameworks of different groups vary and are affected by the level of material and social conditions.[23]

The important point, however, is not the particular way in which various disciplines might decide to cut up the conceptual domain of education. Rather it is that by recognizing that there is a reasonably clear domain for educational studies, the nature of the disciplines and their problematics are altered. A clearer understanding of the domain provides educational studies with a more coherent research program regardless of the particular discipline through which it happens to be articulated at any given time.

Where any particular study may begin is influenced by the background of the researcher, but all of the studies would be designed to inform us about the nature of the knowledge code of a given society and the way in which that code is processed by different individuals and groups. For traditional pedagogical research this means that typical problems of teaching and learning would be examined not only to decide upon effective teaching methods, but also to understand the way in which a given knowledge code influences our understanding of pedagogical ends and means. For example, it would mean that learning theory and research would try not only to account for differences in achievement, but also to account for how those differences influence the way in which various groups of youngsters come to understand their own role in the larger scheme of things. It would examine the way in which knowledge in the classroom is defined for different groups of students, and the influence that this has on their self-understanding – on their understanding of the kind of people and learners they are.[24]

The research program also points beyond the classroom and suggests that the body of research in education should attempt to understand the transmission process in the context of an examination of the knowledge code of a given society and the relationship of different individual and group frameworks to that code. Thus while the school, because of its contemporary influence on transmission, often may be seen as the focus of such studies, it does not define their research programs. Rather, schooling itself is to be understood as a longitudinal system that functions to initiate people from different backgrounds, and with different frameworks, into some aspect of a prevailing knowledge code. Just which code and which aspect of the code must, of course, be determined by empirical research. What is important in this case is the way in which the school interacts with these other frameworks and thus sustains or produces changes in a given code.

It is equally possible to think of other starting points. For example, educational research could also proceed by attempting to understand the process by which different frameworks intersect and are transmitted to members of a new generation that are in the process of coming to understand their individual and social worlds. Rather than beginning with the school, or with the various intellectual debates about appropriate knowledge, researchers could begin with the family or with members of a particular social role or class and attempt to understand what is taken to count as appropriate knowledge for the children of that group. They could then begin to study the changes that this framework undergoes as other institutions, such as schools, join the transmission process. Finally they could begin to examine the way in which certain frameworks are related to the material conditions of groups and the way in which alterations in those conditions influence the particular way in which the frameworks are reproduced.

For example, many small shopkeepers have, over a period of time, experienced a dramatic change in their own self-understanding and a loss of self-esteem that they identify with changes in the power relation between the large corporation and the small business operator. Hence, some small business operators who now believe that they serve as but a conduit between the corporation and the media-conditoned buyer recall a time when the customer looked upon them as a buffer who could advise about both price and quality. In our terms, these retailers view themselves as people whose license as knowing a specific and important area has been removed, and they resent both the corporation for its usurpation and the customer for failing to understand how his or her own best interest has been denied by media manipulation. These perceptions, which on a descriptive level are consistent wth a radical framework, often melt into a more conservative one on the level of prescription where law and order and fewer government "handouts" may be proposed as the solution to the problems of contemporary life. Given this partcular framework, the educational researcher would be interested in knowing how it is altered when it is transmitted to a newer generation growing up in the context of other, more powerful frameworks and whose first-hand experience has not been developed out of the historical context of a personal relationship unmediated by corporate and media manipulation. Given the paradoxical nature of the initial framework, there are a number of possibilities ranging from complete rejection to complete acceptance of the older framework. The description can, for example, be accepted, and the corporation viewed as a usurper, but the prescription can be rejected by challenging the corporate struc-ture. Another possibility is that the description can be rejected (for example, by seeing good reasons for the growth of corporations) and the prescription, more law and order and less handout, can be accepted. Or both the description and the prescription can be rejected, and one can come to believe that the best hope for future and beneficial change will come through working within the corporate enterprises. The first of these alternatives may be seen as consistent with the development of a radical framework of a certain kind, whereas the last seems to be congruent with the everyday activity of school life.[25]

It must not be thought, however, that these frameworks are to be understood just on the political level. Each, for example, has its own way of interpreting the setting in which fundamental human values are to be applied. There are, for example, different rules for truth telling that develop with each situation. For the traditional-minded retailer, truth telling may be appropriate when the customer gives evidence that he is able and willing to listen. Otherwise silent complicity in the interest of a sale (and indirectly of the corporation) may be accepted as an appropriate norm. Within the corporation, truth telling may be appropriate when it involves a strictly technical question or when the potential truth teller will not be perceived as violating the more acceptable norm of corporate trustworthiness. Here the setting largely determines when the truth can be told. Thus certain truths can be told to superiors, but not to subordinates, and others can be shared on a private level, and may even be universally but privately acknowledged as true, but it would be thought "untrustworthy" to share this truth in any of the more public settings, such as committee meetings, even with those who already know it.

Within the corporation, these rules are known and acknowledged to different degrees of commitment, and other rule structures may, from the corporate point of view, "interfere" with the smooth application of the rules. Some people may place a higher priority on personal loyalty than corporate efficiency, whereas others may insist that certain higher principles have priority over corporate rules. Still others may willingly accept the rules but be inept at knowing when to apply different ones, and substructures within the organization may have different sets of priorities.

The process by which the transmission of subordinate frameworks influences the way different groups come to relate to the dominant rule structure is an area that educational research has only begun to explore.[26] Yet for the researcher to capture these various frameworks and the process of their transmission and alteration would be but one task of educational scholarship. Equally important is to understand the process by which such frameworks are established and maintained or diminished and the extent to which answers to these questions are to be sought in the material conditions of different individuals or groups. For example, the paradoxical framework of the small shopkeepers might be understood in terms of both their fragile condition in contemporary society and the extent to which their survival depends upon maintaining at least minimally good relations with the corporations and a competitive advantage over each other.

Ultimately, however, educational scholarship as the study of social reproduction molds the discplines because it recognizes that value considerations cannot be divorced from the way in which reproduction is understood and that the researcher is also a product of a certain set of values that have been socially reproduced. The concepts used, the problems studied, and the factors highlighted are to be understood in part by an understanding of the prominent values and concerns that dominate society. Thus, as we have seen, educational scholarship requires a degree of reflection that some other areas do not, and it requires an ability to capture values that influence the direction of education but that are often concealed in the descriptive posture of social science research.

We saw in the preceding chapter that some historical scholarship has also recognized the important role that values play in guiding educational research. However, this recognition provided little room for critical reflection. Rather, this scholarship gives the impression that the major values that guide historical research exist on a conscious level and require little probing to uncover. Such values, it would seem, belong to historians as individuals and serve only to highlight one set of events rather than another. Thus if one needs to understand anything about the researcher's values it would seem to be only the nature of the individual values that are held by a given historian. In the last analysis, however, it is not even clear why we need to understand this. It is the description of the past, not the values that generate it, that the historian wants us to assess. Yet given conflicting views, each in some way representing an aspect of the past, it is not clear how such assessment is to take place.

The view presented here is different. The most important values associated with educational scholarship do not belong primarily to individuals and they do not always exist at the forefront of consciousness. They are rather to be found in the taken-for-granted way in which skills are clustered to form social roles and in the intellectual categories through which our understanding of social life is organized and understood. Such values are not only attributes of individual thought, they are also attributes of social practice and institutions. They present themselves as *facts* of social life, reinforced by institutional practice, embodied in a language of description, and reproduced by educational procedures. Historical scholarship is in fact useful, not because of the personal biography of the historian, but because historical scholarship can serve to highlight the *constructed* nature of these ''facts.'' It can capture the way in which once abstract values were turned into institutionalized practices, and thereby historical scholarship can set the stage for an evaluation of practice to take place. It can, however, *only* set the stage.

9 The bonding of codes and frames: The case of medical knowledge

This chapter focuses on the area of medicine as an instance of the technical code that has come to dominate educational practice. It is intended to show the salient features of a successful code, one that has been generally accepted by both those who are practiced in it and those who are not, and that thereby has exhibited a close bonding of code and frames. In the chapter that follows this one the technical code is explored on a more extended plain in order to uncover some of the fragile aspects in this bonding, aspects that are revealed as we move from one social context to another. Although in this chapter we are concerned with the more successful stages of code development, we will also explore a few areas that place the code under some stress.

The study of medical knowledge is also useful in exhibiting the relationship between traditional forms of educational research on the one hand – such as that conducted by empirically oriented psychologists and sociologists – and reproduction theory on the other. For example, most studies on professional socialization deal with the process through which students in an area come to take on the identity of a practitioner. Very few have highlighted the structure into which the individual is socialized, and even fewer treat the way in which the general public comes to view a profession and its practitioners. Rather, the fundamental presupposition of a large number of these studies is that the basic structure of the profession is beyond the realm of investigation and generally sound. Educational psychologists do not, for example, tend to study the value of the knowledge taught to medical students, but rather, accepting such knowledge as a given, they then examine the procedure that will most effectively predict success or failure in medical school.[1] Although some recent sociological literature has had a more critical flavor to it,[2] the major tradition in the field has been similar to that found in the psychological studies. The concern here has been to uncover those factors that interfere with effective socialization into the structure of the medical profes-

An earlier version of sections of this chapter was published in Vincent Crockenberg and Richard Labrecque (eds.), *Culture as Education,* Dubuque, Iowa: Kendall/Hunt, 1977.

174

sion and to describe the ways in which students deal with such interference.[3] The important point that needs to be stressed is that in both types of studies the question of the structure of medical education and its relationship to medical practice has been put aside in order to examine the most effective ways to select students for or to accommodate them to that structure. Thus whatever the feelings of the individual researchers may be, their methodology and their research program reveal an implicit statement about the positive value of the structure for which people are being selected and to which they are being accommodated. This orientation of researchers toward the medical profession reflects the general public's acceptance of the knowledge code associated with the professional eminence of the physician.

This chapter examines that aspect of the professional knowledge code by virtue of which a public is willing to grant its practitioners the status of professional. The significant point about such a status is that once it is granted, then the public has effectively handed over its authority to this body which in turn is also authorized to make essential decisions about the selection and training of people into the profession. The focus of this chapter is on the public presentation of medical knowledge and on the relationship between the knowledge code of medicine and other aspects of the medical profession – such as selection, training, and treatment.

The chapter focuses on the area of medicine because of the special status that is granted to the practicing physician in all industrialized nations and in many industrializing ones as well. While the aim of all professions is to further the effective utilization of knowledge, the medical profession is assumed to have accomplished this aim more completely than any other. Thus, if we compare the status of medicine to that of any other profession, it is easy to see that medicine is the paradigm profession. College students do not generally drop out of predental programs and apply to medical school. Rather, it is the other way around. And medical educators do not look toward teacher education as a model to be emulated. Instead those who teach in schools of education look forward to the day, more distant than near, when teacher education will be able to unlock the secret that has served the medical educator so well.[4]

The reasons for these differences are complex, but they depend to a fairly large extent upon the respectful distance that professionals are able to establish between their knowledge code and the understanding of the general public. The extent to which such distance is acknowledged and accepted by the public depends upon the framework through which the knowledge of the practitioner is perceived. Good grade school teachers are supposed to be warm, kind, and understandng. If they are knowledgeable, then that too is nice. However, the "essential" characteristics of their job, teaching Mary or Johnny how to read and write and cipher, while thought to be important, are also thought to be activities that many other people, even many untrained ones, could perform if the time were available to them. Industrial society precludes this, however, and so certain people are chosen. They are "chosen," so it is thought, not because of any unique ability or skill, but rather because the pressures of society make other arrangements inconvenient. Not so the doctor. Those who cannot do, teach! They do not diagnose, prescribe, or operate. Thus the essential characteristic that marks off the paradigm profession from the aspiring ones is the kind of knowledge that its members are assumed to hold and the extent to which such knowledge is thought to be accessible to others in the society. This is a point to which I will return throughout this chapter, but before looking at it in detail, an additional word needs to be said about the relationship between socialization into the structure of the medical profession and socialization into other structures.

Professional and public education

Because medicine is the paradigm profession, an examination of those elements in its structure that lead the public to grant the practitioner the status of a professional should help us to understand the influence that increased professionalization has on the socialization of the population in general. This kind of understanding is particularly important in understanding many of the concerns and problems of public schools. For example, the fact that a person comes to practice a professional role is closely related to his or her performance in school, and for this person, the rewards of the school system are meaningful signs of future status as an adult. However, Stinchcombe explains, for other students,

When the achieved symbols fail to give a satisfactory self-conception, students substitute ascriptive symbols of adulthood. Cigarettes, cars, marriage, dating relations, participation in activities . . . tend to be transformed into symbols of identity. Claims to adult status *outside* the formal achievement ritual of the school provide a meaningful self-conception of those to whom the adolescent self-conception is undesirable. Adolescence comes to be undesirable to students whose future is not attractive enough to justify current subordination. . . .

. . . Commitment to the culture of ascriptive symbols of identity is a reaction against the ritual inadequacy of the achieved symbols which form the culture of the formal organization. By motivated transfer of loyalties from one cultural system to another, the students reduce the punishment to their self-respect in loyalty to achievement symbols. The more active this claim to adult status, the more active is the rebellion against the organization bearing achievement symbols.[5]

In order to understand this situation more fully, we would need to understand the factors by which certain occupations come to achieve the status that they do and the way in which such status is reflected onto students who perform well in certain areas of school knowledge. Once this relationship was known, then we could better appraise the response of those students who rebel against school because they have come to believe that the activity of the classroom is irrelevant to their life chances. The point that needs to be remembered, however, is that insight into various modes of socialization is developed in the context of a tacit understanding of the pattern of interrelationships binding together different occupations.

Although this chapter can only begin to examine the network of relationships that influence behavior in school by looking at certain structural aspects of one profession, it is important for those whose focal concern is in the schools to remember that what schools and teachers are able to do is limited by the occupational structure of the society at large in a number of ways. First, students begin to project themselves into certain occupations and to make judgments about both the desirability of these jobs and the relevance of school knowledge to the requirements that they will eventually have to meet. Second, as we have seen, at some point a school will be judged on the basis of the congruence between its programs and the occupational possibilities that exist for its students. If for such reasons as family background, income, or education the students in a given school are not expected to enter certain of the higher, more academically orientated professions, then pressures are likely to develop against the introduction or the continuation of certain programs and curricula. The absence of such programs of course further reduces the likelihood that such youngsters will be adequately prepared for professional training later on. The resistance to new math programs and the ready acceptance of rigidly structured curricula in certain working- and lower-class schools is an example of the influence that the occupational structure has on educational activity.[6] This does not mean that a public school will necessarily be expected to train students for specific jobs, but it does mean that the training that goes on in primary and secondary school, as well as at the university, and the behavior patterns that are developed, are expected to be reasonably consistent with the occupational pattern in the society.[7] Vocational education is attractive to many people because it is seemingly a direct and visible reflection of this pattern. Yet, as Willis has shown, even the acceptance of vocational education by working-class youngsters depends upon a complex network of understandings and a reasonable congruence between the framework of the teacher and that of the students. In Willis's study of working-class students, teachers were successful in maintaining discipline among those who accepted the basic framework underlying the teacher's presentation. These students accepted control by the teacher because they also accepted the implicit message behind that presentation, a message that was guided by some notion of a fair exchange. Hence, in return for respect, the teachers gave knowledge, which was promised to lead to useful credentials that would lead to meaningful work within the occupational hierarchy. However, for those students who rejected the idea that their worth was to be defined by their place in the hierarchy of work, who perceived that any job that was *truly* possible for them was as good as any other, the relationship broke down. Hence because one old job was perceived to be as good as the next, the credentials provided were seen as useless, the knowledge as inappropriate, and the respect demanded as a bogus imposition.[8] Even liberal arts education, which has been often justified as compatible with and most appropriate for a large number of jobs on the managerial and professional levels,[9] becomes threatened when this justification no longer is acknowledged.

The relationship between education and the higher professions such as medicine is most apparent at the university level, where the final selection for professional training is made, but this is only the most direct and visible point in a long interrelated series. For example, in their classic study *Who Shall Be Educated* Warner, Havighurst, and Loeb argued that the need for more highly trained professionals would have to be reflected in the selection procedures and the curriculum of public schools. Conant's later and equally important studies on the American high school not only echoed this concern, but called for the consolidation of many high schools in order to provide a richer academic program for the 15 percent whom he felt were academically talented and would likely go on to professional or managerial careers. Whatever the merits of consolidation may be, the fact that many smaller school districts chose (or were forced) to implement this proposal is an indication of the influence that professional education has on the very organization of the public schools.[10]

Although the relationship between public education and medical training can be viewed as but a special case of the more general relationship that exists between the public schools and the requirements of professional education, the connections between the two have been established in a more direct way. For example, in his 1925 book on medical education Abraham Flexner devoted a chapter to the subject of general education in the secondary schools.[11] Although the chapter is designed, among other things, to examine the extent to which secondary education serves to keep access to medical school open for talented youngsters, it also implicitly recognizes the extent to which medical education would influence the secondary schools under a well-articulated educational system.

The examination that is offered here focuses on the relationship between medical training and practice and on the bind that ties the two together into a profession, that is, the presentation of medical knowledge. Throughout, one point needs to be kept in mind, and that is that presentation of knowledge functions in two ways. First, it represents the transmission of specific skills needed to carry on an activity; and second, it functions to bind people together into a certain activity – to give them an identity, in this case, as physicians. Concerning the latter function, the mode of presentation, the place of presentation, together with the criteria for deciding who will and who will not receive the knowledge, are all factors that need to be considered.

A brief look at a historical shift in the nature of medical education

If medicine is today the paradigm profession, it was not always so. Early in the century when Abraham Flexner wrote his biting analysis of medical education, one of his suggested models for medical educators was the professor of secondary education. By looking at this comparison we can begin to understand the extent of the change that took place in the status of the medical school. Speaking of the work of the professors of secondary education, Flexner wrote:

> The professors of secondary education in the state universities are evangelists of this auspicious movement. Young, intelligent, well trained, these sturdy leaders ceaselessly traverse the length and breadth of their respective states, stimulating, suggesting, guiding, organizing. It is an inspiring spectacle.[12]

The spectacle was anything but inspiring when it came to the professors of medicine.

> The poor fellow who in an unguarded moment is caught by advertisements, premiums or canvassing agents cannot be taught modern medicine, no matter what investments in apparatus the state boards force. Meanwhile the sole beneficiaries of the traffic are the teachers – as a rule, the small group that constitutes the "faculty," in some instances, however, only the dean who "owns" or "runs" the school. His associates profit indirectly by what is technically known as the "reflex." Their professional dignity impresses the crude boys who will be likely to require with their first case the aid of a "consultant." The "dean" of one such institution was frankly explaining his methods. "What do you give your teachers?" he was asked. "Titles," he replied.[13]

Flexner was commissioned by the Carnegie Foundation to assess the existing standards of medical education and to make recommendations for change. Because the Flexner report is generally associated with the sweeping changes that took place in medical education during the early part of the century, his report can help us to understand the structural changes that occurred and the perception of medical knowledge that propelled them.[14]

Flexner, supported by the Carnegie Foundation, visited each of the more than 150 medical schools in the country and reported on the state of medical education at the time. The last 140 pages of his 300-page report (published in 1910) are devoted to evaluating the quality of each one of these schools. His report on the National Medical University in Illinois is a typical example of his findings:

> The school occupies a badly lighted building, containing nothing that can be dignified by the name of equipment. There had been no dissecting thus far (October to the middle of April), anatomy being didactically taught. Persistent inquiry for the "dissecting room" was, however, finally rewarded by the sight of a dirty, unused, and almost inaccessible room containing a putrid corpse, several of the members of which had been hacked off. There is a large room called the chemical laboratory, its equipment "locked up," the tables spotless. "About ten" oil-immersion microscopes are claimed – also "locked up

in the storeroom.'' . . . The top floor is the "hospital." It contained two lonely patients. [15]

He reported that he found almost a complete lack of acceptable standards among most of the nation's medical schools. With the exception of a few schools such as Johns Hopkins, Harvard, and Michigan, Flexner found the overall situation unacceptable. Most schools supported themselves solely by student fees, and subsequently entrance requirements were designed to maintain a stream of paying "customers." Few of the schools had any substantial connection with a university, although it was not uncommon for a medical school to borrow the name of a nearby campus. The qualifications of the faculty were questionable, the equipment inadequate, and the teaching methods, according to Flexner, didactic and "unscientific." Flexner argued that these schools produced inadequate doctors in large quantities and that this oversupply would have the effect of forcing the few competent physicians out of practice.

Flexner made a number of recommendations that he thought would correct this situation. He suggested that the number of medical schools be reduced from the then existing 155 to 31, and that all the remaining institutions be affiliated with a university and run on a nonprofit basis. In this way he felt that the commercialism of the present situation would be eliminated and the standards of medical education and practice would be raised.

Although Flexner's proposals were basically practical ones, what is of interest to us are the theoretical observations that were used to support them. These observations had to do with changes that he perceived developing in the nature and the growth of medical knowledge. First, he argued that there was a significant lag between advances that had been made in medical knowledge in recent years, on the one hand, and the training of the physician on the other. Medical education simply had not kept pace with developments in the diagnosis and treatment of specific diseases. Second, in addition to the sheer growth in the body of medical knowledge, he observed that there had also been an important change in the mode of medical understanding. Although this shift had been initiated in the area of medical research, Flexner argued that it held many important implications for medical practice as well. However, this change was directly antithetical to the rote learning that Flexner found in the majority of medical schools he visited. These observations bring us to the core of Flexner's view on the nature of medical knowledge, a view that has persisted without great challenge to the present day.

Flexner believed that both medical research and practice had reached the stage where they could operate as scientific activities, and his goal was to establish medicine as a science. Similarly, he believed that medical knowledge, whether exercised in research or practice, was simply a subspecies of scientific knowledge in general and thus to understand the nature of medical knowledge we needed only to look at the nature of scientific knowledge.

Flexner argued that scientific knowledge was to be distinguished from merely empirical knowledge, which was the stage that he believed most medical practice was at in this country. The empirical stage he observed was characterized by rule-of-thumb techniques and by metaphysical assumptions about the causes of disease. It suffered from a number of defects that were often reflected in the inadequacies of medical practice. Among the most serious of these was the tendency to classify diseases with similar symptoms under the same label and then to treat them as the same disease. Other problems resulted from attributing a cure to some medical intervention that was followed by the recovery of the patient in a few, early instances of a disease. As Flexner put it in an example, "The debility of yellow fever . . . Rush explained by 'the oppressed state of the system'; and on the basis of a gratuitous abstraction, resorted freely to purging and bleeding. His first four patients recovered; there is no tellng how many lives were subsequently sacrificed to this conclusive demonstration."[6]

In contrast to empirical medicine was the scientific kind. The goal of science was "simply the severest effort capable of being made in the direction of purifying, extending, and organizing knowledge."[17] All of the sciences strived, according to Flexner, to reach the comprehensiveness of mathematics. This included the "science" of medicine.

Science may be safely treated as a developing conception, moving at different rates and with varying degrees of confidence towards the entire comprehension embodied in the mathematical formula. And in this sense we are entitled to assume not only the science of mathematics and the science of physics, but also the science of biology, the science of psychology, the science of society, the science of agriculture, and the science of medicine.[18]

The comprehension that medical knowledge seeks is to understand, first, the laws that govern the normal functioning of the human organism, and second, the procedures for intervening successfully with abnormal events, such as disease.[19] Here the idea was that the scientific procedures already existed to extend our understanding of human diseases, but that medical practice was not allowing such potential to be realized. In identifying medicine with both the discovery of laws and the procedures for intervening to alter the course of a pathology, Flexner was implicitly merging science and technology.

In addition to being united by the goal of the activity, scientific enterprises were also related in terms of the procedures used, and it is in this sense that Flexner joined together medical research and medical practice.

The clinic is scientific, not merely in so far as it utilizes chemical or physical methods and technique but primarily because it represents a determined, fearless, and painstaking effort to observe, to explore, to interpret, to unravel. It is not saved to science by laboratory methods; it includes them as simply additional weapons to do better what scientific clinicians have always done, viz., observe, explore, unravel.[20]

Flexner's criticism of existing medical education rested not only on evidence that suggested that existing medical schools failed to meet widely accepted standards, but also on his belief that, with few exceptions, where standards were followed, they were the wrong kind. The ideal for medical research and practice was the knowledge of the mathematician, and the problem for medical education was to so organize training as to best approximate that ideal. This meant that medical education had a twofold task. First, it was to further the extension of medical knowledge by preparing a sufficient number of students for research positions in teaching hospitals and elsewhere. And second, it was to select and train students in such a way that the practitioner would be able to keep pace with the ever-expanding developments in medical research.[21]

In order to further these ends, Flexner proposed basic curriculum reforms that included much more laboratory work, the development of experimental procedures in the classroom, and a more thorough and uniform grounding in the natural sciences. In addition, he proposed that the various specialties be thoroughly developed as graduate programs.[22] Finally, in order to assure the flow of high-quality students into medical school while minimizing the influence of a poor public school education, Flexner proposed (in 1925) to deemphasize in the selection process those tests that emphasized subject matter alone. Instead he proposed that wherever it was possible intelligence and industry tests should be used as well.[23]

Progress in medicine and the influence of the Flexner report

For the most part the Flexner report has been looked upon favorably as a landmark in American medical education. Yet its influence on the improvement of medical practice is difficult to assess. In the first place, it is not clear whether the report itself significantly affected the direction of medical education or whether it simply supported trends that would have become dominant whether or not the report had been written.[24] In the second place, although the conditions of the medical schools as Flexner described them were deplorable, it needs to be remembered that most of these schools grew up as complementary to apprenticeship training, and Flexner did not examine this aspect of medical training.[25] Third, there is a natural tendency to associate improvements in the nation's health, at least in some areas, with changes that occurred in medical education, and if we look only at major indices of health, the connection does *seem* to be well established. In 1910, for example, the life expectancy for white members of the population was about fifty years, for nonwhite it was about thirty-five. By 1956 white life expectancy had been extended to seventy years and for nonwhites to sixty-three. Moreover, there had been a steady drop in the infant mortality rate, which was, of course, a major factor in increased longevity rates. However, when we try to factor out the reasons for these improvements, it is difficult to say how much can be attributed to the kind of medical education that Flexner proposed for the practitioner. Clearly medical research has been an important feature in some of the improvements. Diseases that at the turn of the century killed large numbers of people, such as typhoid, diphtheria, whooping cough, and measles, have been rendered generally insignificant by the development and routine application of vaccinations. However, the fact that the application is fairly routine raises some question about the relationship between improvements in health in these areas and changes in medical education for the practitioner. Other diseases such as tuberculosis and syphilis have been controlled (somewhat) by improved sanitation techniques, by education, and by the development of certain "wonder drugs."

   The above is not meant to suggest that intense training is unimportant. Clearly it has improved the capacity of physicians to deal with contingencies that before were unmanageable. It is, however, meant to emphasize that some caution is needed when assessing the cause of improvements in the major areas of health – areas that in the past threatened the largest numbers of people. The reduced importance of these diseases is likely due to a network of factors (sanitation, education, increases in the standard of living), of which improvement in medical education is but one. As with increased rates of cancer and heart disease today, the degree of prominence of certain diseases may be more adequately explained by the general conditions of the time and the age and habits of the population rather than by the technical state of medical education.[26]

Analysis of the principle underlying the Flexner report

The foregoing has been an attempt to introduce some of the historical and contextual considerations that guided Flexner in the writing of his report. In this section I want to abstract the report from the general conditions that guided its development and focus on the principle that seems to be highlighted by it and that remains influential today. This principle relates to three areas that are part of the structure of medical activity, that is, the growth, distribution, and nature of medical knowledge. The relationship between the first and second of these concerns can best be understood by looking at the varying emphasis that was given to them in Flexner's report.

   Flexner's major concern was to provide conditions that would be most conducive to the maximum growth of medical knowledge and to provide the training that would enable the practitioner to work most effectively under conditions of maximum growth.[27] This concern is best understood in terms of the state of medicine at that time. Even before Flexner's attempt to reorganize medical training, many outstanding achievements had occurred in medical science. For example, anesthetics were introduced in the United States in 1846, in 1895 Roentgen described X rays and by 1896 they were being used in diagnosis, and in 1900 blood groups and their incompatibility were discovered. Flexner's concern was thus to organize medical science so that such research could proceed in a rational, organized fashion, thereby accelerating the pace of such discoveries, and to so organize medical training and practice as to assure that physicians could keep pace with such new knowledge. His goal was to achieve an understanding of the nature of as many diseases as possible, of the procedures for preventing them, and the techniques for diagnosing and successfully treating them.[28]

There were three preconditions needed to achieve Flexner's goals. The first can be seen in his concern to establish minimal standards of competence that all graduating physicians would be expected to meet. The second was to close off medical school to all but the most qualified students, and the third was to accelerate the development of medical specialization.

Although Flexner placed great emphasis on the factors that would allow medical practice to be conducted under conditions of accelerated growth in medical knowledge, he placed much less emphasis on the problem of the distribution of medical services. For the most part, he was willing to allow this problem to be solved through the general goodwill of doctors as a group and by their commitment to improved health.[29] His argument here is less than convincing, however. While arguing for a reduction in the number of physicians, he expressed the concern that the presence of many ill-equipped doctors would force the qualified ones to quit their practice. Thus he proposed to reduce the number of medical schools. However, in addressing the question of the unequal distribution of medical talent, he relied not on any structural reform but only upon the goodwill of the physician which, Flexner believed, would take him wherever he was needed regardless of financial reward.[30] The obvious strains in this argument point out the secondary significance that the problem of the distribution of medical knowledge had for Flexner when weighed against the perceived advantages of the principle of the maximum growth of knowledge.

In this respect the Flexner report seems to have anticipated subsequent developments in medicine, for the principle of maximum growth has had a dominant influence on all aspects of medicine from selection and training to research and practice. Yet the principle itself must be understood in terms of Flexner's views about the nature of medical knowledge, and so we need to return briefly to this issue. Once we understand how medical knowledge was and is perceived, we can begin to understand the process of socialization under the maximum growth principle, and we can also begin to generate alternative possibilities for selection and socialization.

In discussing the nature of medical knowledge Flexner focuses most of his attention upon the *process* of coming to know rather than upon the content of knowledge or its structure. The process that Flexner describes is similar to that developed by the philosopher Dewey. It essentially employs the methodology of the sound investigator. One of the primary implications of this focus is to collapse the distinction between the medical researcher and the medical practitioner, hence suggesting that in many respects their training should be the same.

Even granting the merits of many of Flexner's insights on this matter, the question needs still to be raised. What is the nature of the product of this investigation – or, what are the characteristics of scientifically derived medical knowledge? Flexner had little to say directly regarding this question. However, given his reference to mathematics as the paradigm science, and other occasional references to the discovery and utilization of lawlike quality of the findings, one can speculate that Flexner would have accepted the view that the object of medical knowledge was to be found in the discovery of lawlike relationships that link together certain properties. To understand a particular medical problem would be to classify it properly by fitting it into the proper theoretical framework (e.g., bacterial infection of respiratory system), to predict its development through an understanding of certain uniform tendencies exhibited by pathologies of that type, and to decide upon the proper biological intervention in order to restore health.[31]

Flexner's understanding of the nature of medical science is similar to the way such a science is understood today. For Flexner the lawlike relations required for medical education were to be found in the basic sciences such as chemistry, physics, and biology, which he saw as the specific building blocks of all medical studies, and he proposed that these subjects become the prerequisites for admission into medical school. Upon these studies others such as anatomy, biochemistry, and so forth could be developed along with the skills needed for medical intervention. Thus Flexner believed that medical knowledge consisted of understanding the lawlike relations embodied in the prerequisite sciences together with an understanding of the various systems of the human organism and their component parts. Once these are understood, then diagnosis consists of subsuming some particular set of symptoms under the appropriate system as some form of malfunctioning, and treatment is understood as the appropriate intervention for reestablishing normal activity.

Given this view of the nature of medical knowledge, the ideal of maximizing its growth means that the medical profession should be able to specify ever more exactly and in ever-increasing detail the properties of the various systems and the relationships that bind them together along with the causes and treatment of various malfunctionings. The practical outcome is that the medical profession, taken as a whole, should be increasingly able to identify and cure more and more ailments. Yet this view of medical knowledge implies not only a specific form of training, but a specific form of socialization and a specific pattern of reproduction as well, and, as we shall see, these are closely linked together.

Selection and socialization according to the maximum growth principle

The idea of maximizing the growth of medical knowledge has served as the key internal governing principle of the medical profession and as such it influences all of the structural components of the profession from recruitment to research. The task of maximizing the growth of medical knowledge has two sides to it. First there is the accepted need to increase the corpus of medical knowledge and technique at an ever-accelerating pace through the efficient organization of scientific research. And second, there is the need to recruit and select individuals who possess certain attributes, namely those that suggest that they will be able to "absorb" at a high level a certain segment of that corpus and to apply it either in practice or research. Since the existing corpus of knowledge is beyond the capacity of any single individual to grasp, the key to both sides of the task of maximizing the growth of medical knowledge is specialization. The field has to be divided into an ever-increasing number of subspecialties and individuals assigned to the various divisions.[32] The different structural elements of the medical profession, from selection and recruitment, to training and socialization, to research and practice cannot fully be understood without viewing them in the context of the imperative for specialization. In this section, we will look at this imperative as it relates to the selection of students for medical school and to the socialization of those students, a process coextensive with their training.

Although most medical schools consider the same sets of formal papers such as undergraduate grades, recommendations, test scores, and activities, the standards applied vary from school to school. Nevertheless, admission into medical school is a highly competitive endeavor. Usually only those students with high grades and test scores apply, and of these more than half are turned down.[33]

In addition to the formal screening procedures, there are informal ones as well. From our perspective, these are the more interesting because all of the applicants to medical school probably represent but a small proportion of those who might apply given other considerations. For example, the fact that a very high percentage of the medical students in the country are reported to come from parents of high socioeconomic status, with a large proportion of these coming from professional and managerial groups, is a reflection of some of the informal processes.[34] It is first of all a reflection of the fact that medical education is expensive and is not a realistic possibility for a number of students. It is also a reflection of the variations in the quality of public school education that exists for different groups in this society.[35] It is also a result of the curriculum of medical schools which tends to move students uniformly along as a class. Thus, students who might have to work to support themselves, and thereby move at a slower pace than their colleagues, do not generally find a place in medical school. Those who do work outside tend to do so in their later years.[36] One other likely explanation for the high socioeconomic status of medical students is that competition is set at such a high level in undergraduate school that students who need to work to support their education often do not have the grades needed for entrance into medical school.[37]

When we look at these selection procedures in terms of the growth of medical knowledge we can see that factors such as age, income, and time available for medical studies, along with formal indications of medical aptitude, play an important role in making medical education available to a relatively small group of students who give evidence that they are better able than most to absorb the basic content at an accelerated pace. (We will shortly look at just how much of this content is actually absorbed.) Since age is an important factor in the selection of medical students, most finish school sufficiently young so that specialization is a real and usually a desirable option for them.

The desire to maximize the growth of medical knowledge and the high degree of specialization that it has come to entail can be seen to operate in the selection procedure in another way and accounts for much of the discrimination that had been exercised against women in admission into medical school. In many cases where there had been ample evidence that a woman was able to handle the subject matter of medical school she was often denied admission, frequently on the grounds that marriage would likely interrupt her career. Women medical students were not seen as prime candidates for specialization since the tendency had been for them to go into the area of primary health care with a significantly larger proportion than men entering the field of public health.

Increased specialization is an important aspect of the maximum growth principle and is a reflection of the prevailing pattern of reproduction in the medical profession. There is a mutual relationship between the accelerated growth of medical knowledge and specialization. As the corpus of medical knowledge increases, it becomes impossible for any single person to comprehend the various areas of medicine, and this provides a strong professional reason to enter a specialty. Similarly, the higher the percentage of aspiring professionals who are attracted to specialized work, the larger is the pool of talent to select from and the more the number of talented people who will be working on problems peculiar to that specialty. (Here I am treating specialization as a function of the growth in medical knowledge, and putting to one side other important factors in the medical student's decision to enter a specialty, such as income, status, and life style. The reason for putting these aside is that each is explainable in terms of the value that is placed, both within the profession and outside of it, on specialized practice.)[38] Thus once the maximum growth principle is accepted, specialization has a large, internal momentum of its own that may or may not be related to the overall health needs of a society.

The selection of students alone is not sufficient to explain the increased tendency toward specialization. The formal and informal selection procedures only provide a pool of individuals who are likely candidates for specialization should that choice prove attractive to them. Indeed, the decision to specialize does not seem to be one that is made early in the student's career as a medical student, but rather seems to occur only gradually over the course of the years in medical school.[39] In one classic study, for example, when asked whether they planned to go into general practice or specialization, 60 percent of the freshmen class indicated general practice and 35 percent checked off specialization. For the senior class 16 percent indicated general practice and 74 percent indicated that they intended to specialize.[40] Some of the reasons behind the student's decision to specialize are reasonably clear and were addressed in the late sixties by an AMA-appointed committee. In the words of the highly regarded Millis commission, "At present medical schools provide excellent models of the scientist–research scholar and the hospital based specialist, but rarely if ever do they provide models of comprehensive health care or of physicians who are successful and highly regarded for providing that kind of medical service." Yet even if more models of the type suggested were incorporated into the medical schools, the question remains whether, as the Millis commission hoped, significantly more students would choose to follow them. A more recent study of medical education suggests that medical school is but one factor in a student's ultimate choice. This study also sees the movement toward specialization and mal-distribution of physicians continuing.[41] In order to understand the various factors that likely would affect a student's decision to specialize, we need to turn to the process of training as it propels a student toward career decision. For this understanding we need to look at the presentation of knowledge in the medical school.

The presentation of knowledge in medical school serves two functions. First, it provides the occasion for the student to learn the skills, techniques, and general understanding associated with medical practice. And second, it serves to generate and reinforce certain attitudes in the students about themselves and their proper relationship to their profession. It is this second function that will concern us here. In order to understand how the presentation of knowledge relates to the decision to specialize we turn first to the pace of the presentation.

When students first enter medical school they often find themselves confronted with a schedule of lectures and laboratories that may begin at eight in the morning and end at five in the afternoon with but an hour's recess for lunch. In a course such as anatomy, it is not unusual to find students using a text with almost two thousand pages of detailed descriptions and diagrams of the various parts of the body. In the gross anatomy laboratory students are assigned, often in groups, to a cadaver, and are expected to recognize and name the different structures of the body, along with their function and clinical significance.[42] As students dissect the cadaver there is always the risk of hacking up one of the wrong structures, one that they later may be expected to find and identify. Much of the time working with the cadaver is therefore spent in the time-consuming task of carefully cutting away the different tissues so that they can arrive at the portion of the body that they have been called upon to identify and name.[43] The upshot of all of this is that many students come to realize that they cannot possibly absorb everything that is presented to them and they begin to take a very immediate and practical outlook, trying to anticipate what will be asked of them on the examination.[44] Another result, and one that directly relates to the eventual decision to specialize, is that students tend to develop a strong sense of humility with respect to their future profession (although not necessarily toward the patient) as they come to a recognition that the corpus of medical knowledge is too large for any one of them to comprehend. This understandable sense of humility and the felt need to compensate by knowing a small area thoroughly has been reported to play an important role in the eventual decision to specialize.[45]

The pace of the presentation of knowledge is only one of the factors that contributes to specialization and thereby to the practice of medicine under conditions of the maximum growth of knowledge. The setting in which the knowledge is presented is also an important factor. For example, Flexner's proposal that every medical school be associated with a major university and a teaching hospital equipped with the best possible facilities has, to a very large extent, been accomplished. One result is that beginning with the clinical years in medical school, students are introduced to very sophisticated machinery, and significant status is associated with being allowed to use this equipment. During the internship and residency programs, the new doctor comes to acquire greater rights over the operation of the machinery and greater discretion over its use. In the process students also learn to associate high technology with adequate health care.

The trend toward specialization affects many of the secondary aspects of the physician's ultimate situation. Generally, specialists are most effective when they work near specialists from other branches of medicine. Many of the more difficult procedures are best carried out with large supporting staffs and with machinery that is reasonably similar in type and sophistication to that found in the training hospitals. These factors (not to mention climate, scenery, and income) make certain locations more desirable than others, and also add to the tendency to increase the size of hospitals. They also contribute to the inadequate health care facilities reported in many underserved areas of the country.

The bonding of code and frames

If the trend toward specialization contributes to the growth of medical knowledge and to the ability of the practitioner to take advantage of such growth, it also contributes to some of the other, less desirable features of medicine. However, because the commitment to maximizing the growth of medical knowledge has been so widely accepted, many of these features have often gone unchallenged and constitute an area of medicine that the public and the profession has simply taken for granted. For example, it might be expected that one of the most disturbing features about the health care professions would be the fact that they have been a reflection of both the class and caste character of American society. Yet until very recently this issue was rarely raised, and even today only some of these characteristics have been challenged. Doctors by and large have tended to be white and male; nurses tend to be female. But also registered nurses tend to be white, while a much larger percentage of practical nurses are nonwhite. The usual explanation for the exclusion of nonwhites from the ranks of the physician had been that there was a smaller percentage who attend college in the first place, and that those who did attend scored lower than whites on traditional indices such as grades and scores on medical aptitude tests. We will look at the adequacy of this explanation shortly, but for now it is sufficient to note that this explanation does not fit the case of females who have, at least until recently, been the object of conscious and overt discrimination. Until recently a female medical school applicant with the same grades and scores as the average of the entering freshman class usually would have been denied admission. Those few who were admitted usually had grades and scores that were higher than their male counterparts.[46] And until the recent feminist movement began, the general ratio of female to male physicians had been about 1 to 19.[47] The fact that this ratio has improved rather dramatically in recent years may indicate that important changes are underway. However, the failure of blacks to sustain some initial gains made in the early 1970s indicates less than a conscious challenge to the maximum growth principle.

While this situation can be looked upon correctly as one of special privilege and domination by and for white males, the fact that it existed for so long without significant challenge is an indication of the ideological power of the maximum growth principle and of the bond that existed between the code and relevent frames. Thus, if blacks or other minority groups were not entering college in sufficient numbers, or if, for whatever reason, they were not demonstrating high achievement in the scientific studies that are prerequisites for medical school, medical programs did not feel the need to provide prerequisite skills even if in so doing they would be contributing to the improved health of minority communities. On the whole such students were simply screened out of the selection process. (Of course, historically some medical schools screened out blacks and other minorities, such as Jews, even when requirements were met. However, the general abolition of these practices resulted from appeals to the idea of equal opportunity, an idea that under normal circumstances is but the individual prerequisite of the maximum growth principle.) In contrast to various minority groups, women stood on the other side of the maximum growth principle. By and large they were not excluded from medical school because an insufficient number had attended colleges, or because their grades were lower than their male counterparts. To some extent their low numbers are to be understood in relation to the additional fact that prior socialization has influenced female students to pursue nonscientific studies, and that this was reinforced by medical schools, which allocated only 5 percent of their places to female students.[48] Only recently has the treatment of women been challenged as inconsistent with equal opportunity. The wide acceptance of the male/female pattern of domination has been seen as compatible with the general direction of medical practice. In contrast to men who have not been expected to share the burdens of child rearing and housekeeping, women have made unlikely candidates for specialization, and they have been more likely to interrupt their careers or to practice on a part-time basis.[49] Given prevailing social norms, some of which now seem to be changing, it has simply been easier for men to take on the long years of residency that many of the specialties require.

The first fifty years of medical development following the Flexner report saw an ever-closer bonding of the dominant medical code with the various frames through which it was perceived. The more recent challenges from women and minority groups also suggests that the bond may be loosening. However, these challenges, which arise under the general concern for affirmative action, are ambiguous in terms of their fundamental concern. As Mosteller and Moynihan point out:

The Civil Rights Acts of 1964 was on the surface the very embodiment of the former tradition [equality of opportunity for individuals]. In effect it outlawed group identification. No individual was to be labeled: not by race, religion, national origin, nor even for certain purposes by sex. Yet the act arose largely out of concern for the status of a special group: the Negro. Inevitably its enactment and administrative interpretation led to the formal assertion of group rights and interests by the national government.[50]

While the first of these concerns is clearly compatible with the emphasis on maximizing the growth of medical knowledge, the second is less clearly so, depending on the talents or background of the relevant groups.[51]

Although pressure from minority groups and women have, to different degrees, begun to be reflected in the selection procedure of medical schools, the recent Bakke decision by the Supreme Court has placed the future of these procedures in doubt. At the very least, the Bakke decision appears to have given individual medical schools much more discretionary power in deciding whether affirmative action programs will be implemented.[52] While the meaning of these recent challenges remains ambiguous, there is one area in which the bonding of code and frame appears to be firm. This area relates to the opportunities that are closed off to other health professionals.

Perhaps the most obvious and yet the most accepted aspect of medical education is that, given slight variations for individual schools, and except for those few students pursuing joint Ph.D., M.D. degrees, every student is expected to go through the different aspects of the program at the same time and pace as every other student. For the health professional who is not a physician this means that his or her experience in the various areas of health care simply does not count as meeting any prerequisite for medical school. Indeed, because of age barriers, the longer the health professional stays on the job, the smaller the opportunity to enter medical training. This is true even where the fields seem to be closely related. Thus, if a psychiatric nurse wishes to enter psychiatry, or an anesthesiologist's nurse wishes to enter anesthesiology, or a registered nurse hopes to enter general practice, each must begin again and return to the starting point of the first-year medical student.

The justification for these practices is difficult to pin down since they have rarely been addressed in the literature, but there seem to be two that are possible. The first is that assuming that there is some common body of knowledge (presumably scientific and theoretical) that is desirable for all medical students to have, then the selection of relatively older people into the profession would be inefficient. It would reduce the total number of years that an individual could devote to the profession and thereby also reduce the percentage of people who would have the time to devote to a specialty. The second justification would be that the knowledge the physician possesses is different in kind from that possessed by the other health professionals and that the knowledge and skills gained through their experience is not an adequate prerequisite to that required by the physician. The first of these justifications entails a commitment to the idea that medical practice should be undertaken in accord with the conditions of the maximum growth of medical knowledge, and we will return later to evaluate this principle. The second justification requires that we examine again the nature of medical knowledge. However, this justification seems to be intuitively questionable. Thus whether the two years or so that the medical student spends in a clinical setting result in a different level of knowledge than many nurses would pick up through a few years of on-the-job training is an issue that might be investigated much more thoroughly than it has been. It may be, for example, that the skills involved in routine diagnosis and treatment are not that rare among registered nurses, or it may be that if they are not common, it is simply because adequate training has not been made available to them in this area.[53] Of course, we cannot just assume that the range of knowledge practiced by the health professional overlaps sufficiently with that of the physician to make such additional training feasible. However, the important point is that educational research has been so captured by the self-definition and the knowledge code of the medical profession as to preclude a case-by-case examination.

Whether or not a professional caste system of this type is ultimately justifiable would depend upon a detailed examination of the nature of medical training and its congruence with the skills required for medical practice. Whatever the results of such an examination may be, however, the existence of such a caste system creates the impression, rightly or wrongly, both within the medical profession and with the general public, that medical education provides a person, much like the priesthood, with a special kind of insight that years of experience in allied areas cannot yield.

Even here, however, certain groups, such as nurses, have begun to question the present arrangement. Some nurses have attempted to mark off for themselves an area of knowledge that they claim is equal to and independent of that of physicians. Their emphasis has been placed on the nonpathological aspects of health care such as educating the patient as to proper diet and routine. Their hope is that by developing its own knowledge base, nursing would then achieve a degree of autonomy as a profession, and nurses would no longer be percieved as simply the handmaidens of physicians. Pharmacists, in their attempts to gain veto power over physician's prescriptions, provide a similar example of a group of health professionals attempting to establish an independent knowledge base that is separate from that of the dominant profession. In this instance the search for an independent knowledge base is partly a reaction against the rapid loss of independent status as a small business operator as well as a reaction against the downgrading of the profession of pharmacy as a result of the increase in prepared medications. Such attempts represent tensions between the dominant code and relevant frames but do not yet seriously threaten the strong bond that ties them together.

Tensions in the dominant code

The limits of technical knowledge
Despite the relatively tight bonding between the dominant code and its relevant frames, medicine presents a number of issues that could lead to a challenge to the prominence of technical knowledge that the code embodies. Should such a challenge materialize and be successful, it would affect not only access into the profession, as affirmative action programs aim to do, but the socialization and training process itself.

The special status of physicians, the large economic rewards and social prestige that accompanies the occupation, rests upon the general accuracy and acceptance of one major claim. The claim is that the present arrangement is the most adequate way to meet the medical needs of a society and therefore ought to be continued. Any observations about the socialization of the medical profession, about the caste characteristics of the profession, about the special status of physicians, and so forth take on significance only in the context of an acceptance or rejection of this claim. To put it as bluntly as possible, if the highest level of human health could be attained only by training in medical schools white males from upper-middle-class professional backgrounds, then any argument that required that selection be made from other groups would be at a serious disadvantage for it would have to demonstrate that something more important than physical well-being is at stake. It is unlikely that such an argument could successfully be made, but the primary question is whether or not key health care requirements are being met by the present arrangements. Thus, in this section I want to look at certain aspects of health care in the United States and to relate these to the process of medical socialization and and the pattern of medical reproduction. In order to initiate this examination, however, we need to return to observations made earlier and to examine more critically the nature of medical knowledge. It is only by understanding the nature of such knowledge, what it is and what it should be, that we can begin to assess whether or not certain health problems should be considered the responsibility of the medical profession. Thus, we return briefly to the idea of medical knowledge as forwarded by Flexner.[54]

As we saw, one of Flexner's concerns was to make the study of medicine scientific, and he advanced this concern by collapsing the difference between medical research and medical practice and by then subsuming both of them under the classification of scientific knowledge. While there is much in Flexner's treatment of medical knowledge that, with proper amplification, could be accepted today, there is an important feature that he neglected, and that continues to be neglected.

When Flexner argued that medical research and medical practice should both be perceived and developed as scientific activities, he focused his attention on the process of investigation and the methodology that he believed that both research and practice shared. In focusing on the process of knowing, however, he left unexamined the characteristics of medical knowledge itself and simply reinforced the impression that medical knowledge was but a subspecies of scientific knowledge. His emphasis was on lawlike relations. In order, therefore, to understand and to treat a particular medical problem the physician should be able to correctly classify the problem, understand the way it affects the organism, and apply the appropriate biological intervention. In the long run, Flexner believed that medical research would bring us to an ever more comprehensive understanding of the nature of disease in general and of the ways to treat particular diseases. Medical practice was to follow suit with increasingly sophisticated diagnostic and treatment techniques. That this ideal has continued to govern the organization of medical research and practice is evident even in the Millis report, which sought to establish more adequate comprehensive medical care facilities. As the report observes:

The explosion of medical knowledge has been so great that no physician can master more than a fraction of the total. . . . The specialists in the different branches can cooperate most effectively if both in spirit and space they are working closely together. . . . A variety of skills, specialized knowledge in different areas, a more competent corps of paramedical aids, and expensive equipment that the solo practitioner can rarely afford are all brought together for the benefit of the patient who takes his medical problems to physicians based in a hospital or a group practice clinic.[55]

The emphasis on scientific understanding and the growth of medical specialization it entails has led medicine to overlook for many years the need to also understand the particular, nonbiological conditions that retard or advance normal functioning in particular situations. Many of the problems of health are the result of situationally generated factors that do not require a highly sophisticated understanding of the sciences of the human organism to comprehend. If, for example, a child suffers retardation because of poisoning from lead paint, or a heart patient suffers an attack when climbing the stairs to a sixth-floor flat, or a woman cannot alter a destructive diet because of the cultural role that food plays in her family situation, then the problems do not result from a lack of scientific knowledge on the part of a physician. They may, however, entail a lack of situational understanding, an understanding that would entail knowing that these conditions existed, the effects they have, and how they might be dealt with. This latter condition especially presupposes having the kind of relationship with the family or neighborhood that has become increasingly less common among medical practitioners today. Situational understanding is not a major component of the training of the physician.

Given the social and cultural conditions of Flexner's times, it is understandable that he would take for granted the situational component of medical knowledge. It is likely that many doctors did know a good deal more about the life conditions and physical environment of their patients then than they do today. Doctors often lived in the same neighborhoods as their clients, and house calls were not the exception that they are today. Doctors would often have to bid to service the members of immigrant associations, and this likely required a close personal relationship. That doctors were often helpless even with this situational understanding suggested to many that the focal point of medical concern had to be elsewhere. Yet the decline in the number of general practitioners and the increase in the number of specialists have brought significant changes in these areas. Today the doctor is someone we go to, not someone who comes to us, and as the Millis commission unwittingly acknowledged, the advances of modern medicine are available primarily to the person "who *takes* his medical problems to physicians based in a hospital" (emphasis mine). Those who do not have easy access to a hospital, however, or those who are not equipped to understand the bureaucracy of hospitals, are left in a situation that the existing medical structure is increasingly less capable of dealing with.

Physicians see clients in their roles as patients. They do not, as a rule, see them in other capacities. They are expected to be able to evaluate the patient's medical problem and to offer treatment for it. If, however, the patient is reluctant to provide the information that the physician needs to make an adequate diagnosis, or does not follow the prescribed remedy, the patient is often labeled uncooperative, and the physician is not expected to inquire any further. He is absolved of responsibility because situational knowledge is not thought to be a component of medical competence.

The failure to recognize the significance of situational knowledge has implications for medical training. Students are selected for medical school on the basis of their demonstrated achievement in the basic sciences. Little weight, however, is given to their understanding of the health needs of a particular community. Medical schools are dominated by departments of anatomy, physiology, and surgery, not by departments of community and social medicine, departments that are concerned with environmental and preventive medicine rather than treatment. There seems to be no significant correlation between the faculty's evaluation of a student and the extent to which the student feels comfortable with a wide number of patients, many of whose problems fall outside the boundaries of traditional medical concepts.[56] Medical externships and interships are centered in hospitals with a wide array of supporting personnel and sophisticated equipment rather than in smaller community health facilities. Courses in nutrition are rarely taught in medical schools, nor are courses usually given in occupational and environmental health. And because these are not taught, the concerns they represent are not generally incorporated into medical practice. For example, most doctors do not normally ask their patients for a work history even though working conditions, past and present, can constitute an extreme health hazard for many people.[57]

It might be argued that the insights and treatment required by situational knowledge need not be the domain of the physician, and that many of these problems could be handled by others who are more familiar with the cultural and environmental situations affecting individual health. This alternative is attractive in certain respects, and we shall see shortly that there are a number of considerations that speak in favor of it. However, without certain other changes in medical practice, it is unlikely that this emphasis alone will provide the desired results. In the first place, much like the physician, health workers are not selected for their understanding of the needs of a community. Most of them are simply not trained to understand those needs or to serve as effective community health agents. They are primarily trained to perform certain functions for, and under the supervision of, the physician. Perhaps equally important is the fact that the general public expects to be cared for by physicians whom it perceives as having highly desirable technical skills, and many minority people believe that anything less for them would be discriminatory. This expectation is understandable in light of two different factors. In the first place, if physicians do not see the value of situational understanding and incorporate it into the structure of their own profession, it is unlikely that the public will be able to articulate this need, however acutely it may be felt. In the second place, access to highly developed technical competence is important for all people, but even more so for those who can be assured of adequate care at the primary level. Such people tend to be those whose situation the physician is most likely to be familiar with. They tend to be middle-class, to know how to present themselves to physicians, and to be familiar with large bureaucratic structures. They also tend to be more heavily represented by the opinion- and policymakers of the society, and so their concerns are the ones most often and most thoroughly articulated.

The need for greater situational understanding has been felt within those groups that are least like the present population of physicians. Thus if physicians tend to come from white, upper-middle-class professional, suburban homes, the greatest need for situational understanding is to be found among nonwhite, lower- or working-class, nonprofessional, rural or inner-city people.

In order to meet the needs of these groups, the federal government began in the late 1960s and early 1970s to establish affirmative action guidelines for medical schools as a condition for continuing to receive federal support. Under these guidelines many schools set aside a certain number of places for underrepresented minority applicants, and some did the same for applicants from rural areas. Although these programs were not ideal in meeting the situational knowledge required for underserved groups, they were clearly among the most progressive steps taken in that direction. Of course, even with these programs there was a subtle form of racism operating. As one black physician put it:

Black students have another problem. They are the objects of another subtle form of racism. Many institutions are willing to train black students for the ghetto but other students are expected to enjoy a free choice.[58]

One might question just how successful such program might have been in improving the medical services of underrepresented groups. Even those students who came from minority groups and met but minimal standards underwent extremely stiff competition, winning a relatively small number of positions from a wide number of aspirants, both actual and potential. (Among potential aspirants, I include those who have a strong desire to serve in medicine, but who, for one reason or another, do not apply to medical school.) Moreover, when they entered medical school they were subject to the same curriculum as their classmates, a curriculum that required a great deal of sacrifice and discipline from most students. As part of this sacrifice one must also include the large financial debt that many medical students must assume to support their education. For students whose academic background may have been slighted, and who often come from poorer families, the sacrifice is that much greater. Now when mainline students undergo these strains they often develop a sense of ownership, a view that they are in charge of their professional skills and can do with them what they like, and the general public finds no reason to challenge this view. Given the way mobility is accepted by the public for the majority of medical students, it would be reasonable to expect that minority students too would seek to find reasonably comfortable settings in which to practice. How many would choose to return to the poorer areas to practice is but pure speculation, but given problems of living space, schooling, bill collection, crime, and drugs, there are not a great many reasons to think that the numbers would be large. Nor, given the prevailing standards, should such students be blamed if they decided to use their skills to escape the conditions of ghetto life (if that is where they came from). The general pattern since 1950 has been for physicians to migrate out of the inner city into the wealthier suburbs, and barring discriminatory programs that would force minority students to practice in certain areas, there is no reason to think that this trend will not persist.[59] Such speculation is, however, purely academic at this point. The Supreme Court ruled in the Bakke decision that many of these affirmative action programs were unconstitutional and instead *allowed* schools to consider background factors such as race as but one of many factors in determining the desired composition of their entering class. This decision has likely contributed to the decline in the proportion of black students enrolled in medical school. Thus, the health care problem in the United States poses a special dilemma for the treatment of minorities. Without addressing the principle that has governed medical education since Flexner, any proposed solution is likely to discriminate against members of the very groups that it is supposed to help. Before turning again to examine the principle that has governed medical training, it will be useful to look at some of the specific indices of the health care problem in the United States, and thereby begin to understand the basis on which the present mode of medical education can be evaluated.

The nature of the present health care crisis

Any decoupling of the dominant code and relevant frames would have to be accompanied by a wide-scale, if implicit, acknowledgment of a health care crisis and by a recognition that present educational selection and training procedures are not adequate to meet it. In the next chapter we will look at some of the systemic limits that are involved in attempting to address problems of contemporary life, including medical problems, as technical issues alone. Here it remains to document the nature of the present crisis in health care in United States and to assess the actual role of technical knowledge in dealing with it.

There are many people who would deny that there is a health care crisis in the United States, and there are many others who believe that the crisis results only from the pressures that are put on physicians resulting in higher costs in such areas as malpractice insurance. Given a narrow focus, it is not too difficult to find support for this view. One could, for example, look at the increase in medical research since the end of the Second World War to support the point that as a society we have taken Flexner's concern to accelerate the growth of medical knowledge very seriously. Medicine has become a sophisticated technical activity, one that is capable of handling a great many complex contingencies. In many areas of medical practice the skills developed in this country are equal to or better than those found anywhere else in the world, and it is not surprising that we find an occasional news story reporting that some important person from another country has visited the United States for treatment. However, the health care crisis is not primarily at this level, nor would one expect it to be in country that spends about 9 percent of a very large GNP on health.[60] Nevertheless, it would be a mistake to suggest that advances in medical knowledge have only helped the well-off segments of the population and to deny that certain specific advances have not helped the poor as well. The reduction in the death rate from such diseases as polio and tuberculosis have benefited both wealthy and non-wealthy.[61] Moreover, the treatment for such ailments as pellagra has primarily benefited poor people, the group suffering from the dietary deficiency that causes it.[62] Yet it is important to separate these advances, which are the result of medical research and often routine treatment or diet changes, from those which are more closely connected to the increasing sophistication of medical training and practice. Most of the major advances for the poor have in fact come in the areas of preventive medicine rather than in more sophisticated methods of treatment.[63]

Despite the many advances that have been made in such areas as preventive medicine, there are some serious problems in American health that justifiably can be termed a crisis. Some of the problems, such as the number of deaths from heart disease, increased precisely as medicine was becoming more scientific. Moreover, many leading causes of death such as heart disease and cancer strike rich people as frequently as poor. (Part of the reason for this is that these tend to be diseases that strike relatively late in life, and poor people do not live as long as those who are not poor.) These diseases, however, seem to be more a function of increased longevity, life style, and environmental factors, and less a function of inadequate treatment. Yet even though there is a crisis, certain surface factors make it less visible than other past crises.

A number of different types of factors obscure the presence of the crisis. In the first place, the very success of preventive medicine and the control of the most serious contagious diseases means that many problems can be contained among certain sectors of the population and need not be a widely felt concern of all. Secondly, in terms of the percentages among groups that visit doctors, there is not much variation according to income. Poor people seem to visit doctors about as often as wealthier ones.[64] While this may reinforce the impression, especially among physicians, that equal medical care is available to all, there is strong indication that lower-income people need doctors more often. If this is the case, then the similarity in the number of visits is not an indication of similar treatment of similar needs. Moreover, many people are covered by some kind of private or governmental insurance, hence providing the appearance of security for medical illness. However, it is also clear that the burdens of medical care are distributed very unequally and that there are vast differences in the quality of such care.[65]

As the scientific quality of medicine has improved, other problems have arisen that have gone unattended. For example, the very success of improvements in sanitation and the development of scientific medicine has resulted in an increasingly older population. Yet the facilities to take care of the health needs of this population have not kept pace with the increase. Even though programs such as Medicare and Medicaid were organized in the late 1960s to help finance the health needs of the aged, "elderly persons are spending more money out of pocket for their personal health care today than they did in pre-Medicare days." Since 1965 there has been a 429 percent increase in total expenditures for health care for the aged, and approximately 29 percent of this amount is paid for out of pocket by the individuals themselves. Moreover, Medicare has reduced its payment from 50 percent in 1966 to 40 percent in 1978.[66]

What is perhaps most striking is the extent to which the code of scientific medicine has reinforced the perception that significant health care only takes place in a hospital or in a physician's office. This is most clearly reflected in the payment procedures of Medicare for skilled nursing homes and home health services. In the former case Medicare pays all costs for only twenty days and only if the patient enters within thirty days after hospital discharge. It cuts off payments completely after the hundredth day. However, in cases such as stroke the patient has to be certified as showing progress in therapy if payment is to be continued during the first hundred days. Moreover, payments for home health services are allowable only if the individual undertakes such services within fourteen days of discharge from a hospital. Thus, in each of these instances, medical need is defined not in terms of the requirements of care for the elderly. Rather, in the case of nursing homes, it is defined in terms of the possibility for progress as certified by a physician. Moreover, in both the case of nursing homes and home care services need is continuous with care in the institutional setting of scientific medicine – the hospital. The result for many sick elderly people and for their well spouses is that they must declare indigency before they are entitled to funds that will enable their true medical needs to continue to be met.

Because of many factors that obscure the discrepancies in medical care, the nature of the crisis is not always as obvious as it might be. Yet the quality of medical care seems to be a very good indication of a person's social class status. There is, for example, strong evidence to suggest that mortality levels are influenced heavily by factors of poverty and wealth. In one study the age-adjusted mortality rate for poverty areas exceeded that for nonpoverty areas by 40 percent.[67] Moreover, many diseases that public health officials have had reasonable success controlling among the general population, such as tuberculosis, often appear in significant numbers in certain sectors of a city. Since these sections are largely poor, often populated by minority groups, and less visible than middle-class areas, such problems often go unnoticed by the policymakers and the larger public.

Even in areas where significant progress has been made within recent years, such as infant mortality, the large disparity between different sectors of the population causes little alarm. Instead, we are likely to focus on the improvement alone and to see it as but another example of the progress in scientific medicine.

Thus, in recent years, infant mortality rates have improved significantly in the United States, even though it still ranks relatively poorly (sixteenth) among industrialized countries. Some of this improvement is in fact due to advances in scientific medicine and its growing ability to improve the chances of survival for underweight newborns. However, much more of it can be attributed to nutritional factors that have reduced the percentage of underweight newborns and, as one government summary reports, "Nearly all the difference in neonatal morality between white and black infants can be attributed to differences in birth weight distribution."[68]

There are two features of the trend in infant mortality that are most striking. First, the improvement since the late 1960s has been dramatic. "Between 1965 and 1979, infant mortality declined by 47 percent to 13 deaths per 1,000 live births."[69] Moreover, this decline in infant mortality has occurred among both the white and black population. Second, however, the gap between the white and black population remains relatively constant. Thus in 1965 the white mortality rate for infants under one year was 21.5, while the black rate was 40.3; in 1977 the white rate was 12.3, the black 21.7. To put it another way, in 1977 the black infant mortality rate stood a shade higher than the 1965 white rate.[70] Indeed, if only the nonwhite rate was taken into account the United States would rank twenty-fifth among nations in infant mortality. The major problem, as one recent comparison between Norwegian and U.S. infant mortality rates suggests, is not to be found in the scientific advances in maintaining underweight infants, but rather in the higher percentage of underweight infants, that are born in this country than in many other technologically advanced nations.[71] This is likely a function of diet and nutrition.

The above should not be taken as evidence for dismissing the importance of medical technology. The point is rather more modest. It is simply that given a reasonable level of technical knowledge, many health problems are a function of other factors, such as poverty, diet, and the access to knowledgeable health care professionals, many of whom may not be highly specialized. The point is also that the commitment to and acceptance of the significance of the technical knowledge code that has guided medical education and health care have obscured this simple point.

Fragments of a new code: From crisis management to health care

When looking at the general health of a society it is important to keep in mind the fact that medical intervention is but one factor in physical well-being and to remember those factors that retard health that are not generally subject to correction by medical intervention. Childbeating brought about by the tension in a jobless home, homicides resulting from cramped space and insufficient material resources, work-related afflictions, disabilities brought about through automobile accidents, suicides, and many other problems resulting from conditions of modern living are indications of a serious health crisis in this society, but these problems cannot be blamed on the medical profession. Yet the fact that these are rarely included in the catalog of health problems indicates just how much the public has come to accept the general point of view of the medical profession – that the problems of health result from inadequate crisis management. Once the problem is understood in terms of a crisis to be managed, then the solution will be seen in terms of training doctors to handle more contingencies.[72] It is at this point that the dominant code and the relevant frames have coalesced.

The development of a new and more progressive code would have to begin by shifting the focus of concern away from crisis management to a wider emphasis on health care in general. This movement, however, is retarded by the exclusive emphasis given to technical skills in the presentation of medical knowledge.

In medical education the presentation of knowledge serves two functions. First, it allows the student to develop the skills needed for effective practice, and second, it helps to develop certain attitudes that bring the students to share in the ideology of the profession. These attitudes include some general ideas about the relative worth of different kinds of practice, such as primary care as opposed to some specialty. The attitudes have a bearing on where a student eventually decides to practice and, as a result, on who will be the beneficiary of the skills that have been developed. Moreover, the very rigorous selection process together with the strenuous effort that the first years of training involve for many students reinforce a sense of medicine as an elite profession, and this is a view that is shared by physician and public alike. The profession selects people into its ranks primarily on criteria that relate to the effective practice of medicine under the ideal of the maximum growth of medical knowledge, but it is not responsible for the distribution of medical care throughout the society. In general, students are selected because of their demonstrated skill in the basic sciences and little consideration is given to situational understanding or to their demonstrated concern for the health needs of a specific community. Yet both of these are prerequisites for adequate national health care, and the development of any new code would need to take both of these factors into account. Educational research is unlikely to significantly contribute to the development of such a code until it is able to bring into relief and analyze the patterns of skills and consciousness into which medical students are socialized and the code of medical knowledge that the public has come to accept.

The code serves to provide people, both physicians and the public, with a general idea of the kinds of things that physicians do – that is, with an idea of the cluster of activities that we identify as belonging to the domain of the medical doctor. Thus, when we think of physicians in general, we tend to think of what they do in terms of a cluster of activities and skills and we identify that cluster as comprising the role of the physician. Precisely what principle binds a constellation of skills together into a role is difficult to identify. Some factors are probably internal to the nature of the skills themselves, having to do with such things as the complexities and risks involved. Other factors are probably external, having to do with professional dominance, historical accidents, and so forth. Nevertheless, if we reflect on the code and analyze it historically, we can see that the constellation changes. Some tasks are added, others are distributed to the nonphysician. In one historical period, for example, surgery was not considered to be part of the physician's role, whereas in the early days of the American republic, physicians dispensed medicine as pharmacists now do. Not too long ago in this country midwives rather than obstetricians delivered most of the babies, a task which they continue to perform in the Netherlands, which has a lower infant mortality rate than do we. And in times of acute stress, such as war, many functions that otherwise belong to the physician become the prerogative of paraprofessionals.

To a certain extent the medical profession seems to be implicitly giving recognition to some of these considerations by encouraging the development of ''paraprofessional'' training programs, some of them held within the same medical school in which the physicians are trained. Yet at the same time there is a strong control exerted by physicians,[73] and there are few independent authorities who have critically examined the cluster of skills that comprise the code as presently conceived. Thus one of the considerations that educational researchers, who are concerned with social reproduction, might examine is the extent to which skills and procedures now thought of as belonging only to the physician can be reclustered so as to assign greater discretionary activity to other professionals. The use of midwives in the Netherlands (with the third lowest infant mortality rate) is perhaps the most prominent example of a different way of clustering skills, but more research would likely reveal other possibilities. Such research,[74] however, would be as concerned with the distribution of medical knowledge as it is with increasing its rate of growth.[75]

The concern with the distribution of medical knowledge has resulted in some challenges to the code from within the United States. Consumer groups and environmentalists have raised some important issues about the nature of health care in this country, but these have tended to be raised on a case-by-case basis. A more systematic challenge has arisen from within a portion of the nursing profession, especially those trained in four-year university-based programs. Yet this challenge is difficult to sustain with the structure of medicine as practiced in the United States.

The challenge begins with an attempt to separate nursing from the medical profession and to confront the view that the nurse is simply a handmaiden to the physician. Instead it is claimed that nurses are part of the *health care* profession, that they hold professional status in their own right and, along with the physician, comprise equal membership in a health care team. The argument that is used to support this proposed new status begins by challenging the primacy of the physician's knowledge. It is observed that prevention is as important to health as is cure and that an understanding of the life factors of the individual patient that influence the way in which a disease is handled is as significant as sound clinical judgment. Hence, whereas the authority of the physician rests upon knowledge of the biological sciences and the ability to make clinical judgments, the authority of the nurse rests upon an understanding of the social behavioral sciences and upon an understanding of the life situation – the cultural and family background – of the patient.

This argument has resulted in a sharper professional identity for many nurses and for increased understanding of the importance of the nurses' role on the part of some physicians. Yet to a large extent this challenge remains an intellectual one. Although the personal behavior of individual nurses and physicians may be altered by an awareness of the challenge, the new perspective has not been well incorporated into the structure of medical practice. Here the idea of an equal partnership ultimately gives way to the authority of the physician.

We can see the difficulty by looking at two interviews (conducted separately), one of a medical student, the other of a nursing student. Each acknowledges the significance of the aspiring code, but neither is able to incorporate it easily into a key practical issue raised by the interviewer.

In the first interview the medical student began by expressing a good deal of respect for nurses and a recognition of the importance of their new role. In the earlier phase of the interview he had also expressed some strong skepticism about his own training during this, his first year of medical training. For example, when asked about the relationship between the basic science courses that he was now taking and the curative function of medicine, the student responded: "The main one is so that we can pass the medical boards." When later asked about the status of the nurse in relationship to the physician, he responded: "The nurse could easily make many of the simple diagnoses and carry out most of the interventions that are necessary. Unfortunately she has little authority or autonomy. She is legally subordinate to the physician." The interviewer then asked: "Why do you think this is?" And the medical student responded within a political and moral framework that seemed to be at odds with the prevailing code: "Doctors want authority. About the turn of the century the physician became one of the most respected and powerful beings in this country and with this respect came corruption which is almost inherent in any form of power. . . . The situation has partly come about through the efforts of the AMA to increase the power of the physician." And then, seeming to acknowledge the significance of the aspiring knowledge code, he added: "Actually the nurse knows the patient better than the physician does, sees the patient more on a day-to-day basis than the physician does, and interacts more with the patient's family than the physician. So the nurse is probably more qualified on the basis of these factors to make a diagnosis on the basis of these criteria.'' In order to test out this framework and its implications for practice, the interviewer asked the student to respond to a situation in which there was a disagreement between the nurse and physician about whether a dying patient should be told that he was dying and where the nurse in fact did tell the patient against the physician's judgment. The significance of the question is that in this situation the clinical judgment had already been made and that the decision about whether or not to tell the patient would seem to call for the kind of knowledge that this student had attributed more to the nurse than to the physician. The student, however, responded, without hesitation, ''I would probably have her fired. She does not have the authority to act that way!''

A few days later the same question was put to a fourth-year undergraduate nursing student who had expressed strong anger and resentment about the difference in status and income between doctors and nurses. She was asked what she would do if, feeling the patient should be told that he was dying, she found herself at odds with the physician. Her response began: ''Being the person that I am and forward, usually speaking my mind, when I get into that situation, when I feel comfortable in my role, I think I would probably say something to the patient.'' The inverviewer then asked: ''What do you think the consequences would be?'' And the response: ''Probably I'd lose my job – I don't know what I would do if I'd lose my job.'' And then, turning to the interviewer, ''Would I lose my job? If I lost my job – wait a second – that's a different story!'' The interviewer reported the medical student's response that he would probably fire her. The nursing student then ended on a defeated note: ''I probably wouldn't say anything.'' Thus, this nursing student, much like the medical student, acknowledges the intellectual weight of the aspiring code. However, whereas he is unwilling to acknowledge its practical implication, she is able to acknowledge it but is simply not able to address its implications in an institutional setting in which the dominant code prevails. In these cases the dominant code is able to maintain the bond between it and potentially alien frames, but there is obviously significant tension developing. The medical student feels obliged to acknowledge, at least in gesture, the significance of the aspiring code. The nursing student stands outside the dominant code, but is still bound to it by fear.[76]

Among the poor, among minority groups in this country as well as among some allied professional groups, the conditions may well be present for the disengagement of the dominant code and the relative frames. However, the technical success of medicine in advanced societies like our own and the sophisticated institutional network that has developed to support it suggest that fertile ground for the development of a new and equally powerful code will not occur in these areas, and that if new forms are to develop, they are more likely to arise in other areas. It is to education in these that we now turn.

10 Contradictions within the prevailing knowledge code

"Engineering and the hard sciences are the classics of this century."
University of Illinois Professor of Engineering as quoted in the *Champaign–Urbana News Gazette*, Friday, May 2, 1980

In this chapter we will examine the way in which tensions within a given knowledge code, in this case one that emphasizes the importance of technological and scientific knowledge, may develop as its application is expanded to new situations. The focus is on the relationship between developed and developing societies, particularly the way in which material conditions and the different relationships that various groups and nations have to the dominant knowledge code provide the conditions for different frameworks to develop. These frameworks, which in today's world are manifested in the sometimes latent but always seething conflict between the developed and the "developing" world, provide the fragments of a new consciousness that, given proper conditions, could serve as the basis for the successful development of competing knowledge codes.

To begin with, recall that the ideal of technological knowledge is the development of a generalized scheme that outlines various routes to any well-definable goal together with all of the possible contingencies that could arise to direct that one route rather than another would, in any particular circumstance, be the most efficient and least costly way to achieve any particular goal. The totality of technological knowledge can therefore be thought of in terms of the formal anticipation of as many goals and contingencies as possible, and the ideal of maximizing technological knowledge is one that then directs society to invest its educational resources in such a way as to provide at some future point in time the most detailed and comprehensive outline of routes and contingencies.

Figure 10.1 will serve to illustrate this point: AXYB represents the ideal of all possible routes and all possible contingencies, whereas ACB can represent the area of this ideal covered by existing knowledge within a given field and ADB

Sections of this chapter appeared in an earlier form in *Theory and Society*, Vol. 2(2), Summer 1975.

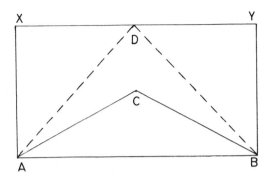

Figure 10.1. Ideal schema for the distribution of knowledge under the maximum growth principle.

represents the maximum growth in this field that can be expected given the most efficient investment of ACB.

Of course, there are many contingencies, such as the requirements that factors of social stability and material resources place on the investment procedures, but these must themselves be considered part of the store of existing knowledge that then helps determine how much growth can be reasonably expected during any given period of time.

Given that the technological code strives to invest existing knowledge so as to maximize the store of future knowledge, the most effective selection procedure is to use the initial years of education to select for subsequent training those individuals who, because of intelligence, cultural background, or appropriate value structures, are able to absorb existing knowledge at an accelerated pace (as determined by the financial resources of the society and the ability of its material base to train and then absorb highly educated manpower). Given this code, what is important in terms of the distribution is that a secure estimate can be made about the subsequent growth of knowledge. However, the growth of knowledge here is indifferent to the actual pattern of distribution among members of the society. If, in other words, the growth of knowledge can best be served by selecting out a few individuals for extra training, the size of the gap that develops between these individuals and the least advantaged members[1] of the society is not a major consideration, except insofar as social stability might be threatened.

The impact of this model on the developed world can best be seen by the way it circumscribes most of the debates about educational selection. For example, in the United States and England, as we have seen, there have been significant and sometimes bitter debates about the merits of IQ examinations as a way to select youngsters for additional schooling, but these debates have generally been carried on within the context of the accepted ideal of equality of opportunity. The debates are about whether or not the IQ exam is an effective instrument for identifying children of talent; they are not about whether the highest level of talent should be the major criterion for determining the level of individual resources or the duration of a person's education, and therefore neither side of the debate offers a challenge to the ideal of maximizing the growth of technological knowledge.

The moral foundation of this code is the belief in equality of opportunity, and in the United States the ideal can be traced back to the beginnings of popular, public education. Jefferson, for example, saw the common school as a way to "rake through the rubble" in order to select a few talented people for leadership positions in the society. James Bryant Conant has argued that the development of American education can be seen as the gradual fruition of the Jeffersonian ideal, and Conant's very influential reports on American education were designed to select out the 15 percent of the school-age population that he considered "academically talented" for rigorous training in high school and college, while the remaining 85 percent would be prepared for suitable vocations.[2] It can also be seen in the almost exclusive emphasis given to the technical aspects of training in professional schools today and the underemphasis on the humanistic perspective on professional practice.

Even those who criticized Conant's specific proposals did so on the grounds that they were not sufficiently adequate to meet the requirements for trained manpower. Thus, for example, the preschool programs that were initiated by the federal government during the 1960s for minority and poor youngsters were called Head Start programs and were partly justified on the grounds that they would allow the nation to meet the need for trained manpower in the years ahead. They were also justified on the grounds that they would further equal opportunity for these youngsters, thus allowing some of them later to better compete for positions that require high-level technical training.

Although the various factors influencing the development of these particular programs are too complex to treat in detail here,[3] the point is that all of these reforms have been carried on within the framework of the generally accepted principle of maximizing the growth of technological knowledge. The acceptance of this principle is not restricted to the United States, however. In England the debates over the eleven-plus examination have not generally been concerned, say, with closing the gap between the least and the most advantaged members of the society, or with maintaining a reasonable level of intellectual development for those who are sorted out of the educational system at an early age. The challenge to this procedure has generally been based on the grounds that selection takes place at too early an age, thus decreasing the probability of identifying the late bloomer.[4]

Although neglect often characterized the educational policies of the Western nations toward "their" Third World colonies, the coming of independence was met with policies that were designed to maximize the growth of technological knowledge within the limits set by the desire to maintain economic and political ties as well as maintaining sources of raw materials and agricultural products. In some cases the enlarged gap between the least and the most advantaged members of the colony was not merely a by-product of this policy, but a conscious and deliberate part of it. This was the case, for example, in Kenya. Here the desire to create an African economic elite who would identify with the expatriate along with the desire to increase the efficiency of farms producing exportable crops, led the colonial government to propose that the rich African farmers be enabled to buy more land and "bad or poor farmers less, creating a landed and a landless class."[5] This goal could not be implemented without an educational strategy that would be designed to increase the efficiency of favored landowners and to prepare the soon-to-be landless class for their new role in an "independent" Kenya.

The extent to which the goal of maximizing the growth of technological knowledge continues as the dominant educational strategy of the Third World is perhaps an open question, one requiring a nation-by-nation analysis. Nevertheless, those who adhere to this code are inclined to explain inequality as resulting from deficiencies in the accumulated store of technical knowledge, whether such deficiencies are found among minority groups within the nation or among other less developed nations. Thus, for example, when T. W. Schultz, the Nobel Prize–winning economist, looks at the difference between the earnings of blacks and whites in the United States, the variation is explained in terms of the difference in the educational facilities, and when addressing the needs of developing nations, he suggests that the major problem is an underinvestment in the development of human capacities.[6] However, for those who hold this view, equality is thought to be only an indirect result of maximizing the growth of technological knowledge.

The assumption that educational growth entails, even as an indirect consequence, educational equality has very weak theoretical support and little, if any, empirical evidence to back it up. One of the intents of this chapter is to show just how questionable the assumption is by showing that except under the most unusual and specific conditions, the principle of educational growth can be expected to produce greater educational inequalities. Moreover, given the principle of educational growth, educational equality can be established within an advanced nation only by encouraging a large degree of educational inequality between nations. In other words, given existing economic relationships, it is illusory to believe that educational growth can, under normal conditions, take place both within and between national boundaries while accompanied by greater intra- and international educational equality. The corollary of this is that given certain traditional conditions of educational growth, if educational equality were to be established within the boundaries of one region, it would have to be balanced by an inequality of education between that region and another. It is perhaps because of the realization of this fact that some Third World countries are beginning to resist the traditional models of growth and are seeking other alternatives.

One of the major reasons for the belief in this mode of development is to be found in the view that the history of technologically advanced nations has established a clear-cut pattern that, it is believed, newly developing technological societies can now follow to their advantage. This view neglects to consider the fact that the very existence of technologically developed nations creates a new condition that renders the older pattern inadequate as a guide for the educational development of newly emerging technological societies. Given this consideration, however, we can begin to see that different histories involve different points of entry into the code and entail different relationships to it and therefore different possibilities for sharing its rewards.

The traditional argument for educational growth

The basic argument for investment in educational growth has been that technological innovation and industrial development require and can sustain the expansion of formal educational institutions. It is argued that technology and industry require the development of new skills that are impossible to acquire in the informal, tradition-based education of the family or the apprenticeship. The development of technological, scientific, and managerial skills requires large outlays of capital and cannot be taught without a formal, vertical structure of schools. In addition to the selection and training of scientific, technological, and managerial talent, it is also recognized that the development of industry entails expanded urban centers, changing patterns of work, and a subsequent decline in the influence of the traditional socializing agencies such as the extended family, the church, and the small local community. It is feared that these factors when taken together will create internal violence and possibly a revolutionary vacuum, thus increasing the possibility of social chaos. Therefore, the argument concludes, formal schools are needed to fill this vacuum by taking over the socialization functions performed previously by other agencies.[7]

Schools, therefore, are thought to serve two key functions in developing technology. They identify and train talent on the one hand while they socialize the less talented into new forms of bureaucracy and work on the other. Moreover, it is argued, these two functions are connected in their service to the ideal of equality. As the older forms of socialization break down, certain accidental characteristics such as race or social class, previously associated with status, theoretically decline in importance and are replaced by the functional considerations of talent and ability. As talent becomes increasingly important for deciding access both to the higher levels of education and to one's position in the economic and status hierarchy, it is believed that the opportunities for the less talented are also increased. Thus, it is argued that as greater productivity develops from the investment in machinery and the training of talent, fewer people are actually needed in the productive process and more people can enjoy the rewards of education both as a vehicle to enhance their employment potential and for the enjoyment of education in its own right.

There is one other conclusion that follows from this argument that is not often mentioned by those who advocate growth but that is essential for the analysis that will follow shortly. The argument for educational growth implicitly recognizes that in modern society the school is the essential instrument for the reproduction of labor, and therefore it is reasonable to conclude that whatever advances are made toward educational equality will depend upon the reproductive needs of the society and the division of labor. We will return to this point later by looking at the specific ways in which different societies with different histories of development may come to relate to the knowledge code. In order to analyze the argument up to this point, however, it is useful to summarize it as follows:

(1) Technological growth or its possibility creates new requirements for education that are related to manpower needs and socialization;

(2) As these educational requirements are met, old inequalities based on social class, race, and other accidental factors are broken down;

(3) A society is developed that increasingly rewards talent and improves productivity; and which then

(4) Frees other segments of the potential labor force; and

(5) Allows for the increased enjoyment of education as a consumer pleasure as well as a source of higher employment possibilities.

Problems with equating educational growth with educational equality

The preceding attempt to summarize the argument for educational growth can be analyzed in the following way. Propositions 1 and 2 deal with the relationship between technological development and educational growth while 3, 4, and 5 deal with the distribution of educational and other rewards in a developed technological society. Propositions 2 and 3, when taken in isolation, have essentially the same content with the latter being the corollary of the former. When these two propositions are placed in the context of proposition 1, they present equal opportunity as a prerequisite for development, but when placed in the context of propositions 4 and 5, they present equal opportunity as the prerequisite for the widest distribution of rewards. The formal problem with the argument is that whereas there seems to be a direct connection between maximizing technological growth and the rewarding of talent, the link between the rewarding of talent and the widest possible distribution of rewards is much more tenuous. This point can be made intuitively clear by rephrasing propositions 1–3 to read:

If maximum technological growth is desired, then reward technological talent.

And then propositions 2–5 to read:

If you desire the widest distribution of rewards to the less able, then reward the most able.

It seems strictly a matter of faith that the wide distribution of social, economic, and educational rewards can be achieved best as an indirect consequence of allowing development to run its course without any direct controls generated by adherence to a policy of equality. The crucial issue then is whether a system, if allowed to develop on its own momentum, governed by the policy of growth, is likely to serve the goal of educational equality well.

In order to determine the extent to which educational growth is compatible with educational equality, we need to look further at the argument for educational growth and at how the dynamics of the system are supposed to work. Here the argument begins by recognizing the fact that efficient production in a technological society entails two disturbing and countervailing movements.[8] On the one hand there is the requirement that complex manual tasks and some clerical tasks be broken down into simpler processes with each worker performing fewer and simpler movements while engaging in an even smaller part of the production process. On the other hand, however, there is the need for more information to be available to managers who need increasingly complex skills in order to translate an ever-enlarging scope of information and to coordinate increasingly complex organizations.

Given these countervailing tendencies, most of the liberal advocates of growth have recognized that unless corrective measures are taken, the direction of advanced technology will be toward absolute intellectual inequality and they have argued that increased schooling is the most likely way to mitigate this tendency. Thus the argument accepts as a given characteristic of industrial society that as the manual (and clerical) tasks become simpler and less demanding, requiring less information and skills, the managerial tasks become more demanding and require more information and greater skills. (This insight has also, incidentally, been the primary theme of many anti-utopian novels such as *1984, Brave New World,* and *The Rise of the Meritocracy.*) Schooling is to mitigate these factors, however, not by challenging the dynamics of production, but by smoothing over its rougher edges.

The argument for increased schooling as a way to correct the tendency toward the inequality generated by industrial society has been supported by two separate platforms. The first has to do with the role of equality of opportunity and the second with the type of curriculum thought by some (usually the liberal–progressive segment of educational reform) to be appropriate for children in industrial societies.

The argument for equal educational opportunity is complex and embraces a number of different factors.[9] However, it is sufficient to note that the argument begins by accepting the given division of labor of technological society as inevitable, and concludes by proposing that the only alternative for the educational system as a whole is to assure that selection into the various slots is based upon the most objective procedures possible.

If the above argument were allowed to stand alone, it would in fact do little to address the issue of intellectual inequality, for it does not attack the structure that generates the inequality but merely outlines a way in which individuals may change positions in that structure. Given the continuation of routine jobs in the primary and the secondary sectors of the economy, the best that this argument can offer is that the least intelligent individuals, as measured by some generally accepted instrument, will be trained for and be employed in jobs where their general abilities are least likely to be challenged and to grow. Thus, the second platform must be raised to address the problem of the intellectual development of those who are destined for slots in the primary and secondary sectors.[10]

Here it is proposed that the function of education in an industrial society is not only to teach specific skills, or even appropriate behavior patterns, but also to bridge the potential intellectual gap by helping each person to understand the complexities of technological society and the interdependent roles that are needed to keep it functioning. Thus, it has been proposed that the youngster who is working in the school shop should learn not only the tools of his trade, or the behavior required by the work situation, but he should learn also such things as the general history of scientific and technological discoveries that underlie his future work as well as the relation of his role to others in the social system and to the overall production and consumption requirements. The purpose of this proposal in our terms is to more closely bind the knowledge code to its relevant frames.

This proposal is offered as a way to equalize the scope of knowledge for different occupational groupings. Yet while proper attention is paid to extending the scope of knowledge, little attention is paid to the level of knowledge that is being developed. What such curriculum proposals offer is ''the opportunity'' to develop a passive understanding of the complex interrelationships of technological society. What they do not offer is any perspective by which to evaluate those interrelationships.

The upshot of this proposal therefore is not to reduce inequality, but rather to help people tolerate their eventual assignment in an industrial complex. One of its most publicized implementations came in the form of the life adjustment movement in the United States, which was rightly criticized for its neglect of intellectual concerns. However, its critics were often even less concerned about the unequal distribution of knowledge and therefore emphasized the selection, training, and occupational placement function of schools. Nevertheless, the fact that movements like life adjustment were designed to attack the problem on the level of attitudes rather than by examining the structures that generated inequalities goes a long way in explaining why such teaching was generally uninspiring, coming to emphasize the fixed, handed-down aspects of knowledge.

The critique of the theory of growth offered so far has challenged the argument that increased educational growth indirectly leads to increased educational equality and suggests instead that the likely correlation is precisely the reverse – that is, that increased growth will lead to greater inequality. What will now briefly be shown is that there is a variety of empirical evidence that supports the counterarguments, after which the link between educational growth and educational inequality will be further explored. Once this link is understood, then we will be in a better position to analyze the way in which intranational equality is likely to affect international equality.

Some empirical support for the counterargument

If the belief that educational growth produced greater educational equality were correct, then we would expect to find the largest degree of equality in those nations that have exhibited the greatest educational growth. However, when educational equality is measured by the number of levels between the most and the least educated, we find that precisely the opposite is the case. In a study using UNESCO data,[11] Johan Galtung and his associates measured the existing relationship between educational growth and educational equality and concluded:

The higher the educational growth, the higher the disparity. Countries with high educational growth show high educational disparity, and countries with low educational growth show low educational disparity – to some extent because they have illiteracy. This conclusion holds for all three measures of disparity, and is not affected by switching from one age group to another. In other words: *educational growth as it is known in the world today does not lead to educational equality.*[12]

One objection to this finding needs to be anticipated. It is that the study fails to consider the number of years that the bottom percentile stays in school under conditions of educational growth. Thus, a critic could argue that even though there is a greater distance between the least and the most educated in areas of high growth, nevertheless the least educated most likely stay in school longer in areas of high growth than they do in areas of low growth.

The force of the objection is that although equality as such may not be a by-product of growth, the less educated members are nevertheless better off under conditions of high growth than they would be under conditions of low growth. This objection suggests that given two societies, we should choose the one in which the least educated stay in school the longest, regardless of the disparity.

This objection cannot be addressed by strictly quantitative instruments because it is based upon beliefs about changes in the quality of individuals due to their attendance in school. Such beliefs usually have to do with the view that an extended tenure in school increases the life chances of individuals by opening them up to new and varied possibilities. Support for these beliefs is usually provided by citing the mobility pattern of school leavers and by drawing a connection between attending school and upward mobility, a connection that has recently been challenged. Some now deny that there has been much significant upward mobility, whereas others suggest that the connection between schooling and upward mobility is much more tenuous than originally thought.[13]

Nevertheless, even if we accept the most optimistic view about the relationship between schooling and mobility, we do not yet have good reason for preferring the society where the least educated spend the most years in school. This is because the view that schooling contributes to upward mobility is generally based upon the career prospects of those who have a lot of schooling, not on those who have only a little. Indeed, given a society with a large correlation between years in school and life chances, we should find that as the distance increases between the actual number of years an individual spends in school and the maximum number of years that could theoretically be spent there, then life prospects should decrease. And this should be true, regardless of how many years are actually spent in school. Although this response only represents a tendency, without the mitigating factors found in advanced societies, the tendency becomes more likely to occur.

Of course, there is another meaning that is given to "increasing the life chances" of individuals that has to do with such things as increasing their powers for human enjoyment and interaction. Given this meaning, the argument for ignoring disparity is that regardless of the distance between the most and the least educated, every year in school is a "bonus" for the development of an individual's humanity. Yet here, the now dated but still insightful journalistic critics of schools – Holt, Kozol, Goodman, and even Silberman – provided some ground for skepticism. The schools they described were not involved in especially humanistic enterprises, and there is little evidence to indicate that conditions have improved significantly. The very fact that their insights have lost their critical force in recent years – as schools have turned to the back-to-basics movement, competency testing, and increased vocationalism – demonstrates again the difficulty of sustaining a humanistic commitment in the context of the dominant technological knowledge code.[14]

The limits to educational equality in developed areas

The central role of the school in a technological society is the reproduction of labor on various levels.[15] The reproductive requirements of a technological society are many, but generally they embrace all of the skills and attitudes that are required in order to maximize production in bureaucratic structures. These include such varied skills as those of scientists engaged in manipulating symbols and managers manipulating organizations as well as the lower-level skills required to follow rigid rules and behavior patterns. Above and beyond the role of reproducing labor, but not incompatible with it, the schools are often given the task of developing individuality, intellectuality, and creativity. However, the extent to which these latter characteristics can be developed by schooling depends upon requirements set by the productive process. To whatever extent production requires or can tolerate individual initiative, intellectuality, and creativity (which I shall refer to as secondary values to distinguish them from the more mechanical primary requirements of production), to that extent the schools can also stress the development of these traits. In general, and just because of the need for trained managers and scientists, the stress on these secondary values will be higher in the more developed regions and will often be found at all levels of the educational system, although not universally. In developing areas functioning under a principle of growth, the stress on these secondary characteristics will generally be restricted to the tertiary level of education and will occur less frequently, even on this level, than in advanced areas.

One key indicator of educational equality is the extent to which the secondary educational values are distributed among different groups within an educational system, and then between systems themselves. Thus, given the principle of growth, we need to determine the limits imposed on the distribution of these values, and for this purpose we turn briefly to examine growth as a concept of economic development.

The general goal of all advanced and developing technologies operating under the principle of growth is to reach a situation such that processing and consumption facilities are operating at peak capacity. In order to reach this state, labor must be distributed as efficiently as materials and, except for some requirements dictated by the need for social stability, this means that labor must be channeled into different levels of the production process. This channeling into different levels places the relationship between education and the division of labor in a light which is not captured by the traditional economic concepts. What is divided is not only skills, but more importantly, different *levels* of skills that bring with them entirely new educational and socializing requirements.

When, for example, the classical economist described the now famous exchange between the butcher and the baker, he was describing an exchange resulting from approximately the same level of productive activity. The work of both the butcher and the baker resulted from approximately the same level of productive activity, involved approximately the same complex of physical and mental skills, and therefore each could be socialized by the same community into a common set of values. However, the skills required to work on an assembly line or to file papers in an office are different in complexity and kind from those needed to manage the enterprise. Indeed, from the point of view of economic theory, the *ideal* line worker or low-level clerk is one whose activities can be described in terms of *movements* rather than skills, a point that the modern educational behaviorist has learned well but that neglects to take into account the fact that workers may *interpret* the productive process differently.

This is not to deny the obvious; different levels of skills exist in non-technological societies as well as in technological ones. However, once the principle of maximizing technological knowledge comes to govern the production and educational process, differentiation becomes a much more deliberate part of planning, dictating that wherever possible, any activity that combines intellectual and mechanical skills is to be divided into two separate activities involving two or more specific individuals. In societies where this principle does not govern production, functional tasks are less specialized and often more fully integrated with spiritual and communal aspects of life.[16]

Because schools take over socialization and educational tasks previously diffused throughout the society, they are themselves a reflection of the intensification of the division of labor. The formal structure of schools will therefore reflect fairly closely the division of labor (or the projected division) of the larger society, and therefore the distribution of the secondary values will be limited by the distribution of higher-level occupational roles. Moreover, the number of higher-level roles is determined by the extent to which the more routine tasks of production can be reduced by one means or another, a point that I will take up later when we return to the question of education in emerging technological societies.[17]

It is only in light of the school's role in reproducing labor that we can understand emphasis placed on testing and vocational counseling procedures in determining which youngsters are more inclined to work with their "heads" and which with their "hands." This emphasis functions first and foremost to provide objective, scientific support for occupational allocations that would otherwise be difficult for many to accept. Of course, this emphasis on testing and counseling can only be sustained by accepting as well the alienation of labor that these procedures are designed to both support and cushion. It is a mistake to believe, however, that if testing were abolished, alienated labor would suddenly disappear, making schools dispensers of sweetness and light. For one thing, tests themselves are not that essential for the maintenance of the system. The essential factors are, first, that whatever the procedures of selection, they should be *perceived* as fair, and second, that the division of labor itself should remain unchallenged. Given these two requirements, then, the reproductive function of the school likely could be preserved simply by the general tendency of parents and others to judge the quality of a school on the basis of their expectations about the occupational possibilities for the child, and such expectations will be heavily influenced by the work requirements that parents experience in their own jobs. As was suggested earlier, even though many parents will look upon the school as a possible vehicle for upward mobility for their children, they will also look upon it as an insurance policy that, if everything else fails, will at least prepare the youngster to assume the work routine of the parent. (This may help explain why, in the previously mentioned study of working- and middle-class parents, the number of parents whose response to an interview could be coded as preparing their children for a passive role in school was more than two-and-a-half times larger for working-class mothers than for middle-class ones.[18])

Given these limitations, it seems reasonable to conclude that the tendency will be for schools to stress the secondary values only in those situations where there is reason to believe that such values will not conflict with the requirements of the child's future work situation, and this itself is an essential factor in maintaining the school's role in the reproduction of labor.

It is not surprising, therefore, that schools do reflect the division of labor, for where else would youngsters acquire the routine demanded by industrial life? Nor, given the complexities of this division in advanced technologies, is it surprising that in some schools and classrooms the emphasis is on teaching the routine of acceptable work behavior and the authority of what Holt called the right answer, whereas in others, greater stress is placed on methods of defining and solving problems. However, the limits of production on educational reform are not absolute for advanced technological systems. They can be stretched to a certain extent, but as we will see, this will have a direct bearing on the educational possibilities for less developed areas.

The limits of educational equality in developing areas

This critique began by challenging the view that developing societies could hope to follow the pattern already laid down by the developed ones. It was suggested instead that the very existence of technologically developed societies presents a significantly new factor that renders the older pattern obsolete. It is now necessary to show why this is so by examining the relationship between production requirements and education as these are governed by the principle of growth. To begin with, we need to look more closely at the possibility that exists for technologically advanced societies to stretch educational reform beyond the limits seemingly set by production. The very possibilities that do exist for developed areas to stretch the hold that production requirements have on educational reform would, if implemented, result in new and stronger limits being placed on possibilities for reform (in terms of the secondary values) in developing areas. In other words, given the principle governing educational policy today, if the advanced nations were to choose to directly intervene in order to temper growth with equality within their own borders, the consequence would be fewer possibilities for educational equality in developing areas. We can see why this is so by looking again at the relationship between education and production.

The basic condition for extending the secondary educational values to citizens within a technologically developed society is to disengage the national labor force from the more tedious and routine production tasks. This condition can be achieved in one of two possible ways (or by some combination of the two). Either machine labor can be substituted for human labor, or else some mechanism can be found for distributing the routine tasks to people who are not a part of the internal political process. In either of these cases, the citizens within the technologically developed society could be freed from the tedious aspects of production and the weight of schooling could be placed on the secondary values.

In an ideal sense, the first of these alternatives would be the most promising, for it seems to provide a way to relieve labor from the more routine tasks of production without depending upon a shadow labor force to take over the work rejected by one's own citizenry. In actual practice, however, automation has been a mixed blessing. Although there seems to have been a trend toward reducing the number of hours that individuals must spend at the tasks of routine production, there are also indications that automation has frequently relegated middle-skill workers to more routine and passive production tasks. For example, in some plants where welding operations have been automated, the average skilled welder's activity is restricted to inspecting the finished work, whereas only the most accomplished welder continues to practice his skill in those jobs where the machine is not proficient.

The reasons for these limitations are open to some speculation, and it is difficult to tell how much is due to the nature of automation itself and how much is due to the nature of the economic structures in which automation is embedded. Clearly, the accepted relationship between political stability and economic growth is one significant factor. When the redistribution of wealth is rejected as a reasonable means for relieving political pressure, then continued economic growth is generally accepted as the only reasonable alternative. It is likely that the ever-increasing demand for new and different consumer goods means that the processes that cannot profitably be automated must become intensified in order to meet demand and to keep prices low. It may also be the case that there are some routine processing tasks that cannot be eliminated by machine labor. Whatever the reasons may be for the limitations that are placed on automation in reducing the need for routine labor, for the purpose of this analysis it is important only to recognize that there are routine tasks that it is unlikely machines alone will be able to abolish.[19] Thus, if the disengagement from routine labor of the citizens of technologically advanced nations is to take place, it will not be accomplished by automation alone.

Given the limitations of machines, the general rule governing the distribution of education is that whenever processing is governed by the need for a radical division of the levels of labor, then, as Bowles and Gintis suggest, the educational system has to turn out people roughly in proportion to the requirements set by this division. In the technologically developing areas there are strict limits on how many people may have access to the secondary and tertiary levels of education. Here primary education often quite literally means that level that prepares people for the primary sector of the economy, and secondary education for the secondary sector, and so on.[20] Of course, to prepare people for a certain level of employment in school does not necessarily mean that jobs will be available for them when they leave.

In more technologically developed societies there will be more demand for scientific and managerial talent, and therefore increasing numbers of people are likely to have access even to the tertiary level, yet not without limit. For those youngsters who are not likely to enter the tertiary sectors of the economy, there is still a demand for an increased number of years of schooling, and secondary credentials become increasingly important for entrance even into the lower levels of economic life. Even though schools for such youngsters have limited educational value, they are functional components in the reproductive process. In both physical appearance and routine, such schools increasingly resemble factories without wages, making it that much easier for new workers to accept the boredom for which they now receive a wage.

Just how long these rigidly structured schools will be tolerated in wealthy societies that pride themselves on open structures is a matter of debate. It is clear, however, that as long as labor cannot be disengaged from tedious and routine production, there will be strong pressures to maintain them, thus intensifying the activities of allied educational industries, such as educational testing, one of the effects of which is to justify an individual's placement. If these efforts should fail, however, yielding to the pressure of rising expectations, or class consciousness, and so on, threatening to destroy the discipline of the school, there are a number of avenues that wealthier societies still have open to them.

The first possibility is to reform the school by relaxing routine discipline, creating open structures, and placing more stress on individual development, thus emphasizing the secondary educational values and the ideal of education for its own sake. In conjunction with this, more places can be provided for working- and lower-class youngsters at the university, and the university curriculum can be reformed to meet their needs. Hence, for example, the emphasis in American society a few years ago on open classrooms, affirmative action in university admissions, and womens' and black studies programs.

All of these are promising short-term methods for relieving political and educational pressure, but at best they can only bring temporary stability. If the tertiary sector of the economy does not expand in proportion to the expansion in education, the result will either be large-scale unemployment or else many people taking jobs below their educational level. This is a situation that has potential revolutionary implications, implications that are unacceptable from the standpoint of the political and educational leadership.[21]

Since such potential instability is intolerable, efforts may be made to change the economic system so as to balance it better with the educational reform. The first step will be, wherever possible, to substitute machines for people, which of course will have an effect on employment possibilities and the school-leaving age. Yet the problem remains of those many routine tasks that cannot be automated, and here, of course, is where the less developed areas come into the picture.

Advanced areas always have an advantage over developing ones because of their greater material base. They can import labor for the routine industrial tasks, or they can export routine processing operations to laborers outside their borders. Thus Yugoslavian workers go to Switzerland, and Japanese TV assembly plants go to Korea and Hong Kong. In both cases possibilities are created for one's own population to advance educationally, leaving the more routine tasks and training to others. Hardly a pleasant prospect if one belongs to the ''others.'' Moreover, the advantage of the developed nations increases the possibility that talented people from the less developed ones will emigrate, thus reducing the benefits that could arise from an educated elite. Galtung has even envisaged the possibility that

ultimately one might end up with the world divided into three types of countries: at the bottom countries with primary education doing extraction work, in the middle countries up to the level of secondary education . . . doing simple processing and at the top, countries where the great majority of people are university graduates engaged in highly research intensive industry.[22]

Thus, given the continuing need for labor in the primary sector, the present pattern of industrial growth allows for only a few possibilities, none of which is particularly appealing on a wide scale. Either we would find, along with a division of labor and education between nations, the intensification of this division within nations as well, or else we would find that as the division within advanced nations is relaxed, the division between nations maintains itself and likely intensifies.

It must be remembered that these possibilities are long-range ones. For the moment, however, there is only slight indication that the more advanced nations are moving toward a situation of equality within their own borders, either in terms of decreasing the distance between the least and the most educated or in terms of extending the secondary educational values. This fact, however, should provide little relief for the developing areas.[23] The need of advanced nations for new markets in order to maintain economic growth and for ever-cheaper sources of routine labor should serve to retard equitable educational development in the peripheral nations of the world even in the absence of a move toward equality in the advanced areas.

Challenges to the dominant code

In 1977 it was reported by an American researcher that the University of Tabriz in Iran had accepted as a general goal "To establish English as a primary language for academic programs in the Faculty of Engineering, the Faculty of Medicine, and all graduate programs by 1980; and in the Faculty of Agriculture and Faculty of Science by 1981; and in the remaining Faculties by 1983."[24] The Iranian revolution followed a little more than a year later and the goal was abandoned.

The goal was developed during a time when a large number of Iranian doctors were practicing outside the country[25] and it could have done little but discourage the entrance into medical school of members of noncosmopolitan, rural populations where the most serious health problems were to be found.[26]

The American researchers who went to Iran to advise the university officials addressed only the practical problems of implementing the objective. It was recommended that advanced-level English-language programs be required for the faculty, that one day each week be set aside as English-language day at the Faculty Club, that students be provided with English-language films, newspapers, and magazines, and that English be rapidly introduced as the medium for lectures and examinations.[27] The goal itself did not come into question. This oversight is perfectly understandable given the force of the technological knowledge code and the fact that so much of the research in medicine is written in English. Equally understandable is the revolution that followed shortly thereafter and that gave dramatic expression to the perceptions of the code from down under.

Challenges to the code have been expressed in less dramatic, often more ambivalent ways. In the United States, for example, recent debates over affirmative action programs and their merits have pressed the formal notion of equality of opportunity, which comprises the moral basis for the code, in significant ways.[28] The justifications for such programs express a significant tension between the idea that individual talent should be the basis for advancement and the less prominent idea that group needs should be served in allocating scarce positions in professional and graduate programs.

Where developing societies have challenged the code in a more progressive and sustained manner it has been through emphasizing the communal features of social life, by encouraging the wider distribution of decision-making authority over questions of production on the local level, and by controlling and reducing the intensification of the division of labor. Societies that have consciously attempted alternative modes of development have not been able to control all of these factors equally well. For example, Yugoslavia has developed procedures for greater decisionmaking among workers in a production unit, but has not been very successful in controlling the intensification of the division of labor. As a result, many decisions have become housed in a managerial class,[29] a development that has reduced the effectiveness of local decisionmaking and increased the strength of the bureaucracy.

If there has been a consistent theme to the different challenges it is a commitment to reduce the gap between the least and the most educated. Few societies have pursued this goal with the persistence and commitment of the Chinese prior to Mao's death. The commitment has not been sustained subsequent to Mao's death. While it lasted, however, it provided a concrete articulation of an alternative code, one that was grounded in a different moral intuition than the idea of equal opportunity.

The following is based on the report of one visitor, Johan Galtung, to the People's Republic, prior to Mao's death, where he visited a number of schools and had extensive discussions with educators and students. It is consistent with the reports of other visitors at the time. He reports that underlying the Chinese educational ideal was a theory of ability, which is strikingly different from notions that are dominant in most technologically developed areas. In developed countries, the dominant emphasis is on *differences* in ability, and the major goal, expressed by the ideal of equality of educational opportunity, is to find a way to accurately assess those differences so that individuals may be granted their "proper" allotment of education – an allotment that is to be in proportion to ability level. This emphasis underlies and is shared by all the major parties to the educational debates regardless of how incompatible they may be on other levels. We have seen that it is this shared emphasis that explains the intensity of the debate over IQ examinations. The argument against such examinations is that they are inaccurate instruments, the use of which results in an improper allocation of educational resources. The alternate point of view to be found in developed societies, one that stresses the need for early experiental education, is not a challenge to the belief that in the long run education ought to be allocated according to ability. Its claim is merely that the IQ test is not an accurate instrument in situations of a deprived environment, and that therefore before an accurate reading can be taken, whether by an IQ test or some other instrument, the environment must be normalized.

For the Chinese during the Cultural Revolution, differences in ability were accepted, but the emphasis was on the similarity in the process of growth. Excerpts from Galtung's interview with leading members of the Revolutionary Committee of a middle school in Peking during the later years of Mao's reign serve to illustrate this point:

Of course people differ in ability. But a student who is weak in one field may be strong in another. And these abilities are not something innate and unchanging. Abilities grow when they are made use of, through practice. Practice is not only a way of testing and developing abilities. Practice arises out of the challenge of a contradiction, and the important thing is that everybody should have access to challenge and practice . . . and grow accordingly.

As abilities grow by being used they are not constant, and it does not make sense to say that a given individual has so and so much ability. Hence we do not have final examinations and diplomas with grades on them in our school. We do make use of examinations during the school year, as a pedagogical method. as a check on students and teachers. Many of these examinations are collective group examinations as the purpose is not to pass judgment on individuals. When students leave school they get a certificate of attendance – almost all of them get this – so that they leave as equals.[30]

Underlying these quotations is the idea that whatever differences in ability there may be, whether genetically or environmentally caused, are minor in relation to how much abilities can grow when challenged. The important stress is on the extent to which this challenge could be equalized and the extent to which the variations in ability that do ultimately exist can mutually reinforce one another to solve everyday human problems without the strict division of labor found in other societies.[31]

It is quite clear that the Chinese model of education was dysfunctional in the context of the more extreme division of labor that exists in developed countries. Recognizing this, Galtung's report at the time indicates that the Chinese made a considerable effort to relax that division. As he describes the practice:

These Chinese have turned their backs to this type of society, partly by rotating individuals between what might remain of the cells, partly by reconstructing the entire system of production in such a way that the whole scheme becomes meaningless. Thus, a People's Commune also has factories and everybody seems to work all places, including administration. A factory worker also works in a commune. An engineer works as a worker, some days a week, one week a month, two months a year or some such formula . . . a worker can get a one year theoretical course to become more like an engineer . . . till they both meet as worker-engineers. At the same time there seems to be considerable flexibility in society, decentralization and delegation of authority downwards (if that term is still meaningful) so as to leave to individuals and groups chances of converting challenges into practice. In short, changes are being undertaken in the economic structure, and have already proceeded very far, of such a kind that traditional division of labor between those who solve problems (the managers, the professionals) and those who implement the solution (functionaries, workers) is, if not totally obliterated, at least blurred less sharp, less full of implications for differential growth?[32]

Although the Chinese experiment has faltered, there are a number of reasons why developing nations might pause before continuing to guide education by a policy that directs them to maximize the growth of technological knowledge. It is misguided to believe that the developing areas can follow the pattern laid down by the developed areas with the expectation that the same possibilities will be open to them. This is because the presence of the already advanced areas presents a new factor that changes the possibilities dramatically.

The fact that already advanced nations constitute a new factor rendering the older patterns of development obsolete cuts more than one way. For one thing, there are often undesirable yet uncontrollable consequences that result from the fact that other nations have decided to modernize. These consequences have to do with such things as the relative influence and power of one nation in comparison to others and the ability of a nation to control events within its borders without undue influence from outside. Moreover, if modernization is viewed simply as a system of techniques that have the potential to satisfy some human needs and to relieve the burden of some human labor, then its appeal is easy to understand and probably not wise to discourage. The problems arise when the techniques of modernization are treated as ends in their own right and when it is simply assumed that growth and development will automatically result in a just and moral state of affairs.

Clearly, neither the decision not to modernize nor the decision to modernize according to already established patterns is a very attractive alternative. To fail to modernize means to fail to create even the possibility of controlling the hazards of everyday life, such as disease and the hazards that come from being in the midst of industrialized nations. To modernize under the traditional pattern, however, means to destroy community ties and to increase the structural violence that arises from urban poverty, slums, and unemployment.

Whether or not this dilemma can be resolved depends largely upon whether the existing pattern of educational and economic development can be altered in such a way so as to control and reduce the disparities that have historically resulted and that are otherwise likely to intensify. It also depends upon whether or not the commitment to technological knowledge and its growth can be contained within a code that provides sufficient expression for other modes of human development and interaction. It is to the nature of one such possible code that we now turn, as we again look at the possibilities for schooling in technologically developed societies.

11 Education and the self-formation of the public

There are two major normative issues in the study of education. The first involves the question of who shall be allowed access into different forms of knowledge. The second involves the issues of what forms of knowledge will be encouraged and carried on. The first of these issues involves questions about the distribution of knowledge such as those raised in the preceding two chapters. These issues largely assume the viability of a given knowledge code. Given this assumption, then questions may be raised on the basis of fairness or efficiency about the access that different groups or individuals have to various levels of the code. It is this issue, for example, that characterizes the debate over IQ tests and that provides the shared ground for the controversy over affirmative action policies. In both instances the technical code of contemporary society is taken for granted and the major issue is how access into the different levels required by the code shall be decided. Yet as we have seen in the preceding chapter, there are structural limits to the level of access, and these limits have more to do with when a group enters the code than with the talent of those who are being selected. Thus there develops a strong tension between the ethical demands of the code itself and the real possibilities that the code creates for different individuals and groups. This tension helps to bring the second issue into focus. Here we are concerned not just with access into the code, but with the very nature of the code itself. In this instance we are concerned not just with the question "Who shall be educated?" but also with the question "Of what shall education consist?"

To raise the latter question already provides some means for answering it. Once we understand education as social reproduction, then we must also understand that to question the nature of education is to question the skill clusters and mode of consciousness that accompany reproduction of a certain kind. Thus, to raise questions about the nature of education within the context of an understanding of the accepted knowledge code of a society is to require a detailed reflection

Sections of this chapter appeared in an earlier version in *University College Quarterly*, Vol. 24(3), March 1979.

on that code. Such reflection, however, is carried on from the standpoint of the existing code itself. In other words, given the kinds of beings that we are, we do not stand outside our own education in order to guide its change. Rather, we stand within that code, while trying to understand its dynamics and to harness it to a clearer understanding of the human enterprise. Reflection does not throw the old code overboard. Rather it builds out of it a new framework of understanding, which then places the existing code in a different context.

The social function of education

Specific modes of education, both formal and informal, grow out of the perceived needs and possibilities of existing societies. The knowledge that is prized and protected by a given code, the formal arguments advanced in its behalf, as well as the pattern of distribution that accompany it can be traced to some historically perceived need and to the ability of some group to capitalize on this need by persuading or coercing others to address it in certain ways. As institutions and practices congeal around the new code, visible and concrete incentives are added to what were but previously abstract arguments or more likely simple and diffuse visions. Such institutions and practices are able to control the structure of rewards, to insert their own socialization mechanisms into older forms of social life, to control the flow of information and the development of skills, and to thus limit and define acceptable forms of individual and group action. The intellectual force of the code can be found in the reasons that provide the shared ground of debate, and the material force can be found in the institutional rewards and sanctions that accompany certain actions.

This general description applies to the development of the technical code that dominates contemporary education. With Flexner, for example, we saw how the articulation of medical need and a vision of the nature of medical knowledge provided the ideational expression for the new organization of medical education and practice and for the material rewards that accompanied it. Similarly, the grounding of the arguments for and against the use of IQ tests has rested upon a shared commitment to the ideal of equality of opportunity. This ideal, which is the individual expression of the general social goal of maximizing the growth of technological knowledge, provides the moral principle for distribution of material rewards and social status. IQ tests are but one convenient way of servicing it.

Yet if the dominance of a specific code can be traced to a historically perceived need, the ultimate judgment as to the appropriateness of that particular code must be informed by the transcendental role of education in the reproduction and development of social life. It is only in the context of this larger requirement that it is possible to achieve perspective on one's own socialization and on the institutions that have guided it. We can easily understand the analysis provided by the ordinary-language philosopher (treated in Chapter 6) as an expression of this concern. Unfortunately the emphasis on the "educated person" and "the forms of knowledge" overstates the function of education for the individual while understating its function in the reproduction of social life. It thus provides no way to bridge the gap between the development of skills and the development of consciousness. Without such a bridge, ordinary-language philosophy, although presented as an abstract, decontextualized system of analysis, reinforces the very distinctions upon which the present system rests. Yet the impulse to find a normative basis for evaluating education is a sound one and, properly directed, can serve as an important corrective to the concealed conservative force of much of the empirical tradition. To provide such an analysis, however, attention needs to be turned away from a focus on individuals and directed toward the general social role of education. This requires that the distinction between "training" and "education" be recognized as a limited one and that the analysis begin by examining the major reproductive functions of educational practice. A normative evaluation of the present code cannot proceed by overlooking the necessary reproductive functions of social life. It must instead consider the constraints and possibilities that these provide.

Two paradigms of education

Thus we must begin by distinguishing two major social functions of education, two paradigms that can begin to provide an understanding of the possibilities that exist for progressive change. The first of these involves those areas that provide deliberate instruction into a code of knowledge, a set of principles and techniques designed to further the participation of an individual in the market through the mediation of skills that possess an exchange value. Ordinary-language philosophers would prefer to identify this kind of education with training, but *mere* training is not sufficient to cover the many different kinds of instruction that are carried on under this form of education. It would, for example, include not only all those performances that involve simple rote procedures in which one has been instructed, but also those performances that involve the ability to deal with contingencies through the application of well-grounded scientific understanding. Hence this category would include not only the simplest kind of vocational training, but education into a craft or profession as well, and it is primarily concerned with the transmission of technologically exploitable knowledge at some level. The second function is concerned with those forms of instruction primarily intended to further social participation as a member of the public through the development of interpretive understanding and normative skills. This form of instruction is often called general education. It is that component of education that prepares students for a common life, regardless of the nature of their vocation, and it is often thought that, because general education projects a life in common, an arena in which decisions are to be made regardless of calling, it requires a common curriculum. However, I want to leave this issue aside and suggest only that the minimal common element required by general education consists of the skills that are implied by interpretive understanding and normative appraisal. Given these two models, which are not intended to be exclusive, what we often call liberal education is a condition for the kind of public participation implied by general education. In liberal education we are considering that form of instruction that involves the development of free persons, persons who are, at least in principle, capable of making unmanipulated judgments on the basis of reason and theoretical understanding, but who also find solidarity with their fellow human beings.

Thus, we begin with two forms of education: One that is defined by its tendency to differentiate, a second that is defined in terms of its concern to unify. The differentiation entailed by specialized education implies not only a difference in skills, but also a difference in outlook and point of view. Moreover, as skills are divided in contemporary society, they also entail differential well-being and expectations, as implied by terms such as "unskilled laborer," "craftsman," and "professional." In short, the differentiation entailed by a vocationalized education system is the preparatory phase of the differentiation that is entailed by the class system in general.

In the university, in contrast to the lower forms of schooling, the specialized form of education is primarily the training into a profession, and the tension between this and general education can easily be understood as a conflict between two different systems of knowledge. The more esoteric and specialized the knowledge system, and the more exclusive the entrance requirement into that system, the higher is its professional status, and the greater is its exchange value. Moreover, "a profession" has come to imply a depoliticized set of expert practices, practices that are to be judged only by the rules that the profession establishes for assessing competency and officially known only to other professionals in the same field. Of course, professions differ in their ability to disengage their practice from political debate, and we have seen that the successful ones, such as medicine, then become a model for those that are less successful, such as teaching or social work.

In contrast to the knowledge system of the professions, which is a system based on differentiation and exclusion, general education, as education for participation in a public, ideally implies a community of equals, active partners engaged in a process of self-formulation. Its ideal is a process free from domination and manipulation where arguments are heard and judged on their own merits and where all have equal access to the debate.

Granted this is an idealized concept of the goal of general education, aspects of it can be found in many of the established statements on the subject. The 1945 Harvard report, for example, while not emphasizing the self-formative role of the public, did see the idea of general education as that of creating a common purpose, a way to "balance . . . the forces which divide group from *group*."[1] A more adequate expression is found in the writings of the Italian Marxist Antonio Gramsci. In commenting on the existence of special and separate schools for ruler and ruled, he wrote:

If one wishes to break this pattern one needs, instead of multiplying and grading different types of professional schools, to create a single type of formative school . . . which would take the child up to the threshold of his choice of job, forming him during this time as a person capable of thinking, studying, and ruling – or controlling those who rule.[2]

For Gramsci, the introduction into this self-formative process provided an essential criterion for determining what subjects should be included in the curriculum and for determining how they should be taught. In arguing for the importance of Latin, for example, he observed that with this subject "an historical process is analyzed from its source until its death in time. . . . Not only the grammar of a certain epoch . . . or its vocabulary are studied but also, for comparison, the grammar and the vocabulary of each individual author and the meaning of each term in each stylistic 'period.' Thus the child discovers that . . . the same nexus of sounds does not have the same meaning for different periods and for different authors."[3]

Quite naturally this twofold function of education presents certain stresses and strains within any system that has a reasonably advanced and uncontrolled division of labor. The more highly developed this division is and the larger the variation in rewards and life chances between those at the bottom and those at the top, the greater is the pressure exerted on the general function of education by the exchange function. It is probably in recognition of this tendency that John Stuart Mill, in his inaugural address before the University of St. Andrews, could write:

The proper function of a University in national education is tolerably well understood. At least there is a tolerably general agreement about what a University is not. It is not a place of professional education. Universities are not intended to teach the knowledge required to fit men for some special mode of gaining their livelihood. Their object is not to make skillful lawyers, or physicians, or engineers, but capable and cultivated human beings.[4]

What Mill was likely concerned about was the neglect by professional training of the ends and value of human activity and its tendency to view a career in exclusively technical terms. Although Mill's discussion of the role of university education was still governed by Locke's earlier vision of the English gentleman, a man of culture whose personal taste and judgment were thought to be wedded inextricably to the common good, he nevertheless saw university education as preparation for life as a member of the public. He believed that professional training, if begun prematurely, could do nothing but undermine this role. Gramsci, in discussing the proliferation of vocational schools, goes beyond Mill's vision and, although not disavowing professional training, extends the rationale for general education beyond the limits of a privileged few. He writes:

The labourer can become a skilled worker, for instance, the peasant a surveyor or petty agronomist. But democracy, by definition, cannot mean merely that an unskilled worker can become skilled. It must mean that every "citizen" can "govern" and that society places him, even if only abstractly, in a general condition to achieve this.[5]

The words of Mill and Gramsci remind us that when we consider the question of influences on general education in contemporary society we must count as one of those influences the growth of professional training, especially in its de-politicized form. The conflict between the two forms of education is captured in a conversation reported by Bledstein between Andrew White, the president of Cornell University in the late 1800s, and Leo Tolstoy:

White recounted his advice to a Russian student of engineering at Cornell. The student should "bear in mind" . . . that building railways and telegraphs was the means to a better civilization and to the "enlightenment of the empire." Never, under any conditions, should the student divert his energies and "conspire against the government." Tolstoy and White stood face to face. Tolstoy said "the advice was good," but that he would have also advised the young man to speak out his ideas, whatever they might be. He said that only in this way could any advance ever be made; that one main obstacle in human progress is the suppression of the real thoughts of men.[6]

Although many people have attempted to find a way to amalgamate professional with general education, when the conflict becomes one of a depoliticized professional program, as opposed to a program that functions to prepare students for a political role as members of a public, there can be no amalgamation. Either professional and technical education on all levels must begin to examine questions of human norms and values as related to its practice and hence recognize its political nature, or else that which goes under the name of general education must become depoliticized, that is, it must overlook the political features of its own practice.

Mill in his inaugural address could simply take it for granted that professional education had no place in a university, and hence the question of the mutual influence of the two forms of education need not be raised. Today, not only has professional education found a place within the university, but in its depoliticized form it continues to exert an ever-stronger influence over those components that are normally associated with general education. Thus, for example, *Newsweek,* in an issue on renewed support of language teaching, could cite, as a primary reason for such support, the fact that multinational corporations cannot find enough college graduates who are qualified for the positions that are opening abroad.[7] Whatever one might think about the activities of multinational corporations, this reason is a far cry from that of Gramsci or even of the 1945 Harvard report on general education. In other words, it minimizes the interpretive function of languages while emphasizing the exchange function. Yet with regard to the Harvard report, it is useful to remember that only a dozen years after it was submitted to then Harvard University President James Conant, Conant himself was praising the importance of language study and science, and other areas associated with general education, for national defense and the space race. Conant's vision was one that argued for the importance of a dual education system: One that would prepare the academically talented for high-level jobs in industry, government, and the professions, and another that, among other things, would defuse the "social dynamite" that he found in the slums by providing each high school graduate with an employable skill. Thus Conant too subordinated the interpretive and critical functions of education to the exchange function.

These examples suggest that what counts as general education is not to be derived simply by adding up courses in different areas in order to see whether they have been increased or diminished. Equally important is the code through which such subjects are presented and the frame through which they are received. In this respect, there is strong initial reason to believe that much of what goes on under the name of general education is perceived, within an institutional framework, not as having value in providing interpretive and normative skills leading to participation in an enlightened public, but rather as skills that will lead to successful market participation. For Gramsci, vocational education was perceived as a way to negate the possible development of working-class intellectuals. However, a vocationalized education system, operating under a technical knowledge code that subsumes under it general education, likely can serve this function even better. Thus, the major question for contemporary education is how the interpretive and value functions of general education can be reestablished at a time when the dominant code provides legitimacy to the idea that public participation is reducible to market participation.

Conclusion

To begin to address this issue it is important to notice that the tendency to subordinate public participation to market participation is not totally accidental, but is given credence by much of contemporary political science. Thus, for example, the influential report of the Trilateral Commission views many of the recent problems of Western Europe, Japan, and the United States as resulting from an excess of democratic participation, in what Samuel Huntington calls the democratic distemper of the 1960s and the perceived decline in governmental authority.[8] The report is itself consistent with some contemporary American theories of democracy that, ironically, suggest that political inactivity and alienation on the part of a sizable proportion of citizens is essential for the continuation of the democratic process as we know it. Usually, of course, the alienation that is seen as desirable is to be found among the poor and lower-class groups in the society.[9] Thus there is advocated in much of the recent literature in political science very definite limits to the idea of public participation.

Related to this is a tendency to build into the very language used to describe educational practices a vocabulary that links schooling directly and naturally to market considerations. Without great effort we speak of a population in a Third World country as being "overeducated," which means that more people have been trained for middle- or high-level jobs than there are positions to be filled. The concept is now being applied more frequently to the situation in the United States and Western Europe as well. Of course, only through the understandings provided by general education can the normative implications of this concept be revealed and evaluated.

Perhaps an even more subtle political and ideological influence is to be found in the accepted notion that political democracy can function adequately in isolation from economic democracy. Thus there is perceived to be little role for a public in everyday life, and where the public does take charge, as on election day, it is as single citizens cast in a monolog with a voting machine. In addition, the rewards for technical talent within modern society are high; and because the possession of one form of knowledge is often the condition for receiving the benefits of another, the penalties for not possessing technological skills can be severe.

These external influences provide a strong internal pressure upon universities and other parts of the educational system to function to maximize the growth of technological knowledge, and hence to develop experts who, at least in theory, are able to anticipate and respond to any and all contingencies. Within this kind of system, general education has its place, but it is clearly a subordinate one. Most professional schools have little room in their own curriculum for the kind of debates about purpose that would characterize a politically aware public, and the socialization process within such schools tends to narrow normative issues to a few well-established and safe principles of professional ethics. For the student training for a professional degree, this often means that the general education curriculum will be seen as just one more hurdle that needs to be overcome before the "true business" of education can get under way. For the curriculum designer who is intent on mitigating some of the potential divisiveness of vocational education, the general education curriculum is seen as a mechanism to impose unity by reinstating in each generation the fundamental principles of Western civilization, with of course a nod now and then toward whatever other culture or group is demanding a hearing. Here general education becomes a way to gloss over significant social and cultural differences and serves as a legitimizing mechanism bypassing the interpretive and normative issues it should be designed to address.

This is not surprising given the absence of many of the conditions that would allow general education to be meaningful as preparation for participation in the life of an active public. Three of these conditions seem, in conclusion, worth mentioning.

safe education brings up things that are acceptable knowledge code.

First is a political condition that the distribution of power in a society be such as to allow no group to be able to impose its will independently of an understanding of the perspective of other groups.

Second is an economic condition that, while consistent with minimal requirements for individual incentive, would maintain a distribution of wealth that is consistent with the development of unmanipulated judgment.

Third is a knowledge condition that provides that different forms of expert knowledge and scientific understanding be developed and exercised in the context of interpretive and normative understanding. As Gramsci put it:

> The last phase . . . must be conceived and structured as a decisive phase, whose aim is to create the fundamental values of "humanism," the intellectual self-discipline and the moral independence which are necessary for specialization – whether it be of a scientific character . . . or of an immediate practical productive character.[10]

Gramsci was here speaking of the common school rather than the university, but given the American setting, the advice would seem reasonable for both.

 These conditions provide a general outline of the features required for the study of education. To understand education it is not sufficient to know the existing level of material conditions or to develop a catalog of the existing skills. Education also requires that such understanding be articulated in terms of a concern for the development of an unmanipulated judgment and for the kind of dialog that makes the self-formation of a public possible.

Notes

1. Introduction: Educational studies and the disciplines of educational understanding

1 See, for example, Paul Hirst, "Liberal Education and the Nature of Knowledge," in Reginald Archambault (ed.), *Philosophical Analysis and Education*, Highlands, N.J.: Humanities Press, 1972, pp. 113–38.

2 Samuel Bowles and Herbert Gintis, *Schooling in Capitalist America: Educational Reform and the Contradictions of Economic Life,* New York: Basic Books, 1976.

2. The empirical tradition and its limits for understanding education

1 The first of these issues is addressed in a volume by Eric Bredo and Walter Feinberg (eds.), *Prediction, Interpretation, and Criticism: Knowledge and Values in Social and Educational Research,* Philadelphia: Temple University Press, 1982.

2 For an example of this approach and a more elaborate treatment of conceptual analysis see P. H. Hirst and R. S. Peters, *The Logic of Education,* London: Routledge & Kegan Paul, 1970, chapter 1. See also Chapter 6 of this book for an analysis of this tradition.

3 For an interesting statement on the same tendency of educational sociology to take its perspective from the problem of the schools see the introduction to Michael F. D. Young (ed.), *Knowledge and Control: New Directions for the Sociology of Education,* London: Collier-Macmillan, 1971.

4 See Bredo and Feinberg, *Prediction, Interpretation, and Criticism.*

5 For an important challenge to this belief, see Jurgen Habermas, *Knowledge and Human Interest,* Boston: Beacon Press, 1971.

6 See Bredo and Feinberg, *Prediction, Interpretation, and Criticism,* and also Jon Hellesnes, "Education and the Concept of Critique," *Continuum,* Vol. 8, No. 1, Spring–Summer 1970, pp. 40–51.

7 See, e.g., Imre Lakatos and Alan Musgrave, *Criticism and the Growth of Knowledge,* Cambridge University Press, 1970.

8 I am indebted to Helen Freeman for discussions regarding the distinction between the practical and theoretical frame.

9 Acknowledgments are extended to Ned Block, Eric Bredo, Landon E. Beyer, Fred Coombs, Rupert Evans, Ernest Kahane, Brian Mimmack, Bruce Stewart, and the mem-

bers of the University of Illinois Department of Educational Policy Studies who read and commented upon earlier drafts of this section.

10   See Walter Lippmann, "A Future for the Tests, IV" *New Republic,* Vol. 33, November 29, 1922, p. 10. For further discussion of Lippmann's contribution to this debate, see Walter Feinberg, *Reason and Rhetoric: The Intellectual Foundations of Liberal Educational Policy,* New York: Wiley, 1975, pp. 77–8.

11   For one of the most comprehensive and penetrating criticisms of this kind, see N. J. Block and Gerald Dworkin, "IQ Heritability and Inequality," parts 1 and 2, *Philosophy and Public Affairs,* Vol. 3, No. 4, Summer 1974, pp. 331–409 and Vol. 4, No. 1, Fall 1974, pp. 40–99.

12   Given the racial overtones that have often accompanied debates about IQ tests, this oversight is perfectly understandable. In the context of the contemporary debate, to focus on the extent to which a certain treatment can be derived from a certain IQ score could too easily be read as implicit agreement with the more obviously problematic claim that different groups possess different levels of intelligence and that a score on an IQ test is a measure of that difference. This point echos that of Noam Chomsky, "Language Development, Intelligence, and Social Organization," in Walter Feinberg (ed.), *Equality and Social Policy,* Urbana: University of Illinois Press, 1978, pp. 163–188. Another word of caution is necessary here. In order to highlight the normative issue we have bracketed out of consideration many of the problematic scientific claims of the testers, claims that have been thoroughly criticized by others. These criticisms should, however, be kept in mind. Moreover, in considering the normative issue, we begin by revealing an ambiguity in the claim that IQ tests measure intelligence and by criticizing one interpretation of that claim. We have done this in order to show how, through a linguistic oversight, the testers have avoided the crucial normative questions, not as an endorsement of the other interpretation.

13   Arthur R. Jensen, "How Much Can We Boost IQ and Scholastic Achievement," *Harvard Educational Review,* Vol. 39, No. 1, Winter 1969, pp. 110–11.

14   Ibid., p. 111.

15   Ibid.

16   Ibid.

17   Ibid.

18   Ibid.

19   Ibid., p. 112.

20   Ibid., p. 113.

21   Ibid., p. 114.

22   Ibid., p. 115.

23   Ibid., pp. 115–16. It should be mentioned that in this passage, Jensen makes two very questionable claims. The first is that schools developed primarily with a middle-class orientation, and not, as Michale Katz and others suggest, as instruments to control the working class. The second questionable claim is that schools emphasize primarily cognitive skills and neglect associative ones. It is at least as likely that the kinds of skills that schools emphasize is a function of the social class of the children in those schools. See Michael Katz, *The Irony of Early School Reform,* Cambridge: Harvard University Press, 1968. For an analysis of Katz's book see Chapter 7 of this book.

24   Jensen, "IQ and Scholastic Achievement," p. 116.

25   Ibid., pp. 116–17.

26   See report of the work of Sandra Scarr as reported in *Chronicle of Higher Education,* September 12, 1977, p. 5.

27   Indeed, J. P. White has argued somewhat convincingly that except in the most extreme cases, there is no evidence to support the claim that IQ exams measure some upper limit for learning and, more interestingly, that in fact no evidence could conceivably be given. See J. P. White, "Intelligence and the Logic of the Nature–Nurture Issue," *Proceedings of the Philosophy of Education Society of Great Britain,* Vol. 8, No. 1, January 1974, p. 45.

28   This is suggested, for example, by Jensen when he speaks of an IQ score as measuring an individual's *capacity* for abstract reasoning, where capacity implies some kind of intellectual limiting factor. And it is again implied by him in discussing De Lemo's study of Australian aborigines' performance on a variety of Piagetian conservation tasks, linking their lower performance to genetic factors analogous to those that he believes are tapped by IQ tests. (See Arthur R. Jensen, "Reducing the Heredity-Environment Uncertainty: A Reply," *Harvard Educational Review,* Vol. 39, No. 3, Summer 1969, pp. 450–51.) The idea of a measurable limit is suggested even more strongly by C. Burt when he writes: "The degree of intelligence with which any particular child is endowed is one of the most important factors determining his general efficiency all throughout life. In particular it sets an upper limit to what he can successfully perform, especially in the educational, vocational and intellectual fields." Quoted in White, "The Nature–Nurture Issue."

29   Of course, it must be recognized that either external factors, stemming from environments other than the school, or internal ones, stemming perhaps from the natural way in which the mind orders its world, might intervene such that children who are taught in an associative manner in school actually pick up some important conceptual skills along the way. This is an empirical issue. Suffice it to say here, however, that if conceptual skills do develop in this manner in low-IQ youngsters, then Jensen's dichotomy between Level I and Level II skills is simply wrong right off the bat. However, given these radically different styles of teaching, it is likely that certain conceptual skills would simply not be available for the child who is to be taught associatively. For some evidence that IQ tests indicates speed of learning rather than a conceptual limit the work of Benjamin Bloom is suggestive.

For a more detailed account of conceptual development see A. R. Luria, *Cognitive Development: Its Cultural and Social Foundations,* Cambridge: Harvard University Press, 1976.

30   It needs to be mentioned here that there are two questions that should be kept separate from one another. The first question is whether or not there are some conceptual skills that certain individuals, try as they may, simply will not be able to master. The second question is, if there are such absolute limits, whether a score on an IQ examination can in fact be thought to identify them and then tell us something about the level of conceptual development beyond which any individual cannot be expected to reach. It is the second of these two questions that this section is intended to address.

In my own research I could find nothing in the test manuals that correlated a given score with a certain level of conceptual development. Thus, although this claim is often implied by testers, it does not appear to have been sufficiently systematized to allow for rigorous examination.

31   This approach was first suggested in a seminar paper by Wells Eddleman.

32   Jensen, "IQ and Scholastic Achievement," pp. 110–11.

33   Ibid., p. 111.

34   Of course, this criterion, as stated, is probably too hard, allowing for the elimination of only forward-direction digit span; the memory for sentences (Stanford–Binet), where the subject is expected to repeat verbatim a sentence that the examiner reads to him; and perhaps a few other items. The criterion can be softened somewhat to read that there should be nothing in the response that the child has not at some time received both in form and in content from some other source. Given this expanded criterion, we can then eliminate such items as naming the days of the week (S-B VIII), picture vocabulary (S-B II), identifying objects by name (S-B II), and other similar items, most of which are to be found in the Stanford–Binet.

In all, thirteen subtests were eliminated from the Stanford–Binet L-M series from age 2 to superior adult III for testing rote learning. From the Wechsler one item, the digit span, was eliminated and no items were eliminated for calling for rote responses from either the Raven Progressive Matrices test or the Cattell Culture Fair Test.

35   When it came to eliminating items that seemed to duplicate those that either in form or content were to be found on achievement tests, there was no formal criterion that could be applied. The general guide was whether it was thought that an intelligent layperson would be likely to identify correctly which items belonged to IQ tests and which ones belonged to achievement tests. While there was obviously a subjective element in this procedure, there was little question that it could be formalized. In addition, if there was reason to believe that an item was likely to be taught in school, it was eliminated from consideration.

The following are all examples of the kinds of items that we eliminated from consideration on one test: "Who discovered America?" "What does the stomach do?" "In what direction does the sun set?" "Why does oil float on water?" "What is the main material used to make glass?" "What causes iron to rust?" "How far is it from New York to Los Angeles?" The above examples are from David Wechsler, *Manual for the Wechsler Intelligence Scale for Children – Revised,* Information Test, New York: Psychological Corporation, 1974, pp. 67–8.

Similar kinds of questions on an achievement test were:

Columbus sailed on his first trip across the Atlantic Ocean because of the idea that:

(a) people should worship as they choose

(b) a democracy is the best government

(c) the earth is round

(d) engines can move ships

We see the moon because of light from the:

(a) sun

(b) North star

(c) planets

(d) big dipper

Which of these is not burned for fuel?

(a) wood

(b) paper
(c) stone
(d) coal

Stanford Achievement Test, Intermediate I, Complete Battery, Form Y, New York: Harcourt, Brace and World, 1965, pp. 24, 28)

Other items seem similar not only in type, but in content as well. In the following illustration each item in the two-pair series comes from a different type of test, one from an achievement test and one from an IQ test:

(A) 1. What is the thing to do when you cut your finger?
(Wechsler, *Manual* Part 9, Comprehension, p. 97)

   2. Which one of these is wrong to do if your clothes catch on fire?

    (a) roll on the floor
    (b) put water on the clothes
    (c) wrap a blanket around yourself
    (d) run as fast as you can

    (*Stanford Achievement Test,* Intermediate I, Form Y, Science, p. 28)

(B) 1. What are you supposed to do if you find someone's wallet or pocketbook in a store?
(Wechsler, *Manual,* Part 9, Comprehension, p. 97)

   2. If you buy something, and as you are leaving the store, you discover the clerk has given you a nickel too much in change –

    (a) it is best for you to return the money
    (b) you should keep it so the clerk won't be fired
    (c) you may keep it because the store expects to lose some money this way
    (d) you may keep it because it is only a small amount

There were a large number of items like the above that were eliminated from the standard IQ tests that we looked at because they were indistinguishable from those used on achievement tests.

Using our somewhat intuitive guidelines for determining the overlap between IQ tests and achievement tests, we eliminated from consideration eight subtests from the Stanford–Binet IQ test and four subtests from the Wechsler. There were:

Rote Tests	*Duplication*
I. Stanford–Binet	
Repeating *n* Digits	Comprehension
Memory for Sentences	Definitions
Naming Objects from Memory	Vocabulary
Memory for Designs	Abstract Words
Repeating *n* Digits Reversed	Memory for Stories
Memory for Stories	Minkus Completion
Copying a Bead Chain from Memory	Finding Reasons

Rote Tests	Duplication
Naming the Days of the Week	Arithmetical Reasoning
Picture Vocabulary	
Identifying Objects by Name	
Naming Objects	
Picture Memories	
Word Naming	

II. Wechsler

Digit Span	Information
	Arithmetic
	Vocabulary
	Comprehension

III. Raven Progressive matrices

None	None

IV. Cattell's Culture-Fair

None	None

Although a number of test items from Stanford–Binet and Wechsler were eliminated because they either tested rote learning or because they were duplicated on achievement tests, no items from the two "culture-fair" tests were eliminated. One point should be made before reporting on the conceptual skills that seem to be called for by the remaining items on IQ exams. To eliminate from consideration those items that are duplicated on achievement tests does not mean that, everything else being equal, some index of achievement could not also be used as an indicator of intelligence. Indeed, if one held constant such factors as motivation, health, the quality of schooling, family background, and so forth, one would likely expect that the higher a person's achievement, the greater, in some sense, might be his or her intellectual capacity. However, given simply a score on an achievement test, there is little that we can presume about the cause of such a score. It might be a function of the intellectual capacity of a given child, but it could just as easily be a function of motivational or health factors, or of the quality of the school itself. To say, however, that everything else being equal achievement might well be taken as an indication of intelligence is simply to say that intelligence never operates in the abstract – that it always is expressed through something else, and is likely best gauged by the quality of a person's activity over a range of different kinds of situations, including performance in real-life situations.

Some additional remarks are in order here. First, both the tests and the test manuals often fail to provide any clue as to the processes that the authors believe are being called for by a particular item. Therefore, in many instances it was not possible to check the analysis given here against the author's intent. By and large, however, this problem is a minor one since the question of what an item tests calls for an analysis of the item itself, not for an analysis of the author's intent in writing the item.

Indeed, in some cases where the author does state the particular process that an item is supposed to test, the statement itself appears to be misleading and subject to challenge. For example, on the Stanford–Binet test for 2-year-olds, there is an item where the examiner builds a four-block tower and then says to the child: "You make one like this, make yours (pointing) right here." The directions for scoring then reads as follows:

> The child must build a tower of four or more blocks in imitation of E's tower and in response to E's request, not spontaneously either before or later. It is purposive behavior in which we are interested rather than spontaneous play activities involving manipulation of material. (*Stanford–Binet Intelligence Scale Manual for The Third Revision*, Form L-M, Lewis M. Terman and Mauda Merril, eds., Boston: Houghton Mifflin, 1960, p. 68)

One could easily take exception to the radical distinction that is made here between spontaneous behavior on the one hand and purposive behavior on the other. Imagine as an example the child who does not respond to the direction until after the examiner has moved on to the next item, and only then builds a rather elaborate structure with the blocks at hand. Are we to assume that this behavior is not purposeful? Or would it be more appropriate to assume that purposeful behavior is only a secondary criterion for grading this item? More significant would be the willingness to follow directions and the ability (as mentioned in passing) to imitate the activity of the tester.

Second, even though the following analysis proceeds by giving the tests the benefit of the doubt by assuming that there is some specific conceptual process that is being tested even when an item is very obviously deficient, this procedure should in no way be taken as an endorsement either of the items themselves or of the view of intelligence that seem to be suggested by them. Rather, the procedure should be viewed as simply a way to demystify the tests and to help reveal the idea of intelligence that they embody. Thirdly, even though the aim of this analysis is to understand some of the conceptual skills that are being called for, a number of the items are deficient in very obvious ways, and it would be irresponsible not to point out at least some of the deficiencies. However, in selecting items for analysis we did so not because of the deficiencies that they entail, but rather because the conceptual skills they call for seem to be reasonably available to analysis.

36 In demonstrating such an ability, different types of characteristics appear to be acceptable, such as those dealing with function – as, for example, different modes of mobility structure (birds have wings) and shape. And only those characteristics that apply to all or most of the members of the species seem to be acceptable.

37 Although some of the items clearly seem to require the kinds of specialized knowledge that a youngster would learn in school (e.g., "In what way are the numbers 49 and 121 similar?" where a maximum score involves recognizing that they are both perfect squares), other less complicated items (e.g., In what way are beer and wine similar?) would seem to require only that the youngster have picked up the kind of "context-independent" classification scheme that the test item calls for.

The similarities test appears on the Stanford–Binet at age 11. However, like the Stanford–Binet difference test, no distinction is made between "fundamental" and "superficial" similarities.

38 Terman and Merrill, *Stanford–Binet Intelligence Scale Manual*, Form L-M, Average Adult.

39 Ibid.

40 Ibid., Year XIV.

41 Ibid.

42 Luria, *Cognitive Development*.

43 This is from Lewis E. Terman and Maud A. Merrill, *Stanford–Binet Intelligence Scale,* 1972 Norms Edition: *Manual for The Third Revision,* Form L-M, © 1973. Published by The Riverside Publishing Company.

44 If we were to judge different tests simply on the basis of the ingenuity and comprehensiveness of the questions, the Wechsler test would be judged superior to the Stanford-Binet. The test systematically attempts to cover a reasonably wide range of behaviors, which it then divides into two groups, verbal and performance, and many of the items appear to be thoughtfully constructed. This does not, however, mean that there are not some very obvious problems with the test, such as the question that asks why we need policemen and allows as a correct answer "in order to protect property" but disallows "because of drugs," or "because people fight around here." *Wechsler Manual,* pp. 177–89).

45 David Wechsler, *The Measurement and Appraisal of Adult Intelligence,* Baltimore: Williams & Wilkins, 1958, p. 78.

46 Ibid., p. 186.

47 Actual items from this test could not be reproduced.

48 For spotting many of the problems in these items I am indebted to my daughters, Deborah and Jill.

49 Wechsler, *Manual,* p. 76.

50 This sample is reproduced courtesy of The Psychological Corporation from the *Wechsler Intelligence Scale for Children—Revised.* Copyright, 1974 by The Psychological Corporation. All rights reserved.

51 Jensen, for example, dismisses the gains that occurred in IQ scores in some compensatory programs by noting that such gains have not been demonstrated in what he calls "relatively non-cultural or non-verbal tests like Cattell's Culture Fair test and Raven's Progressive Matrices" (Jensen, "IQ and Scholastic Achievement," p. 101).

52 It should be mentioned that one of the tests, the Raven, describes itself as "a test of observation and clear thinking" (J. C. Raven, *Guide to Using the Colored Progressive Matrices Sets A, Ab, C, Revised Order, 1956,* London: H. K. Lewis, 1960, p. 1). In contrast to Jensen, the testmaker cautions that "By *itself,* it is not a test of 'general intelligence,' and it is always a mistake to describe it as such" (ibid., p. 1). After raising this caution, however, the test manual goes on to say that as a test of general intelligence, "it should be used in conjunction with a vocabulary test" (ibid., p. 1). Given the cultural problems surrounding vocabulary tests, we find this claim difficult to accept. (It is unfortunate that items from the Raven were not allowed to be reproduced.) In contrast to the Raven, the Cattell test is labeled as a test of *g.*

53 This also renders doubtful the Raven's weaker claim that it is "a test of observation and clear thinking."

54 For challenges to this assumption, see, e.g., Rosalie A. Cohen, "Conceptual Styles, Culture Conflict, and Non-verbal Tests of Intelligence," *American Anthropologist,* Vol. 71, 1969, pp. 828–56. Also see R. L. Gregory and E. H. Gumbrich, *Illusion in Nature* *and Art*, London: Duckworth, 1973, and John W. Berry, "Temne and Eskimo Perceptual Skills," *International Journal of Psychology*, Vol. 1, No. 3, 1966, pp. 207–30.

55 This is from Raven, item B8.

56 This and the following figures are taken from the *Culture Fair Intelligence Test*, Scale 2, Forms A and B, copyright, 1949, 1960 by the Institute for Personality and Ability Testing, Inc., Champaign, Illinois. Reproduced by permission.

57 Here presumably 2 and 5 are linked because in each the shapes are the same and colored black. Boxes 1 and 3 are linked because in each the shapes are different and not colored. Box 4 is odd man out because the figures are different and the area is colored black.

58 In a survey that was done of the literature on teaching conceptual skills to children who had scored low on IQ tests, a number of programs were found that seem to have successfully taught many of the skills that were identified here as required by the IQ tests. Most of these studies were not *designed* specifically to measure the development of the skills that we extrapolated from the tests, and hence any conclusions from these studies must remain tentative. (I am especially indebted to Linda Houghton for the survey of this literature.) Therefore, it would be uninformative to dwell on these studies now. What is more instructive is simply to note the way in which a prior commitment to the idea of an IQ test as a true measure of fixed intelligence can lead one away from issues of this kind. Jensen admits rises in IQ scores have taken place. However, he dismisses the significance of programs that have produced them on the grounds that they have not been duplicated on any large-scale basis. Yet if the increase in IQ scores could be taken to indicate an improvement in conceptual ability, even though the program be small, then it would seem that the appropriate thing to do would be not to argue for more associative methods of teaching, but rather to examine why such gains have not been duplicated in any program instituted on a large scale. The research program of the tester, committed as it is to the idea of an intelligence that is largely fixed, precludes such a question.

3. Values and empirical research

1 As quoted in J. P. White, "The Nature–Nurture Issue," *Proceedings of the Philosophy of Education Society of Great Britain*, Vol. 8, No. 1, January 1974.

2 Note that Butcher reports that "Eysenck . . . has just published an important article in which he draws attention to a finding by Furneaux. This is to the effect that *speed* in attaining the correct answer is the main individual difference in measured intelligence," a difference that, if the test items do vary in conceptual requirements, would seem to speak more in favor of speed rather than conceptual limits as the overriding factor. See H. J. Butcher, *Human Intelligence: Its Nature and Assessment*, London: Methuen, 1968, p. 35. Eysenck has been one of the staunch defenders of Jensen's research program and fails to consider the potential implications that this observation could have for educational selection and training. See H. J. Eysenck, *The IQ Argument: Race, Intelligence, and Education*, New York: Library Press, 1971.

3 David Wechsler, *Manual for the Wechsler Intelligence Test for Children – Revised*, New York: Psychological Corporation, 1974, pp. 175–88.

4 See John T. Chandler and John Plakos "Spanish Speaking Pupils Classified as Educable Mentally Retarded,'' Stanford, Calif.: Mexican American Education Research Project, Division of Instruction, n.d., p. 1.

5 The extent to which testers have been unwilling to question their own framework is illustrated by one of the earlier and most peculiar publications in the testing literature, Catharine Morris Cox's *Genetic Studies of Genius,* Stanford, Calif.: Stanford University Press, 1926, in which she estimates the IQ scores of several historical figures. The scores range all the way from a low of between 100 and 110, which is found among such figures as Copernicus and Michael Faraday, to John Stuart Mill's high, estimated between 190 to 200. Cromwell, Haydn, and Bach fell between 110 and 130. If the study were in fact accurate, then the only reasonable conclusion would seem to be that IQ tests measure nothing of any significance, but the author seemed unable to draw such a conclusion. Rather than recognizing that this study is a significant commentary on the tests, the author thought it was in fact a commentary on historical genius.

6 See Richard H. Weller, *Humanistic Education: Visions and Realities,* Berkeley, Calif.: McCuchan, 1977, p. 279, for an interesting observation about the use of categories such as ''retarded'' and ''learning disabilities'' to classify children of different races.

7 Antony Flew, *Sociology, Equality, and Education: Philosophical Essays in Defense of a Variety of Differences,* New York: Harper & Row, 1976, p. 68.

8 Eysenck, *The IQ Argument,* p. 138.

9 Ibid.

10 Ibid., pp. 138–39.

11 Arthur Jensen, *Educational Differences,* London: Methuen, 1973, p. 405.

12 It is instructive that Jensen does not argue for a restrictive interpretation of Heber's study.

13 I am framing the issue in the terms used by researchers like Jensen even though it is important to note that genetic and environmental factors cannot be treated quite in this way. Although the concept of the range of reaction illustrates that the product of specific environmental factors and specific genetic ones is a function of the particular mix (and not necessarily a linear one), the technical issues involved here are not necessary to treat in order to analyze the entitlement question.

14 See David Wechsler, *The Measurement and Appraisal of Adult Intelligence,* 4th ed., Baltimore: Williams & Wilkins, 1958, p. 63.

15 Ibid., p. 14.

16 See Herbert Gintis and Samuel Bowles, ''The Contradictions of Liberal Educational Reform,'' in W. Feinberg and H. Rosemont, Jr., *Work, Technology, and Education: Dissenting Essays in the Intellectual Foundations of American Education,* Urbana: University of Illinois Press, 1975, pp. 92–141.

17 Jensen, *Educational Differences,* pp. 223–24.

18 Ibid., p. 225.

19 Ibid., pp. 228–29.

20 Ibid., p. 235.

21 Ibid., p. 236.

22 Ibid., pp. 252–53.

23 Ibid., p. 260.

24 Pierre Bourdieu and Jean-Claude Passeron, *Reproduction in Education, Society, and*

Culture, London: Sage, 1977, p. 207. Bourdieu and Passeron are making an important point about the nature of social science research and the tendency among researchers to isolate attitudes and aspirations from the class culture and objective conditions that produce them. Indeed, their analysis could be used as a critique of Jensen since one of the most important of these conditions is perceived to be the different way in which the very use of examinations themselves serve as an instrument of class domination whereby social classes differentially select or exclude themselves from certain forms of education, according to their relationship to the dominant culture. Thus it is not the failure rate per se that is the most important aspect of the admissions test, but rather the extent to which different classes perceive their chances of passing and choose thereby to compete or not.

25 The comparison may be mitigated by reading Bourdieu and Passeron's analysis as a critique of class society in general. However, there is little in the book other than suggestions of the need for compensatory programs, which would mandate such a reading or which ultimately would challenge the meritocratic visions that underlie Jensen's different evaluation of tests.

26 Jensen, *Educational Differences,* p. 267.

27 Ibid., p. 254.

28 Ibid.

29 Richard Herrnstein, "IQ," *Atlantic,* Vol. 228, No. 3, September 1971, p. 51.

30 Ibid., p. 64.

31 Jensen, *Educational Differences,* p. 254.

32 See Bourdieu and Passeron, *Reproduction in Education.*

33 See Michael A. Wallach, "Tests Tell Us Little about Talent," *American Scientist,* Vol. 64, No. 1, January–February 1976, pp. 57–63.

34 The same analysis that holds for medicine likely also holds for legal training as well. In many black ghetto areas, for example, the prime cause of death among young male adults is gunshot or knife wounds. In part this problem exists because in our bureaucratically organized structures there is often no immediate and mutually respected source for resolving conflicts in a neighborhood. This function has been lost to many communities. In today's society such a role would entail knowing a good deal about the nature of the larger legal structure, whether one were a lawyer or not; but if one were a lawyer, it would entail maintaining one's roots in a community and its conflicts. As things now stand, however, the socialization process for most professions, legal and otherwise, is one that brings individuals out of their roots in a community and enables them to "escape" it.

35 Jensen, *Educational Differences,* pp. 270–71.

4. Educational research and classroom knowledge: The case of behavioral theory

1 See Leon J. Kamin, *The Science and Politics of IQ,* New York: Wiley, 1974.

2 For a more detailed examination of the issues involved here see Eric Bredo and Walter Feinberg, *Prediction, Interpretation, and Criticism: Knowledge and Values in Social and Educational Research,* Philadelphia: Temple University Press, 1982.

3 Robert F. Mayer, *Preparing Objectives for Programmed Instruction,* San Francisco: Fearon, 1961. p. 11.

4 B. F. Skinner, *Science and Human Behavior,* New York: Free Press, 1965, p. 6.
5 Noam Chomsky, "Review of Skinner's *Verbal Behavior,*" *Language,* Vol. 35, No. 1, January–March 1959, p. 38.
6 Skinner, *Science,* p. 257–58.
7 Ibid., p. 257.
8 Skinner, "Behaviorism at Fifty," in T. W. Wann (ed.), *Behaviorism and Phenomenology,* Rice University Semicentennial Publications, Chicago: University of Chicago Press, 1964, p. 85
9 Norman Malcolm, "Behaviorism as a Philosophy," in T. W. Wann (ed.), *Behaviorism and Phenomenology,* pp. 150–51.
10 Skinner, *Science,* p. 6.
11 Malcolm, "Behaviorism," p. 153.
12 P. F. Strawson, "Review of Philosophical Investigations," *Mind,* Vol. 63, 1954, pp. 87–88.
13 Ibid., p. 88.
14 I am indebted to Stella and Willie Applebaum for this example.
15 I am indebted to Robert Revak's description of his teaching of science for this example.
16 Charles Taylor, "Interpretation and the Science of Man," *Review of Metaphysics,* Vol. 25, No. 1, Issue 9, September 1971, pp. 3–51.

5. Empirical research and the goals of the educational system

1 See Chapter 2.
2 Edward Banfield, *The Unheavenly City: The Nature and the Future of Our Urban Crisis,* Boston: Little, Brown, 1970.
3 Charles Silberman, *Crisis in the Classroom,* New York: Random House, 1970.
4 Lawrence Cremin, *The Transformation of the School,* New York: Vintage: 1961.
5 See Paul Willis, *Learning to Labour:* Farnborough, England: Saxon House, 1978, for a more detailed understanding of what appears to some as simple passivity.
6 For a more elaborate treatment of these remarks by W. T. Harris see my *Reason and Rhetoric: The Intellectual Foundations of Twentieth Century Liberal Educational Policy,* New York: Wiley, 1975, chapter 1.
7 For an example of the first kind of study see Melvin L. Kohn, *Class and Conformity: A Study in Values,* Homewood, Ill.: Dorsey Press, 1969. For an example of the second study see Walter Brandeis and Basil Bernstein, *Selection and Control: Teacher Ratings of Children in the Infant School,* London: Routledge and Kegan Paul, 1974. Some recent work by Paul Willis, *Learning to Labor, How Working Class Kids Get Working Class Jobs,* suggests that some working-class youngsters are less passive and more resistent to authority than the above literature suggests. To some extent this difference can be explained by methodological variations, and to some extent by the specific focus of each study, parents on the one hand and school-age youngsters on the other. However, a closer analysis of these variations is needed.
8 See Ray C. Rist, "Student Social Class and Teacher Expectations: The Self-Fulfilling Prophecy in Ghetto Education," *Harvard Educational Review,* Vol. 40, No. 3, August 1970, pp. 411–51.

9 See Harry Braverman, *Labor and Monopoly Capital,* New York: Monthly Review Press, 1974.

10 For a general discussion of the role that schools play in teaching functions like these, see Robert Dreeben, *On What Is Learned in School,* Reading, Mass.: Addison-Wesley, 1968.

11 Johan Galtung, Christian Beck, and Johannes Jaastad, *Educational Growth and Educational Disparity,* UNESCO Current Surveys and Research in Statistics, Paris-UNESCO, 1974.

12 Both of these items are found in the Wechsler exam. For a treatment that focuses on the early testers see Clarence Karier, "Testing for Order and Control in the Corporate Liberal State," in C. Karier, P. Violas, and J. Spring (eds.), *Roots of Crisis,* Skokie, Ill.: Rand McNally, 1974.

13 For a more detailed look at this difference see my *Reason and Rhetoric,* chapter 4.

14 See Braverman, *Labor and Monopoly Capital.*

6. The philosophical tradition and its limits for educational understanding

1 In this chapter the term "education" is used in different ways. When, for example, discussing traditional empirical research, it is often used to mean schooling. When discussing ordinary-language philosophy, it often carries a normative sense, and later, in discussions of domain, it is used to suggest social reproduction. Generally, the meaning should be clarified by the context, but occasionally this is not the case and in such instances I have tried to spell out the sense in which the term is being used.

2 See R. S. Peters (ed.), *The Concept of Education,* London: Routledge and Kegan Paul, pp. 1–3.

3 See J. L. Austin, *How to Do Things with Words,* Cambridge: Harvard University Press, 1975.

4 See John R. Searle, *Speech Acts: An Essay in the Philosophy of Language,* London: Cambridge University Press, 1978, pp. 3–4.

5 See Peter Goldstone and Donald Tunnel, "A Critique of the Command Theory of Authority," *Educational Theory,* Vol. 25, No. 2, Spring 1975, pp. 131–38.

6 Peters, *The Concept of Education,* p. 2.

7 Ibid., p. 4.

8 R. S. Peters, *Ethics and Education.* Glenview, Ill.: Scott, Foresman, 1967, p. 5.

9 Ibid., p. 3.

10 John Wilson, "Education and Indoctrination," in T. H. B. Hollins (ed.), *Aims in Education,* Manchester, England: Manchester University Press, 1967, p. 26. This section on indoctrination owes much to discussions with Henry Rosemont, Jr. A version of this section was presented at the Philosophy of Education Society Annual Meeting, Kansas City, 1975, and published in *Proceedings of The Philosophy of Education Society 1975 Meeting at Kansas City.*

11 Ibid., p. 28.

12 Ibid.

13 Ibid., p. 34.

14 Ibid., p. 35.

15   Richard M. Hare, "Adolescents into Adults," in Hollins (ed.), *Aims in Education,* pp. 47–69.

16   This criticism is essentially the same as that made by Henry Rosemont, Jr., in "On the Concept of Indoctrination," *Studies in Philosophy and Education,* Vol. 8, No. 3, Spring 1972, pp. 226–37. Rosemont's essay is especially valuable for the qualifications that it raises about the application of ordinary-language analysis.

17   Wilson, "Education," p. 41.

18   Hare, "Adolescents," p. 57.

19   Paul H. Hirst, "Liberal Education and the Nature of Knowledge," in Reginald Archambault (ed.), *Philosophical Analysis and Education,* Highlands, N.J.: Humanities Press, 1972, pp. 113–38.

20   Ibid., p. 126.

21   Ibid., p. 123.

22   Ibid., p. 124.

23   Ibid.

24   Ibid.

25   See Willard Quine, *From a Logical Point of View,* Cambridge: Mass.: Harvard University Press, 1953; see also John Dewey, *The Logic: The Theory of Inquiry,* New York: Holt, 1958, and Stephen Toulmin, *Human Understanding.* Princeton, N.J.: Princeton University Press, 1972.

26   See D. C. Phillips, "Perspectives on Structure of Knowledge and the Curriculum," in P. W. Musgrave (ed.), *Contemporary Studies in the Curriculum,* Sydney: Angus and Robertson, 1974, pp. 15–29.

27   Hirst, "Liberal Education," p. 125.

28   See Thomas Kuhn, *The Structure of Scientific Revolutions,* Chicago: University of Chicago Press, 1968; and Imre Lakatos, *Proofs and Refutations: The Logic of Mathematical Discovery,* ed. John Worrall and Elie Zahar, London: Cambridge University Press, 1976. Lakatos, for example, documents the ad hominum and spurious arguments that were used to establish a sophisticated and finally accepted mathematical theorem. He argues from this example that many new theories that are struggling for recognition must take on a protective belt that, though appearing irrational, serves to protect the theory from criticisms that could prematurely destroy it before its fruits were realized. Yet Lakatos's examples, confined as they are to the arguments among academics, are mild when one considers the external political factors that often determine the kinds of issues that will be taken as problematic and thought worthy of knowledgeable investigation, and that are often influenced heavily by the power relationships that exist in a society. Hirst, of course, might decry these features of knowledge, but a full examination would take them into account.

29   See Paul Hirst, "The Logic of the Curriculum," in *Journal of Curriculum Studies,* Vol. 1, No. 2, Fall 1969, pp. 142–58.

30   See Wilson, "Education," p. 35. It is possible that Wilson might address this criticism by noting that any rational person from another culture would have to take into account the necessary social functions that such interpretations served before his judgment could be definitive. If this were his response, there would be little argument, but also the distinction between education and indoctrination that he wants to make would have to be maintained on different grounds.

31 Ibid., p. 28.

32 For those who believe that "indoctrination" should be more restrictive than this, involving the presence of an indoctrinator, we make a distinction between indoctrination 1, which involves an indoctrinator, and indoctrination 2, which does not. We will not have occasion to use this distinction.

7. History and the interpretive understanding of education

1 Clarence J. Karier, *Shaping the Educational State, 1900 to the Present*, New York: Free Press, 1975, pp. xvi–xvii.

2 Ibid., p. xvii.

3 Arthur Schlesinger, Jr., "America: Experiment or Destiny?" *American Historical Review*, June 1977, p. 505, quoted in Donald Warren (ed.), *History, Education, and Public Policy*, Berkeley, Calif.: McCutchan, 1978, p. 3.

4 See, for example, Diane Ravitch, *The Revisionists Revised: A Critique of the Radical Attack on the Schools*, New York: Basic Books, 1978. See also the responses to this in *National Academy of Education Proceedings*, Cambridge: Harvard Printing Office, 1980.

5 Quoted in Michael B. Katz, *The Irony of Early School Reform: Educational Innovation in Mid-Nineteenth Century Massachusetts*, Cambridge: Harvard University Press, 1968, p. 288.

6 As quoted in Colin Greer, *The Great School Legend: A Revisionist Interpretation of American Public Education*, New York: Basic Books, 1972, p. 13.

7 Katz, *The Irony*, p. 112.

8 Greer, *The Great School Legend*, pp. 23–24.

9 There are some problems with Greer's evidence that should be mentioned. For example, the statistical evidence that Greer cites to show that these developments have not generally occurred is drawn from employment statistics from a few unnamed cities; see ibid., p. 27. Perhaps more significant is a study conducted by the National Opinion Research Center in Chicago and supported by the Ford Foundation. The report, authored by Reverend Andrew Greely, found Jews and Irish Catholics to be the most financially successful groups in metropolitan areas, and these two groups ranked similarly high in terms of the number of years of education. Polish and Italian groups ranked about the national average on these indexes. If correct, the findings are significant since so much of Greer's argument rests on his belief that, except for the Jews, these groups have done relatively poorly in American society.

10 Ibid., p. 107.

11 Ibid., p. 108.

12 Ibid., p. 85.

13 Lawrence A. Cremin, *The Transformation of the School: Progressivism in American Education, 1876–1957*, New York: Vintage, 1964, p. ix.

14 For a discussion of Dewey's views on this see my *Reason and Rhetoric: The Intellectual Foundations of Twentieth Century Liberal Educational Policy*, New York: Wiley, 1975, chapter 5.

15 Katz, *The Irony*, p. 213.

16 Ibid., p. 214.

17 Ibid.

18   Michael B. Katz, *Class, Bureaucracy, and Schools: The Illusion of Educational Change in America,* New York: Praeger, 1971, p. 135.
19   Ibid., p. 136.
20   Ibid., p. 139.
21   Greer, *The Great School Legend,* p. 154.
22   Quoted in Oscar Handlin, *Immigration,* Englewood Cliffs, N.J.: Prentice-Hall, 1965, p. 17.
23   See Greer, *The Great School Legend,* p. 13.
24   Ibid., p. 95.
25   Ibid., p. 85.
26   Ibid.
27   Ibid.
28   For a more traditional treatment of the conflict between the Protestant advocates of public education and the Catholic dissenters see R. Freeman Butts and Lawrence A. Cremin, *A History of American Education in American Culture,* New York: Holt, 1953.
29   Katz, *The Irony,* p. 78.
30   Ibid., p. 82.
31   Ibid., p. 89.
32   See ibid., pp. 89–90.
33   For a statement of what some of these limits are, see Feinberg, *Reason and Rhetoric,* chapters 3 and 4.
34   W. T. Harris, "Educational Needs of Urban Civilization," *Education,* Vol. 5, May 1885, p. 447.
35   Arthur E. Bestor, *Educational Wasteland,* Urbana: University of Illinois Press, p. 58.
36   See Clarence Karier, "Testing for Order and Control," in Clarence Karier, Paul Violas, and Joel Spring, *Roots of Crises,* Skokie, Ill.: Rand McNally, 1973, for these items. I am indebted to Lamont Weich for pointing out these items in the Stanford Binet test.
37   For a description of what some of these limits have been, see Feinberg, *Reason and Rhetoric,* chapter 4.
38   Katz, for example, comments about the fact that only the children of the well-to-do could use the high school to advance their social position, hence criticizing the schools at this point for failing to live up to the value of equal opportunity. Yet he also decries the fact that school reform was imposed upon the local community. (See *The Irony,* pp. 90–91, for the first of these points and see the treatment of Katz's ideas on imposition in the earlier parts of this chapter for an example of the latter.) Greer, leaning on Katz's analysis, points out that the early critics of school reform were rightly concerned that the increasing professionalization and centralization of schools "would interfere with community interests and lead toward too much state interference in the life of the individual" (Greer, *The Great School Legend,* p. 72). Thus, here Greer affirms the value of participation and local control even in light of his criticism of the schools for not achieving equal opportunity.
39   Lawrence Cremin, "Public Education and the Education of the Public," in Warren, *History, Education, and Public Policy,* pp. 26–27.

8. The domain of educational understanding: Education as social reproduction

1 See, e.g., Pierre Bourdieu and Jean Claude Passeron, *Reproduction in Education, Society, and Culture,* trans. R. P. Nice, London: Sage, 1977. See also Michael Apple, *Ideology and Curriculum,* London: Routledge & Kegan Paul, 1979.

2 Samuel Bowels and Herbert Gintis, *Schooling in Capitalist America: Educational Reform and the Contradictions of Economic Life,* New York: Basic Books, 1976.

3 I am indebted to Eric Bredo for pointing out this issue to me. For a critique of Bowles and Gintis along these lines, see Donald J. Light, Jr., "Raising Consciousness: A Review of Schooling in Capitalist America," *School Review,* Vol. 85, No. 2, February 1977, pp. 312–21.

4 Quoted in John W. M. Whiting, "Socialization: Anthropological Aspects," in David L. Sills (ed.), *International Encyclopedia of the Social Sciences,* New York: Macmillan and Free Press, 1968, p. 545.

5 Ibid.

6 I am indebted to conversations with Eric Bredo for helping me to this point.

7 Here I am following some ideas developed by Charles Taylor in "Interpretation and the Science of Man," *Review of Metaphysics,* Vol. 25, No. 1, Issue 97, September 1971, pp. 3–51.

8 The example of the physician comes from a symposium presentation by Samuel Gorovitz on medicine and education presented at the 1978 meeting of the American Educational Studies Association.

9 This has been one of the major sources of criticism of the new sociology in Britain. By failing to make this distinction, and to indicate that their concern is not to elaborate a criterion for true knowledge, this school of thought has been vulnerable to the charge that its findings rest upon a naive cultural relativism. For a possible defense against this charge see Helen Freeman, "Authority, Power, and Knowledge: Politics and Epistemology in the 'New' Sociology of Education," *Proceedings of the Thirty-sixth Annual Meeting of the Philosophy of Education Society,* Normal, Ill., 1981.

10 See, for examples of the relationship between formal scientific structure and institutions, Thomas Kuhn, *The Structure of Scientific Revolutions,* Chicago: University of Chicago Press, 1962, and also Imre Lakatos and Alan Musgrave, *Criticism and the Growth of Knowledge,* Cambridge: Cambridge University Press, 1970.

11 I am indebted to some comments by Charles Lemert before the Social Theory Group at the University of Illinois for helping me to see the idea of a role in terms of the possibilities that it entails.

12 For an excellent examination of this process see Magali Safatti Larson, *The Rise of Professionalism: A Sociological Analysis.* Berkeley: University of California Press, 1977.

13 Quoted in Dennis Smith, "Power, Ideology, and the Transmission of Knowledge: An Exploratory Essay," in Earl Hopper (ed.), *Readings in the Theory of Education,* London: Hutchinson University Library, 1971, p. 253.

14 Paul Willis, for example, has examined a group of rebellious students who held practical knowledge superior to theoretical knowledge. Ultimately, however, this group posed no threat to the dominant culture because their idea of valuable knowledge was woven into a sexist, racist culture that directed hostility away from the dominant group. See Paul Willis, *Learning to Labor: How Working Class Kids Get Working Class Jobs,* Farnborough, England: Saxon House, 1978.

15 See Max Weber, *Essay in Sociology,* ed. H. H. Gerth and C. Wright Mills, New York: Oxford University Press, 1958, pp. 416–45.

16 Ibid., p. 416.

17 Ibid., p. 431.

18 Ibid.

19 Ibid., p. 432.

20 Ibid., p. 437.

21 Ibid., p. 439.

22 This is of course what Bowles and Gintis's study attempts to do.

23 For an interesting attempt at such an approach, see A. R. Luria, *Cognitive Development: Its Cultural and Social Foundations,* Cambridge: Harvard University Press, 1976.

24 A number of scholars have begun to look at these questions in the context of the classroom. See, for example, Michael Apple, *Ideology and Curriculum.* Also see Nell Keddie, "Classroom Knowledge," in Michael F. D. Young (ed.), *Knowledge and Control,* London: Collier—Macmillan, 1971, pp. 133–60; Ulf P. Lundgren and Sten Petterson, (eds.), *Code, Content, and Curriculum Processes,* Stockholm: Stockholm Institute of Education, Department of Educational Research, 1979.

25 See, for example, Robert Dreeben, *On What Is Learned in School,* Reading, Mass.: Addison-Wesley, 1968. Educational scholarship has only recently begun to examine the way in which particular frameworks are transmitted and altered in the reproductive process. For one recent attempt to understand some of the factors in this process see Paul E. Willis, *Learning to Labor.*

26 For one example of this kind of research see Bourdieu and Passeron, *Reproduction in Education.*

9. The bonding of codes and frames: The case of medical knowledge

1 For a review of this literature see Donald E. Super and Paul Bachrach, *Review of the Literature on Choice and Success in Scientific Careers,* Scientific Careers Project, Working Paper No. 1, New York: Teachers College, Columbia University, November 1956, chapter 4. See also Edward Gottheil and Carmen M. Michael, "Predictor Variables Employed in Research on the Selection of Medical Students," *Journal of Medical Education,* Vol. 32, February 1957, pp. 131–47; Judith A. Dawson, "The Complexities of Selecting Medical Students: A Search for Criteria and Predictors," Urbana, Ill.: School of Basic Medical Sciences, College of Medicine, University of Illinois, n.d.

2 See, for example, Eliot Friedson, *Professional Dominance: The Social Structure of Medical Care,* New York: Atherton Press, 1970.

3 For a good example of this literature see Howard S. Becker, Blanche Greer, Everett C. Hughes, and Anselm L. Straus, *Boys in White: Student Culture in Medical School,* Chicago: University of Chicago Press, 1961.

4 I am indebted to a comment by Donald Arnstein for reminding me of this fact. One fairly recent expression of this is a major address by Robert Howsam (of the University of

Houston) before the American Association of Colleges of Teacher Education, Chicago, March 1976. Howsam called for a Flexner plan for teacher education.

5 Arthur I. Stinchcombe, *Rebellion in a High School*, Chicago: Quadrangle Books, 1964, pp. 131–32.

6 For an analysis of some of the dimensions of education that can be influenced by class characteristics see Basil Bernstein, *Class, Codes, and Control*, Vol. 3, *Towards a Theory of Educational Transmissions*, London: Routledge & Kegan Paul, 1975. Also, for a most suggestive treatment of the different pedagogical styles found in schools with children from different social classes see Jean Anyon, ''Social Class and the Hidden Curriculum of Work,'' *Journal of Education*, Vol. 162, No. 1, Winter 1980, pp. 67–92.

7 For an elaboration of this point see Herbert Gintis and Samuel Bowles, ''The Contradictions of Liberal Educational Reform,'' in Walter Feinberg and Henry Rosemont, Jr. (eds.), *Work, Technology, and Education: Dissenting Essays in the Intellectual Foundations of American Education*, Urbana: University of Illinois Press, 1975, pp. 92–141.

8 For an analysis of some of the pitfalls of direct and visible approaches see W. N. Grubb and M. Lazerson, ''Rally Round the Workplace: Continuities and Fallacies in Career Education,'' *Harvard Educational Review*, Vol. 45, No. 4, 1975, pp. 451–74. For other kinds of problems see Paul Willis, *Learning to Labour: How Working Class Kids Get Working Class Jobs*, Farnborough, England: Saxon House, 1978.

9 The fact that some of these opportunities have been reduced in recent years has, quite naturally, been used as a reason for scaling down the importance of the liberal arts areas.

10 For the first of these studies see W. Lloyd Warner, Robert J. Havighurst, and Martin B. Loeb, *Who Shall Be Educated? The Challenge of Unequal Opportunity*, New York: Harper, 1944. For the second, see especially James B. Conant, *The American High School Today*, New York: McGraw-Hill, 1959. For a more detailed analysis of both these works, see my *Reason and Rhetoric: The Intellectual Foundation of Twentieth Century Educational Policy*, New York: Wiley, 1975, chapter 4.

11 See Abraham Flexner, *Medical Education: A Comparative Study* (hereafter *1925 Study*) New York: Macmillan, 1925, chapter 3.

12 Abraham Flexner, *Medical Education in the United States and Canada: A Report to the Carnegie Foundation for the Advancement of Teaching* (hereafter *1910 Report*), New York: Carnegie Foundation for the Advancement of Teaching, Bulletin No. 4, 1910, p. 40.

13 Ibid., pp. 88–89.

14 The very fact that Flexner was not a physician and yet was commissioned by the Carnegie Foundation to undertake this study indicates the precarious state of the medical profession at the time.

15 Flexner, *1910 Report*, p. 213.

16 Ibid., p. 52.

17 Flexner *1925 Study*, p. 3.

18 Ibid., p. 4.

19 See Flexner, *1910 Report*, p. 83.

20 Flexner, *1925 Study*, p. 7.

21 See Flexner, *1910 Report*, p. 25. This ideal continued to guide his judgments and observations in many ways. For example, his *1925 Study* criticizes France for not sufficiently encouraging original medical research and commends Germany for furthering this end.

22   See Flexner, *1910 Report,* p. 104.

23   See Flexner, *1925 Study,* p. 80. In light of recent criticisms of IQ tests, some may think this proposal rather naïve. Yet if we are to understand that the problems with these tests represent more than simply technical difficulties, we need to see just how many people, in proposing their use, believed that they were acting in accord with a general principle of fairness whereby many poor but "talented" children would be allowed to compete. That such a principle spoke little to the needs of the less talented, however, seemed to go unnoticed. (See Chapter 3.)

24   For an attempt to place the Flexner 1910 report in the perspective of the times see Robert H. Ebert, "The Medical School," *Scientific American,* September 1973, especially p. 140.

25   See ibid., p. 139.

26   I am indebted to Allan Chase for this insight. It is interesting to note, in this regard, that historically dramatic declines in certain diseases have occurred prior to the development of vaccination and were more closely associated with such things as improvements in sanitation or a rise in the general standard of living.

27   We can see what some of these conditions were by understanding the appeal that the German university had for Flexner and, by derivation, the German medical school. In a reference to Flexner, Joseph Ben-David describes some of these:

> Three conditions are mentioned in the literature in explanation of German scientific superiority in the nineteenth century: (1) the relative excellence of laboratory and hospital facilities for research and faster recognition of the importance of new fields of research, especially physiology; (2) the clear recognition of the aim of the university as a seat of original research, and efficient organizational devices to achieve that aim; . . . (3) the existence of a large number of academic institutions which made possible the mobility of teachers and students, and resulted in an atmosphere of scientific competition that did not exist elsewhere. (Joseph Ben-David, "Scientific Productivity and Academic Organization in Nineteenth Century Medicine," *American Sociological Review,* Vol. 25, 1960, p. 833)

As we have seen, because of the nature of American medical schools, this last condition had to be modified in Flexner's early work. Nevertheless, the passage from Ben-David points out the importance that Flexner gave to so arranging conditions that medical knowledge could grow at the fastest possible pace.

28   This is not to overlook the fact that Flexner gave priority at times to certain diseases over others, and it is worth looking briefly at this to see how other than scientific or strictly humanitarian factors have often influenced the organization and pursuit of scientific research. His treatment of the health problems of blacks is interesting in this regard for it indicates the ways in which he was both ahead of and limited by the climate of his times. In the 1910 report he devoted a couple of pages to medical training for black physicians, as well as an additional page or so to women physicians. In these remarks he simply assumes that blacks will continue to be trained in all-black medical schools. He emphasizes the fact that the black person often lives in close proximity to white people, and that therefore there is a special need to prevent communicable diseases among this group. He does mention that the physical well-being of blacks is important in its own right (a statement that puts him significantly ahead of many educational leaders of his time). However, the emphasis is on communicable diseases that can invade white as well as black communities, rather than on some diseases, perhaps equally debilitating, that might have been unique to blacks as a group.

29 See Flexner, *1910 Report,* p. 44.

30 See ibid., pp. 44–45.

31 For an interesting discussion of the nature of medical knowledge see Samuel Gorovitz and Alasdair MacIntyre, "Towards a Theory of Medical Fallibility: Distinguishing Culpability from Necessary Error," *Hastings Center Report,* Vol. 5, No. 6, December 1975, p. 15.

32 See Bernard R. Blishen, *Doctors and Doctrines: The Ideology of Medical Care in Canada,* Toronto: University of Toronto Press, 1969, p. 14.

33 In 1978–79 the acceptance percentage was 45.1, which in fact was a considerable jump from previous years. The reason for this jump in acceptance is largely a function of the decrease in the number of applicants. See "Datagram: Applicants for 1978–79 First Year Medical School Class," *Journal of Medical Education,* Vol. 55, January 1980, p. 74.

34 The 1977–78 applicants reported that 52.6 percent of their parents had incomes of $20,000 or more. The largest group of students fell in the category of parental income between $25,000 and $49,999. Moreover, as parents income rises the chances for acceptance increases in most categories. Thus in 1977, 50.4 percent of entering class had parents with incomes of more than $26,000. Moreover, 45 percent of the 1977–78 entering class came from professional or managerial households. Travis L. Gordon, "Study of U.S. Medical School Applicants, 1977–78," *Journal of Medical Education,* Vol. 54, September 1979, pp. 677–702.

35 The question of how this differential is best explained is an open one. That much of the variance cannot be explained by differences in IQ scores seems to be strongly suggested by the analysis provided by Gintis and Bowles, "The Contradictions of Liberal Educational Reform," especially pp. 110 and 112.

36 For the years 1974–75, 14 percent of the first-year class reported that they worked. The median number of hours was 10 a week. Twenty-six percent of the senior class reported that they worked. The average number of hours worked was 10 a week for this group. The largest number of students (75 and 64 percent) listed their own savings and earnings and gifts and loans from family as sources of funds. When all the various categories of loans are added up, the proportion of students listed in these categories is 85 percent. This is an extremely important source for working- and middle-class students, and the recent rise in interest rates together with the increase in medical school tuition will almost surely result in restricting access to many potential students from these groups. For the 1974–75 figures see Association of Medical Colleges, *Survey of How Medical Students Finance Their Education,* Washington, D.C.: U.S. Department of Health, Education, and Welfare, Public Health Service, Health Resource Administration, Bureau of Health Manpower, December 1975. In some countries the idea of paying medical students for their studies has been proposed by certain groups, although such an idea has not received much attention in this country. However, given the persistence of other factors such as the different quality of public school education for different sectors of the society, it is debatable whether this procedure would serve more to open up opportunities for poorer segments of the society or simply to provide another subsidy for the wealthier ones. In any event, at this writing a few private medical schools have raised tuition to $15,000 a year, and others are following suit. Even without the cutbacks in loans by the Reagan administration, new physicians often begin their practice with such high loans that they are unlikely to settle in areas of need if those areas cannot support their educational mortgage.

37   Even without challenging the existing standards, there are serious questions about whether the competition need be so intense. Many medical schools must turn away at least the equivalent of one fully qualified class of students each year. Existing standards, however, require an additional analysis of the populations whose basic medical needs go underserved.

38   The trend toward increased specialization is easily discernible when we look at the ratios of general practitioners (GPs) to specialists over a period of time. In 1949, for example, there were 1.8 GPs for every specialist. In 1967 there was but 1 GP for every 2.8 specialists. (Howard W. House, *Objectives in Medical Education: A National Survey of Medical Faculty Opinions,* Iowa City: University of Iowa, Health Care Research Series, 1971, p. 63.) Today approximately 80 percent of physicians are specialists of some kind. Although estimates vary and definitions of different specialties are rather loose, one informed guess is that somewhere between 15 and 25 percent could be classified as *engaged* in primary care such as pediatrics, obstetrics, gynecology, or internal medicine. (From interview with Ernest Drucher of the Montefiore Medical Schools.) One 1974 study projected 11 percent of physicians would be engaged in general practice in 1980 (*The Survey of Health Manpower: 1970 Profiles and Projections to 1990,* Washington, D.C.: DHEW NO [HRA] 75-38, table 35.) Although one of the most recent government reports on medicine predicts a surplus in most areas by 1990, the surplus predicted in the primary care disciplines is described as trivial when compared to that in most specialties. See *Summary Report of the Graduate Medical Education National Advisory Committee to the Secretary, Department of Health and Human Sciences,* Vol. 1, Washington, D.C.: U.S. Dept. Health and Human Services, September 30, 1981, p. 23.

39   See, for example, Robert K. Merton, George C. Reader, and Patricia L. Kendall (eds.), *The Student–Physician: Introductory Studies in the Sociology of Medical Education,* Cambridge, Mass.: Harvard University Press, 1957, p. 155. See also Howard S. Becker, Blanche Greer, Everett C. Hughes, and Anselm L. Strauss, *Boys in White: Student Culture in Medical School,* Chicago: University of Chicago Press, 1961, p. 63.

40   See Merton et al., *The Student–Physician,* p. 156.

41   "The Millis Report: Must Reading – a *ME* Condensation from the Report of the Citizen's Commission on Graduate Medical Education," *Medical Economics,* January 9, 1967, p. 266. For a later report see *Summary Report of the Graduate Medical Advisory Committee.*

42   For a description of the student's first year see Becker et al., *Boys in White,* chapter 6 and especially pp. 81–83.

43   See ibid.

44   See ibid., pp. 65–184.

45   See Merton et al. *The Student–Physician,* pp. 153–176. It should be noted, however, that this humility is not often revealed to the patient. Whereas revealing one's ignorance to another medical student or a teaching physician is seen as a virtue, the same revelation is looked upon differently when communicated to a patient.

46 See John Kosa and Robert E. Coker, Jr., "The Female Physician in Public Health: Conflict and Reconcillation of the Sex and Professional Role," in Athena Theodore (ed.), *The Professional Women,* Cambridge, Mass.: Schenkman, 1971, pp. 195–206.

47 See ibid., p. 196. By 1976–77 the ratio was improving significantly. It is reported that at that time almost 25 percent of the students were women ("Minorities and Women in the Health Fields: Applicants, Students, and Workers," in *Health Manpower References,* DHEW Publication No. [HRA] 79-22, October 1978, figure 4). This trend, along with an initial but now leveled-off increase in the number of medical students from minority groups, seems to be a response to the feminist movement and the civil rights movement and is now already a few years old. By 1971, for example, 13 percent of the first-year class were women and 7 percent were from minority groups. See Robert H. Ebert, "The Medical School," *Scientific American,* September 1973, pp. 143–44.

48 Ibid., p. 196.

49 See ibid., p. 198. Of those women who do enter medicine as physicians and then go on to specialize, they have tended to concentrate in the areas of pediatrics, public health, preventive medicine, and psychiatry (ibid., p. 202).

50 Frederich Mosteller and Daniel P. Moynihan (eds.), *On Equality of Educational Opportunity,* New York: Vintage Books, 1972, p. 7.

51 For a more extended treatment of this issue see W. Feinberg (ed.), "Introduction," *Equality and Social Policy,* Urbana: University of Illinois Press, 1978.

52 Regarding these recent changes, some medical schools have given special weight to minority status. It is reported that minority students do well despite the fact that a number of them have significant deficiencies in their undergraduate preparation and that the school loses no more of these students than it does of those admitted on a regular basis. A few schools have given special weight to students from rural areas who agree to return to rural settings to practice for at least four years. The effect of the Supreme Court decision in *University of California Regents* v. *Bakke* on these programs has yet to be fully appraised.

53 The move toward a larger number of paramedics does not meet this issue, because the paramedic is blocked from medical school in the same way as has been the registered nurse.

54 Here I want to express some misgivings about the major theme of what is sometimes an insightful although overly general, unsystematic evaluation of the medical profession, Ivan Illich's *Medical Nemesis,* Toronto: Bantam Books, 1976. Illich's major theme, that the medical profession is a threat to health, is often supported by explaining away some of the fundamental contributions of research and sophisticated medical technology. Indeed, much of Illich's case seems to be made on the basis of the celebration of pain and death, an approach that when taken to the extreme (which is easy to do with Illich's unqualified style) is unacceptable. The major difficulty that I have with Illich's work on medicine, as with his work on schools, is that it focuses attention away from the distribution mechanism. The question is not whether the medical profession is a danger to the nation's health, but rather, given the limitations of resources, where ought health priorities to be placed, and how should skills be clustered and distributed.

55 "The Millis Report: Must Reading," p. 254.

56 See William Martin, "Preference for Types of Patients," in Merton et al., pp. 189–205.

57 I am indebted to Ernest Drucker for many of these observations. Indeed, the failure of physicians to be concerned about the relationship between work and health may have a significance that is wider than the problem of immediate work hazards. In one fifteen-year study, job satisfaction was shown to be the best predictor of longevity. Of course, this problem involves more concerns than just those of the physician, but the fact that medical associations have not been concerned with addressing this problem points out the way the physician's role has been limited to that of a crisis manager. For the report on studies of work and longevity see Special NEW Task Force, *Work in America,* Cambridge: MIT Press, 1971, p. 77.

58 N. Alfred Haynes, "Problems Facing the Negro in Medicine Today," *JAMA,* Vol. 209, No. 7, August 19, 1969, pp. 1067–69.

59 To see the pattern of physician migration in one large city see Donald Dewey, *Where the Doctors Have Gone: The Changing Distribution of Private Practice Physicians in the Chicago Metropolitan Area, 1950–1970,* Chicago: Chicago Regional Hospital Study, 1973.

60 Alain C. Enthoven, *Health Plan,* Reading, Mass.: Addison–Wesley, 180, p. 13.

61 It is interesting to note, however, with the introduction of the polio vaccine and its uneven administration according to social class, the percentage immunized in the poor population has dropped relative to the percentage immunized among the wealthier groups (interview with Ernest Drucker). The policies of the Reagan administration can be expected to widen this gap.

62 See Allan Chase, *The Biological Imperatives: Health, Politics, and Human Survival,* New York: Holt, Rinehart and Winston, 1971.

63 There is a sense in which this statement applies to the nonpoor as well, whose improved health is likely more the result of a higher standard of living then of sophisticated forms of medical intervention.

64 See Martin S. Feldstein, "The Medical Economy," *Scientific American,* Vol. 229, No. 3, September 1973, p. 157.

65 For information on the distribution of the financial burden, see ibid., p. 158. Feldstein also points out some interesting factors about the nature and distribution of medical insurance that generate this unequal financial burden. For example, he reports that individual insurance is most adequate for hospital care, with insurance companies paying about 80 percent of consumer expenditure in 1972 (see p. 191). However, he reports that this is much higher coverage than for ambulatory care and general treatment (p. 151). One of the results of this, of course, is that the same expense, say $1,000, for ambulatory care will be absorbed with much more difficulty by lower-middle-income people than by upper-middle-income ones. Another consequence, one reported by Feldstein, is that the pattern of insurance tends to distort the number of people who are hospitalized for an illness who could otherwise be handled on an ambulatory basis. There is anther implication to these remarks that is reasonable to draw. Given these factors, it is not difficult to understand one of the reasons why members of different social classes tend to define differently a set of symptoms as a disease. Those whose income makes ambulatory care too expensive, and who cannot afford hospitalization, are likely to overlook symptoms that others would seek out care for. For a report of the different ways in which different classes of people define disease see E. L. Koos, *The Health of Regionville,* New York: Columbia University Press, 1954, p. 32, as reported in Bernard Blishen, *Doctors and Doctrines,* Toronto: University of Toronto press, 1969, p. 19.

66 Shirley H. Wattenberg and Leona McGann, "Medicare/Medigap/Medicaid: Helping Elders Meet their Health Care Needs," paper presented at the Seventh National Association of Social Workers, Professional Symposium, Philadelphia, November 18–21, 1981, pp. 1–2.

67 See Monroe Lerner, "Social Differences in Physical Health," in John Kosa, Aaron Antononvsky, and Irving Kenneth Zola (eds.), *Poverty and Health,* Cambridge: Harvard University Press, 1969.

68 "The Recent Decline in Infant Mortality," in *Health: United States, 1980,* Hyattsville, Md.: U.S. Department of Health and Human Services, Public Health Service, Office of Health Research, Statistics, and Technology, December 1980, p. 31.

69 Ibid., p. 29.

70 "Annual Summary for the United States," *Monthly Vital Statistics Report,* Vol. 26, No. 13, December 7, 1978; Vol. 27, No. 13, August 13, 1979, pp. 8–9.

71 T. David Erickson and Tor Bjerkedal, "Fetal and Infant Mortality in Norway and the United States," *JAMA,* Vol. 247, No. 7, February 19, 1982, pp. 987–91.

72 For a good treatment of the problem of crisis management see Chase, *The Biological Imperatives.* It is worth noting that until about the age of 35 the major causes of deaths are such things as motor vehicle accidents (number one for whites until age 30–34), homicides (number one for black males from about 15–34), and suicides.

73 See, for example, "The Millis Report," p. 254, for an example of the view that paraprofessionals must be centralized under the control of the physician. Also witness the attempt by the AMA to define other accepted professionals as paraprofessionals to bring them under the control of the physician. A recent example is attempts by the AMA to usurp the authority of the clinical psychologist.

74 In addition to the benefits that would arise from the more equitable distribution of medical knowledge, serious research on the clustering of medical skills would have an additional advantage. It would create the conditions under which debates about the conduct of medicine in an open market could be carried on in a serious fashion. Presently, of course, such discussions are a charade since an open fee structure does not make for an open market when the professional association alone controls the number of people who can enter the profession. Whether the open market is desirable, and if so, in what form, is a subject that warrants much debate. For those who seriously believe that it is desirable, the greater distribution of medical knowledge would seem to be a first and necessary step in its realization.

75 In this country dentists have traditionally enjoyed an autonomy from the medical profession that could serve as a loose model for other areas. However, dentistry itself could involve the same kind of analysis in terms of expanded roles for dental assistants. It is worth noting in this regard that dental problems are one of the most widespread in the United States and that the differences between different socioeconomic classes is striking. (See Lerner, "Social Differences," pp. 108–12.)

76 These interviews were conducted by the author among medical and nursing students in a large metropolitan area.

10. Contradictions within the prevailing knowledge code

1   The term "least advantaged" members is borrowed from John Rawls, *A Theory of Justice,* London: Oxford University Press, 1972.

2   See James B. Conant, *The American High School Today,* New York: McGraw-Hill, 1959, and James B. Conant, *Slums and Suburbs: A Commentary on Schools in Metropolitan Areas,* New York: McGraw-Hill, 1961. Conant's career reflects a continuing influence on both educational and national policy. From 1933 to 1953 he was president of Harvard University. From 1947 through 1952 he was a member of the general advisory committee of the Atomic Energy Commission. In 1953 he was appointed U.S. High Commissioner to West Germany and later ambassador. The two books mentioned above were financed by the Carnegie Corporation, which has played a major role in steering American education throughout much of this century. The project was administered by the Educational Testing Service, which is a national organization that oversees most of the development and administration of educational assessment techniques. This organization has a large but informal influence in determining curriculum and selection through its College Boards testing program.

3   For a more extended discussion of the reason behind educational reform in developed countries see Walter Feinberg, *Reason and Rhetoric: The Intellectual Foundations of Twentieth Century Educational Reform,* New York: Wiley, 1975.

4   One consequence of the failure to address the gap between the most and the least talented members of society is perhaps seen in the pattern of IQ scores for individuals over a period of time. Except for those individuals who score very high, the tendency is for IQ scores to begin to decline somewhere between 20 and 30 years of age and to continue to decline until death. For those who score high on the initial exam, however, the evidence suggests that their IQ scores will continue to improve until well into middle age. There is, however, no evidence to indicate that the intellectual clocks of the average person are programmed to run down faster than the intellectual clocks of the high-IQ person, and one might reasonably speculate that these differences could have something to do with the kinds of work situations and social structures that the high-IQ child is likely to be selected into as opposed to the child with an average or below average IQ score. Regarding the rise and fall of IQ scores, some of the relevant research is: D. Wechsler, *The Measurement and Appraisal of Adult Intelligence,* 4th ed., London: Bailliere, Tindal and Cox, 1958, and J. D. Nisbet, "Intelligence and Age: Retesting with Twenty-Four Years Interval," *British Journal of Educational Psychology,* Vol. 27, 1957, pp. 190–98. See also K. Lovell, "A Study of the Problem of Intellectual Deterioration in Adolescents and Young Adults," *British Journal of Educational Psychology,* Vol. 46, 1955, pp. 199–210.

5   Colony and Protectorate of Kenya, *A Plan to Intensify the Development of African Agriculture in Kenya,* comp. R. J. M. Swynnerton, Nairobi: Government Printer, 1955. For an analysis of this and other development policies see Ann Seidman, *Comparative Development Strategies in East Africa,* Nairobi: East African Publishing House, 1972.

6   See T. W. Schultz, "The Concept of Human Capital," in M. Blaugh (ed.), *Economics of Education,* Middlesex, England: Penguin Books, 1968, especially pp. 16–21.

7   The function of the school in reducing the likelihood of violence in industrialized and industrializing societies has been a long-standing theme among educational leaders. In the late 1800s William Torrey Harris, the United States commissioner of education, asked: "Why educate the children of the common labourers?" and he answered:

For your own well-being and the well-being of your children, the children of all must be educated. If you wish property safe from confiscation by a majority composed of communists, you must see to it that the people are educated so that each sees the sacredness of property, and its service to the world in making available to each the industry of the entire population of the earth. (William T. Harris, *Why Educate the Children of the Common Laborer?* Cambridge: Harvard University, Weidner Library Collection, (n.d.)

Harris's views of the "responsibility" of white civilization to the "subcultures" of the world is worth mentioning also. He wrote:

The White man proves his civilization to be superior to other civilizations just by this very influence which he exercises over the people that have lower forms of civilization, forms that do not permit them to conquer nature and to make the elements into ministers of human power. (W. T. Harris, "An Educational Policy for Our New Possessions," *Educational Review* [reprint], 1889, p. 15)

The general theme that schools must be used to reduce the possibility of violence in a rapidly expanding industrial society has continued as a major platform of many of the most influential studies of education in the United States. The influential book, *Who Shall Be Educated? The Challenge of Unequal Opportunity* (New York: Harper, 1944), by W. Lloyd Warner, Robert J. Havighurst, and Martin B. Loeb, has as a subtheme the message that schooling and selection must be so designed as not to strain the social order while at the same time meeting the ever-expanding need for highly skilled manpower. Both the life adjustment movement that arose in the United States after the Second World War and the Conant volumes that are generally critical of the life adjustment movement were concerned with reducing the alienation and potential violence of the poorer urban masses. Echoing W. T. Harris, Conant stressed the urgency of his educational proposals for the children of the slums:

I do not have to remind the reader that the fate of freedom in the world hangs very much in the balance. Our success against the spread of communism in no small measure depends upon the successful operation of our own free society. Conant, *Slums and Suburbs*, p. 34)

He then went on to propose an education for slum children that emphasized citizenship training and vocational skills and deemphasized academic training.

Similar concerns have been important in developing educational policies for the former colonies, especially as independence came obviously closer. In the 1952 Nuffield Foundation–sponsored conference on African education the need for compulsory education in the urban areas of East and Central Africa was stressed in the context of the disengagement of individuals from their traditional culture and the accompanying rise in juvenile delinquency. (See *African Education: A Study of Educational Policy and Practice in British Tropical Africa*, produced on behalf of the Nuffield Foundation and the Colonial Office by Charles Batey, Printer to the University, Oxford: Oxford University Press, 1953, especially pp. 129–30.)

8 With varying emphases this argument has been put forth by a number of liberal theorists such as Warner, Dewey, and Mannheim.

9 For a more detailed analysis of some of these factors see W. Feinberg, *Reason and*

Rhetoric: The Intellectual Foundations of Twentieth Century Educational Policy, New York: Wiley, 1975.

10 It should be observed that these two platforms are not always advocated by the same people, but that together they make a composite by which advocates of growth have addressed the problem of equality.

11 Johan Galtung, Christian Beck, and Johannes Jaasted, *Educational Growth and Educational Disparity* (mimeo), Oslo: University of Oslo, p. 16, Paris: UNESCO, 1974.

The six stages of education reflected the UNESCO tradition and were reported as follows (p. 14):

    I. No schooling
    II. Incomplete primary education
    III. Complete primary education
    IV. Incomplete 1. cycle, secondary level education
    V. Incomplete 2. cycle, secondary level education
    VI. Post secondary education

12 Ibid., p. 17. (emphasis in original)

13 For an example of the first point of view see Colin Greer, *The Great School Legend: A Revisionist Interpretation of American Public Education,* New York: Basic Books, 1972. For an example of the second point of view see Christopher Jencks et al., *Inequality: A Reassessment of the Effects of Family and Schooling in America,* New York: Basic Books, 1972.

14 It is most instructive to compare Charles Silberman's *Crisis in the Classroom: The Remaking of American Education,* New York: Random House, 1970, to the articles for the *Forum* written by John Maynard Rice in 1892–93. Both their criticisms and their proposals, with minor exceptions, are the same. For a more detailed analysis of this see Walter Feinberg and Henry Rosemont (eds.), *Work, Technology, and Education,* Urbana: University of Illinois Press, 1975.

To cite the journalistic evidence regarding the rigid nature of schooling is not to be taken in this chapter as an endorsement for deschooling or for no schooling. Although the advocates of deschooling, such as Ivan Illich, are quite correct in drawing our attention to the distinction between education and schooling and to the fact that education can take place without schools, there is little reason to believe that with the absence of schools other agencies would not be found to reproduce labor and distribute work according to the present patterns. Indeed, many conservative critics of schooling have proposed that the school-leaving age be lowered in order to enable lower-class youngsters to experience the discipline of work at an earlier age. It is quite clear that these people do not believe that the present distribution of work is a problem, and their proposals are not designed to address that distribution. (For an analysis of this point of view see the treatment of Edward Banfield's *The Unheavenly City* in Chapter 5.)

The problem is not schooling per se but that the inequitable pattern of work forces itself onto and is reflected in the structure of schools.

15 In this discussion I am following somewhat the points made by Herbert Gintis and Samuel Bowles, "The Contradictions of Liberal Education Reform," in Feinberg and Rosemont, *Work, Technology, and Education.* I differ slightly in emphasis, however, for whereas their stress is on the reproductive role of the school in a capitalist society, my stress is on this role in a technological society. The reason for this shift is that the reproductive function as described in the following section is found in more than those nations commonly thought of as capitalistic and includes, for example, the Soviet Union. The essential factor seems to be less the nature of the economic market determining the distribution of goods, and more the principle of efficiency as it underlies the production of goods.

16 For an expansion of this point see M. D. Shipman, *Education and Modernisation*, London: Faber & Faber, 1971, pp. 60–61.

17 In the established literature the concern with matching schooling with the labor requirements of the society is expressed most directly in the discussion of the selection function of schooling. Thus the authors of the influential *Who Shall Be Educated?* wrote in 1944:

> If too few people are selected and promoted through the educational system, the upper levels will be filled through other agencies and perhaps not filled with people as well-equipped by skill and training for the positions. If too many people are selected and pushed up through the educational system, competition will become fierce for the higher level jobs, and some people will have to take positions below the level for which they have been trained. Doctors will have to take jobs as laboratory technicians, engineers as factory workers, and teachers as clerks. This will cause feelings of dissatisfaction with the social order, and the social structure may be strained beyond its tolerable limits. (Warner et al., *Who Shall Be Educated?* p. 150)

Although the discussions of the selection function of schooling have generally taken the existing division of labor as the major factor determining various levels of educational attainment, it is to the proposals on program and curriculum development that one must turn in order to get an idea of what the acceptance of this limitation meant for the value structure of the schools. These limitations are more often than not implicit in other proposals, but they are present in both conservative and liberal discussions of schooling. On the more liberal side, for example, John Dewey's proposals for curriculum development differed significantly depending upon whether or not he was discussing schooling for middle-class or lower-class children. Although these differences have been almost universally overlooked by commentators on Dewey, they are nevertheless present, and the fact that they have been overlooked is as good an indication as any about how widely they are shared. In *Schools of Tomorrow*, written with his daughter Evelyn in 1915, the Deweys examined an all-black school in Indianapolis where the curriculum stressed vocational education and citizenship training to the neglect of academic subjects. After praising the school for its program, Dewey remarked how such a program was especially useful for black, immigrant, and poorer youngsters. The same kind of treatment is given in this book to the schools of Gary, Indiana, which were largely educating the children of the working class to enter the steel mills of that city. (See John Dewey and Evelyn Dewey, *Schools of Tomorrow*, New York: Dutton, 1915.) The point to notice here is just how much the taken-for-granted division of labor was reflected in the schools and the extent to which even the liberal Dewey was unable to perceive this as problematic. On the more conservative side of this issue are James B. Conant's recommendations for the children of the slum schools. The following will serve to illustrate the emphasis on order and control that is found throughout his study:

Many educators would doubtless be shocked by the practice of on-the-spot demotion of one full academic year, with no questions asked, for all participants in fights. In one junior high school I know of, a very able principal found so intolerable a situation that he established that very rule. As a consequence, there are fewer fights in that school. (Conant, *Slums and Suburbs,* p. 22)

Of course the particular distribution of primary and secondary educational values will depend upon the political and economic factors prevalent at the time. The passage above from Warner et al. is a clear indication of some of these factors, and it is unlikely that Conant's decision to label 15 percent of the school-age children as academically talented was not taken without a consideration of how much academically trained manpower the society needed and would be able to absorb. (For a discussion of some of the particular ways the distribution of primary and secondary educational values have been influenced by economic, social, and political factors in educational reform in the United States see Feinberg, *Reason and Rhetoric,* chapter 4.)

18   See Walter Brandis and Basil Bernstein, *Selection and Control: Teacher Ratings of Children in the Infant Schools,* London and Boston: Routledge & Kegan Paul, 1974, Appendix, pp. 139–157, and especially p. 145. This finding may appear to contradict the recent study by Paul Willis, *Learning To Labor: How Working Class Kids get Working Class Jobs,* Farnborough, England: Saxon House, 1977, but the point is not whether parents accept the message of the school, but their reasons for doing so. Thus the creative element that Willis views as primary in the youngsters' rejection of schools may well be present in those who conform to its standards but do so for different reasons than the school presents. In other words, some groups may discount the viability of equality of opportunity but conform to school norms because they understand this to present the only prospect for secure employment.

19   The question of whether or not these limitations are imposed by the economic structure on the development of automation or whether there are simply some routine processes that the machine cannot be expected to perform is a very important issue in terms of understanding the extent to which economic structures limit or enhance technological progress. However, for an understanding of the relationship between education and production it is simply necessary to see that there are limits to the extent to which the machine can accomplish the routine production tasks.

20   See Galtung et al., *Educational Growth,* p. 8.

21   See note 7.

22   Galtung et al., *Educational Growth,* p. 9.

23   See ibid., p. 14, for an elaboration of this point. Also, for an interesting look at the perpetuation of inequalities among the children of immigrant laborers see Stephen Castle's "The Social Time-Bomb: Education of an Underclass in West Germany," *Race and Class,* Vol. 21, No. 4, Spring 1980, pp. 369–87.

24   George E. Miller, *Report on Visit to Iran – June, 1977,* Chicago: University of Illinois, p. 2. That education is no safe business should be obvious from the Iranian's execution of Esfant Farroktiv-Parsa, the former minister of education under the shah.

25   A. Shahmaee, *High Level Health and Manpower Situation in Iran: An Overview,* Population and Manpower Bureau, Planning Division, April 1976. This report placed the proportion of graduates practicing outside the country at the time of publication at 75 percent.

26   Ibid.
27   Miller, *Report on Visit to Iran*, pp. 2–3.
28   See W. Feinberg, *Equality and Social Policy*, Urbana: University of Illinois Press, 1978, Introduction.
29   For an analysis of the advantages and disadvantages of the Yugoslav system see Mihailo Markovic, ''The Relation between Equality and Local Autonomy,'' in ibid., pp. 82–98.
30   Galtung et al., *Educational Growth*, pp. 26–27.
31   See ibid., p. 28.
32   Ibid.

11. Education and the self-formation of the public

1   *General Education in a Free Society: Report of the Harvard Committee*, Cambridge: Harvard University, 1945, p. 14.
2   Antonio Gramsci, *Selections from the Prison Notebooks*, ed. Quintin Hoare and Geoffrey N. Smith, New York: International Publishers, 1971, p. 40.
3   Ibid., p. 39.
4   John Stuart Mill, *Inaugural Address Delivered at the University of St. Andrews, Feb. 1st, 1867*, Boston: Littell and Gay, n.d., p. 3.
5   Gramsci, *Selections*, p. 40.
6   Burton J. Bledstein, *The Culture of Professionalism: The Middle Class and the Development of Higher Education in America*, New York: Norton, 1976, p. 142.
7   *Newsweek*, December 5, 1977, p. 56.
8   See Michael J. Crozier, Samuel P. Huntington, and Joji Watanuki, *The Crisis of Democracy: Report on the Governability of Democracies to the Trilateral Commission*, New York: New York University Press, 1975, p. 102.
9   For a fuller treatment see W. Feinberg, *Reason and Rhetoric: The Intellectual Foundations of Twentieth Century Educational Policy*, New York: Wiley, 1975, chapter 6.
10   Gramsci, *Selections*, p. 32.

Index